Will Rogers, Performer

White
Studio
N.Y.

Will Rogers, Performer

An Illustrated Biography with a Filmography

by Richard J. Maturi *and*
Mary Buckingham Maturi

FOREWORDS BY
Will Rogers' son Jim Rogers
Steven K. Gragert, Director, Will Rogers Memorial Museum

21st Century Publishers
Cheyenne, Wyoming

ALSO BY RICHARD J. MATURI
AND MARY BUCKINGHAM MATURI

Cultural Gems: An Eclectic Look at Unique United States Libraries

Beverly Bayne: Queen of the Movies: A Biography and Filmography

Francis X. Bushman: A Biography and Filmography

Wyoming: Off the Beaten Path

Nevada: Off the Beaten Path

ALSO BY RICHARD J. MATURI

Triple Crown Winner: The Earl Sande Saga

"Many racing critics are calling it the best book of its kind ever written."
— *Tulsa World*

www.triplecrownwinnerearlsande.com

Cover Photo: Will Rogers in *Young as You Feel* 1931 (courtesy Will Rogers Memorial Museum)
Frontispiece: Will Rogers in vaudeville (authors' collection)

Library of Congress Control Number: 2007933361 (paper)
Library of Congress Cataloguing-in-Publication Data

Maturi, Richard J.
Will Rogers, performer: an illustrated biography with a filmography /
by Richard J. Maturi and Mary Buckingham Maturi ;
forewords by Jim Rogers and Steven K. Gragert
p. cm.
Filmography: p.
Includes bibliographical references and index.
ISBN 0-9607298-8-7, 978-0-9607298-8-3 (revised, paper edition)
1. Rogers, Will, 1879-1935. 2. Entertainers—United States—
Biography. 3. Humorists, American—Biography.
I. Maturi, Mary Buckingham. II. Title.
PN2287.R74M39 1999 (hardback)

792.7'028'092—dc21 99-14629 CIP

1 2 3 4 5 6 7 8 9 0

21st Century Publishers, 1320 Curt Gowdy Drive, Cheyenne, Wyoming 82009, 307-638-2254.
Copies may be ordered from publisher. Quantity discounts available.

Cover design and layout by Lee Lewis Walsh, Words Plus Design, www.wordsplusdesign.com

To Will Rogers, who left an indelible mark
on the world's landscape as humorist,
unofficial ambassador, columnist and author.
His performances ranged from Wild West shows,
vaudeville, Ziegfeld Follies, radio and stage
to the silver screen.

To the folks at the Will Rogers Memorial
in Claremore, Oklahoma, who are keeping
Will's legacy alive in the nation's heartland.

"Most thorough source to date on Rogers' film work...recommended."
—*Choice*

"An interesting and informative chronicle of Rogers' experiences as a movie actor. Filled with many famous Rogers' quips and some less famous that are equally interesting."
—*Claremore Progress*

"Packed with brilliantly produced photos...well-researched."
—*Nostalgia Westerns*

"Hard to argue with the folk wisdom Rogers dispensed."
—*Denver Post*

"Rogers' legacy lives on in this excellent book. A book for the true Rogers fan."
—*Bookviews*

"Packed with photos and Will Rogers' quotes."
—*Laramie Boomerang*

"Rogers was the master of every entertainment medium that came his way... a fine book on a fine fellow."
—*The Virginian-Pilot*

"A well-done piece of scholarship."
—*Under Western Skies*

"What a book this is. One that's certain to get a lot of acquisitions by movie history classes."
—*Rapport*

"This book is a keeper."
—*Roundup*

"Rogers remains a man for all times. This heavily illustrated work provides a detailed look at all aspects of Will Rogers' performing career."
—*Shelwing, Ltd.*

Acknowledgments

Special thanks to all of the folks at the Will Rogers Memorial in Claremore, Oklahoma, for their invaluable help. Their generosity in providing background material, access to Will Rogers' files and papers, and copies of lobby cards, photographs and films can never be adequately repaid.

We offer our gratitude to Jim Rogers, who took the time to visit with us at his ranch in California to share his insight into the man that was Will Rogers: famous humorist, screen legend, husband and father.

We also extend our thanks to the staffs of the following film resource centers for their aid in our research of Will Rogers and his career: the Academy of Motion Picture Arts and Sciences, the Billy Rose Library at the Lincoln Center for the Performing Arts, the Museum of Modern Art, the USC Film Library and the Wisconsin Center for Film and Theater of the State Historical Society of Wisconsin.

Richard J. Maturi
Mary Buckingham Maturi
Cheramie, Wyoming

Table of Contents

Foreword

Jim Rogers

When I learned that Richard and Mary Buckingham Maturi were writing a book about Will Rogers and his films, I was very pleased, for I have always believed that Dad's movie career never received the attention it deserved. It was sort of a first step on the road from being a famous *Follies* star to becoming a national celebrity. Having films playing in theaters all over the country made his name and face recognized in households from coast to coast.

Dad really liked working for Goldwyn. The money was great and the movie making schedule gave him more time for his family. Besides that, his horses were on the backlot, and he could ride down Washington Boulevard and rope goats at Walter Cameron's.

Even though I was at the studio a great deal and appeared in three pictures as a five-year-old, I don't remember much about them. I have read that Dad's silent films were not successful, but after reviewing the ones we still have prints of and prints from other sources, I think they were very good. The reviews of the day, as presented in this book, bear this out. Dad's fling as a producer was financially unsuccessful, yet during that brief time he produced *The Ropin' Fool* and *One Day in 365,* both of which are popular showings every day at the Will Rogers Memorial in Claremore, Oklahoma. I do not know how much money he lost producing movies, but I doubt if it could have been more than $40,000 — a setback but not a disaster.

As you read about Dad's activities through 1928, it is easy to see that he was a workaholic. Even living in the Rogers household, I didn't realize the killer schedule he kept. I never felt that either Dad or Mother didn't have time for us, nor do I recall ever hearing Bill or Mary saying that Dad or Mother were too busy for them. When Dad went to Fox, we were older and more aware of the things he did: his writings, countless benefits, trips to Europe, radio appearances. No matter how great his success, he continued with all of these activities.

I know that I am prejudiced — he was my pop — but I still get a lot of laughs and enjoyment from his films with Fox. Will Rogers made twenty-one films while under contract with Fox. One, by error, did not have its copyright renewed, four were released by Fox for home video, but the remaining sixteen remain buried in the film vaults. Judging from the information I get from the Will Rogers Shrine in Colorado Springs, Colorado, the Will Rogers Memorial in Claremore, Oklahoma, and the Will Rogers State Historical Park in California, there are a lot of folks who would dearly love to see them. I want to thank Richard and Mary for writing this book and helping to revive interest in Dad's movies and his movie career.

Foreword

Steven K. Gragert
Director, Will Rogers Memorial Museum

When Rick and Mary Maturi told me that they planned to republish *Will Rogers, Performer* in soft cover, I was pleased. I was especially excited they decided to make a trip to Claremore to undertake new research. I looked forward to their visit because one of my great pleasures since joining the staff of the Will Rogers Memorial Museum has been the opportunity to become personally acquainted with the researchers and writers whose books on Will Rogers I have read and used. Perhaps it's the subject matter common to each that just seems to attract the most decent of sorts, but for whatever reason, I have come to feel, "I have never met a Rogers researcher I didn't like."

The Maturis proved no exception. They bring to their work strong intellects, expert research skills, curiosity, thoroughness, and professionalism. They have written on many topics, but when it comes to the man in question their *Will Rogers, Performer* shows they understand how an intelligent, down-to-earth Cherokee cowboy from Indian Territory became one of the foremost communicators of his time. He achieved it in diverse ways, using with great success every medium to touch people: vaudeville, Broadway extravaganza, syndicated writings, magazine serials, sound recordings, radio, and of course, motion pictures. (One wonders what he would have accomplished with a blog?)

This edition of *Will Rogers, Performer* helps you appreciate and understand the movie career of an all-time box-office favorite and is timely with the Twentieth-Century Fox release of eight Rogers' sound films in state-of-the-art digital format. Eager Rogers fans await release of the other thirteen from the Fox vaults.

After enjoying the Fox re-releases and this expanded *Will Rogers, Performer*, consider a visit to Will's old stomping grounds. The Will Rogers Memorial offers the world's most complete one-stop, panoramic view of Will Rogers, his life and times. Visitors to our twelve-gallery museum in Claremore and the Will Rogers Birthplace Ranch near Oologah can learn first-hand how this rope-spinning cowboy with a wide grin and an "aw-shucks" demeanor captured the imagination and respect of a nation and brought it hope and laughter during some of its darkest days.

Our galleries relate his multi-faceted stardom in print, on stage, over the air, and on screen. Visitors can watch his films, both silents and talkies, and enjoy the artistry of Will Rogers motion picture posters in the Gordon Kuntz collection. Celebrate with us as we honor Will's birthday on 4 November with our activity-packed Will Rogers Days. Or join us in August during the annual Will Rogers and Wiley Post Fly-In, a time for remembering their deaths in a horrific airplane crash in Alaska on 15 August 1935, and recognizing their incredible contributions to civil and commercial aviation. This edition of *Will Rogers, Performer* includes a special section, Will Rogers, Aviation Enthusiast. We invite you to visit. You will leave with a smile, just as Will would have hoped.

Author's Note

Richard J. Maturi

As far back as I can remember, Will Rogers held a special place in my life. In this age sorely in need of heroes, Will Rogers is my hero. Will continues the habit of entering my life from time to time. I first ran across him in my early childhood as I prowled through my parents' library in search of interesting reading material. Time and again I read *Will Rogers: Ambassador of Good Will, Prince of Wit and Wisdom* by P. J. O'Brien and *Will Rogers: His Wife's Story* by Betty Rogers, and they shaped my personal philosophy of treating all people with respect, working hard and holding up my end of a bargain.

Why these two particular books were in my parents' reading collection is anybody's guess, but my father had been a small aircraft pilot in his youth and during the days when Will was busy barnstorming the country on lecture tours and promoting flying. That probably had something to do with it. I also saw a lot of Will in my father. Like Will, my father believed in honesty and good character. I remember my father never saying anything bad about somebody else, except, of course, us kids when we got out of hand. Will Rogers was known for his generosity to his friends and others in need, and like Will, Dad was generous to a fault.

A simple story will illustrate what I mean. As Dad ran a road construction project one summer, a beat-up truck pulled up to us alongside the highway. Several ragamuffins peered out of the dilapidated truck's window. Out crawled an overweight, middle-aged man who addressed my father, "Mister Boss, how about a job for a poor migrant worker who needs some money to get back home?"

My father put him to work and at the end of the day, the worker again came up to Dad and asked for an advance on the week's check in order to get his truck fixed and buy food for his family. Without a bit of hesitation, my father took out his wallet and gave the man several days' wages in cash. The next day the man failed to show up for work.

I asked Dad why he had given the long-gone worker the money, when he probably realized the man would not return for work again. Dad replied simply, "Because he needed it."

From my reading, I developed an admiration of Will and his wife, Betty Rogers. Our visit with their son Jim Rogers confirmed that Will and Betty created a loving family environment that fostered strong bonds. Jim Rogers said, "Nobody could have a better set of parents. Both were level-headed with their feet on the ground. They were very understanding and supportive of anything we wanted to try. They loved us very much." That perfectly captures how I feel about my parents and how they raised us kids.

Will Rogers again surfaced in my life decades later as I journeyed to Texas in 1979 in search of work. Along the way, I made a slight detour in order to stop by Claremore, Oklahoma. I know the year because I still wear the Will Rogers Centennial belt buckle I purchased while visiting the Will Rogers Memorial on that trip. Several years later, hoping to pass along some of my feelings about Will Rogers and his philosophy, I took my two sons to the Cleveland theater district in order to see James Whitmore perform in *Will Rogers' U.S.A.*

Nearly a decade after my father had passed away, tears crept down my face as my wife, Mary, and I watched *The Will Rogers Follies: A Life in Revue* at the Palace Theatre on Broadway. The date was September 5, 1992, and we were with our dear friend Roz, who was fighting a courageous battle against cancer. Roz knew how much I loved Will Rogers and had purchased the tickets as a special treat for our visit to New York City. I never saw her as happy as that evening. After the show let out she literally skipped out of the theater humming one of the tunes. We lost Roz exactly two years later.

After years of Will hovering in the background of my life, I find it fitting to take a more active role in his by writing this book with Mary.

We have recently had another bittersweet experience. We had enjoyed watching Will's movies on video with my mother and sweetly sharing interesting tidbits about Will Rogers with her. Coincidentally, she lived in Hibbing, Minnesota, where we unearthed a photo of a 1937 Will Rogers snow sculpture that dwarfed the Hibbing Winter Snow Carnival queen and her court. The bitter part came as we continued our work on the Will Rogers book, knowing that Mom was slipping away from us.

Once again Will Rogers provides some bits of wisdom: "It's only the inspiration of those who die that makes those who live realize what constitutes a useful life." And furthermore: "If you live right, death is a joke to you as far as fear is concerned."

Introduction

Will Rogers stands as a unique figure in American history. While definitely a man of his times, he remains a man for all times. Much of his political and social commentary remains as valid today as when he first spoke or wrote it. Many excellent books and articles extol Will Rogers as humorist and philosopher.

Will's wit and social wisdom stemmed from his own experiences and flowed over into his life as a performer. In *Will Rogers, Performer,* we direct our attention to a review of his professional career with a particular emphasis on his work in films.

Will was one of the few movie actors who successfully made the transition from silent films to the talkies. His brand of humor and the way he talked particularly suited the new medium. Will never shied away from new adventures, was always game for new experiences and looked for ways to improve on his previous performances. From hours and hours of practicing new rope tricks to meticulously poring over the newspaper to develop timely material for his vaudeville and Ziegfeld *Follies* appearances, Will was the ultimate perfectionist. He never took himself seriously, but he approached his work with great seriousness.

Over the years, Will Rogers wrote thousands of newspaper articles and gave hundreds of dinner speeches and radio talks. Newspapers of the day quoted him uncounted times as he traveled across the country and around the world in pursuit of adventure. In *Will Rogers, Performer,* we include a select sprinkling of his quotes and anecdotes, portions of articles by and about him and capsule comments of reviews that pertain to Will's movie career.

While most people know about the humorist Will Rogers and recognize his sayings, many do not realize that Will Rogers had a very successful film career that spanned nearly two decades before being cut short by his untimely death. Will started out his movie career in the silents and after a brief return to the *Follies* made a successful transition into the talkies with twenty-one Fox pictures. A number of his films earned the distinction of being voted among the best productions of the year, and Will often received applause for his fine performances. In 1934, he was voted the top box office draw, outranking even Shirley Temple and Clark Gable.

We hope that our book increases your knowledge about Will Rogers and your regard for him as a consummate performer. We hope, too, that it will entice you to read some of the excellent books that cover other aspects of this amazing American's life.

Chapter 1

The Formative Years

The Yen to Travel

Even if you're on the right track, you'll get run over if you just sit there.

William Penn Adair Rogers made his first appearance in Indian Territory near what is now Oologah, Oklahoma, on November 4, 1879. As Will explained his ancestry, "My father was one-eighth Cherokee and my mother one-fourth Cherokee, which I figure makes me about an eighth cigar-store Injun." William P. A. Rogers became a citizen of the Cherokee Nation upon his birth. He received enrollment number 11384.

"My ancestors didn't come over on the Mayflower, but they met the boat." From those unique beginnings, Will Rogers emerged as America's unofficial ambassador to the world and the nation's "poet lariat." He made his mark as friend of the common man as well as crony of presidents, kings and titans of industry. His gum-chewing, homespun philosophy hit home with good, common sense. His generosity to those less fortunate set a fine example of public spiritedness and genuine concern for his fellow man and bolstered the spirits of people hit hard by droughts, floods and economic disaster. When Will Rogers and aviator Wiley Post died in an airplane crash near Barrow, Alaska, en route to Russia, the shock reverberated around the globe. Will left this earth as he approached life: seeking new adventures and searching out new friends.

"Everybody is ignorant ... only on different subjects." Will's natural curiosity and desire to learn of the world around him sent him on travel adventures early in his life. He ranked among the honor-roll students during his early schooling, even earning a medal for elocution at Willie Halsell College in 1894. He enrolled at Kemper Military Academy in Boonville, Missouri, in January 1897 but left Kemper in the early part of

Will Rogers as he appeared in the Ziegfeld *Follies* (courtesy Will Rogers Memorial).

1898 to work on ranches in the Texas panhandle.

Referring to his schooling, Will said, "My father was pretty well fixed, and I being the only male son he tried terribly hard to make something out of me. He sent me to about every school in that part of the country. In some of them I would last about three or four months.... At one school I spent two years there, one in the fourth grade, and one in the guardhouse. One was as bad as the other. I spent ten years in the fourth grade and knew more about *McGuffey's Fourth Reader* than McGuffey did.... There has always been some curiosity about how I left Kemper Military Academy ... whether I jumped or was I shoved. Well, I can't remember that far back. All I know is that it was a cold winter and Old Man Ewing's ranch on the Canadian River near Higgins, Texas, wasn't any too warm when I dragged in there."

After Will spent his time traveling, he eventually returned to Oologah to operate his father Clem's ranch later in 1898. On July 4, 1899, Will won his first money in a roping contest, earning $18.10 by tying his cow in 52 seconds.

Will later recounted this momentous occasion in one of his 1932 weekly articles: "It was the first one I ever was in, the very first thing I ever did in the way of appearing before an audience in my life. Well, as I look back on it that had quite an influence on my little career, for I kinder got to running to 'em, and the first thing I knew I was just plum 'honery' and fit for nothing but show business. Once you are a showman you are plum ruined for manual labor again."

At St. Louis in October 1899, Will participated in steer-roping contests and riding contests with Zach Mulhall's troupe. In March 1900, Will's father traveled to New Mexico with the purpose of setting up a stock farm there in charge of his son. That plan never materialized, but Clem did stake Will to a small herd of his own. On a trip to San Francisco, Will and a stockman bedded down in a hotel for the night. They improperly turned off the gas and were found in bad condition the next morning. Rogers recuperated at Hot Springs, Arkansas. (This was Will's second brush with death. Four years earlier, his Winchester rifle had accidentally discharged with the bullet passing through his hat, leaving a scalp wound.) Will teamed up with the Mulhall troupe again in October 1901, appearing in steer-roping contests at the Des Moines Seni-Om-Sed Carnival.

But wanderlust drew Will and, in March 1902, he sold off his herd of cattle and announced plans to go to South America with the intention of entering the cattle business there. The resulting two-year adventure took Will across the ocean several times and set the stage for his breaking into the entertainment business as a performer.

Will Rogers in school (authors' collection).

As Will later recounted in a Fox Film press release, "I left the ranch down in Oklahoma, Indian Territory, ... and started out to show the world what a cowboy looked like. I had $5,000, representing cattle I'd sold off the ranch."

Will and his friend Dick Parris left from New Orleans on March 19, 1902, on the steamship *Comus.* That began the first of many of Will's unpleasant experiences with boat travel. He wrote, "Our baggage was searched for tobacco and spirits; they did not find any in mine for I don't chew and my spirits had left me on that boat."

In New York, Will and Dick transferred to the SS *Philadelphia* en route to England. After London they made their way on board the *Danube* to stops in Spain, St. Vincent, Brazil and Uruguay before Will and his friend finally arrived in Argentina on May 5, 1902. Parris and Will then traveled 500 miles by train and another 300 miles overland into the interior of Argentina from Buenos Aires. They eventually landed jobs punching cattle on the Pampas but their time with the gauchos did not work out as planned, and Parris returned to the States on May 24. Broke but not despondent, Will sailed on August 5, 1902, for South Africa, tending pack animals en route to the Boer War as payment for his passage on the *Kelvinside.*

Will related his South American experience as follows: "I was sorter itching to show these Gauchos how I could rope and tie down a steer. One day they wanted to catch one to put the brand on him, so I takes down my little manila rope. I even went so far as to pick out the exact spot I was going to lay the steer down. Well, I hadn't even got close enough to start swinging my rope when I heard something go whizzing over my head. A guy running about twenty feet behind me had thrown clear over my head and caught the steer. Why, he could rope a steer better'n I could shoot a guy with a Winchester."

Knowing that his father did not approve of his way of life and was refusing to send Will money with which to return home, Will wrote:

> I never cared for money, only for what pleasure it was to spend it, and I am not afraid of work, and so as I am now I feel better than I ever did in my life, and am in good health, so don't you worry about me because I am not making money. For if I did I would spend it and as long as I dont I cant.... I cannot help it because my nature is not like other people to make money, and I

> dont want you all to think I am no good simply because I dont keep my money. I have less money than lots of you and I dare say I enjoy life better than any of you, and that is my policy. I have always delt honestly with everyone and think the world and all of you and all the folks, and will be among you soon as happy as any one in the world, as then I can work and show the people I am only spending what I make.

Upon arriving in South Africa, Will garnered work on Piccione's horse farm and later drove a herd of mules to Ladysmith, where he found Texas Jack's Wild West Show and Dramatic Company. He applied for a position with the show by showing Texas Jack his skill at roping, executing the Big Crinoline (an 80-foot loop twirled in a great horizontal circle). Texas Jack gave him a job on the spot with the grand salary of $20 per week and a sleeping car in which to bed down. Unbeknownst to Will, Texas Jack had made a standing offer of 50 pounds for anyone who could perform that rope trick. In five years Texas Jack never had a taker. Unfortunately, once Will was an employee, he was no longer eligible for the award. Will was billed as "The Cherokee Kid, the World's Premier Lasso Thrower" and rode and roped his way across South Africa.

Will's own words and wit captured his experience with Texas Jack's show: "There are four of us who ride bucking horses, but I do all the roping and am called the Cherokee Kid on the programs. I have learned quite a bit about fancy roping and it takes fine over here where they know nothing whatsoever about roping."

Will left Texas Jack's show in August 1903, hoping to work his way around the globe and eventually back home. Upon his departure, Texas Jack gave Will a letter of recommendation: "I have the very great pleasure of recommending Mr. W. P. Rogers (The Cherokee Kid) to circus proprietors. He has performed with me during my present South African tour and I consider him to be the champion trick rough rider and lasso thrower of the world. He is sober, industrious, hard working at all times and is always to be relied upon. I shall be very pleased to give him an engagement at any time should he wish to return."

Will often credited Texas Jack with teaching him to develop his roping act for the stage and knowing how to work an audience — always leave them wanting more.

Will then journeyed from South Africa to New Zealand and Australia, where he used Texas Jack's recommendation letter to get a job with the Wirth Brothers Circus, again billed as "The Cherokee Kid." The *Auckland Herald* described Will as a "gentleman with a large American accent and a splendid skill with lassos." Will stayed with Wirth Brothers, playing various engagements in Australia and New Zealand, through the end of 1903 and early 1904 before returning home in April.

Years later, Will looked back upon his first international travels: "I started out first class. Then I traveled second class, then third class. And when I was companion to the she cows, was what might be called no class at all. It took me two years to get enough money to get back home on, and Old Glory sure looked good to me when I sighted it outside of Golden Gate."

Roping and Riding

Well, in five minutes I was opening his show. I dident have time to get scared.

Back home, Will acted on plans to perform with Zach Mulhall's Wild West Show in conjunction with Cummins' Congress of North American Indians at the 1904 St. Louis World's Fair. In preparation for the opening of the fair, Will and the rest of the troupe trained at the Mulhall Ranch in Oklahoma. They spent their time rehearsing rope tricks, rough riding, bronc busting, pony express relay racing and reenacting stagecoach holdups. It was at the Mulhall Ranch that Will met and struck up a lifetime friendship with cowboy, and later western movie star, Tom Mix.

The Vinita *Daily Chieftain* reported on Will's travels: "He had seen a lot of the world but had hardly made his fortune.... Yet he had acquired something else ... a kind of surefootedness ... which comes to a feller who has learned to paddle his own boat."

However, Will's father was less convinced, confiding to friends that "no boy who wasted his time around Wild West circuses could ever amount to anything."

Zach Mulhall's Wild West Show at the St. Louis World's Fair lived up to its name. After the last show one evening, Mulhall and the stable boss got into an argument. They took to shooting at each other as the people were streaming out of the main entrance. For his troubles, Mulhall spent a few days in jail for wounding three people, and his show was barred from the World's Fair.

The unexpected shutdown of Mulhall's Wild West Show contributed to Will's making a move he had been pondering since Texas Jack back in South Africa hinted that Will should consider taking his roping act on stage. Will teamed up with fellow Oklahoman Ted McSpadden and made arrangements to perform roping demonstrations at the Standard Burlesque Theatre in St. Louis. He impressed well-known theater owner Colonel Hopkins enough with his first indoor stage appearance that the colonel wrote a letter to J. J. Murdock, owner of the Chicago Opera House. Murdock responded with an offer for an engagement starting at $30 per week. Will left St. Louis for Chicago on October 16, 1904, but upon arriving discovered his engagement had been canceled. Not savvy to the customs of vaudeville, Will had neglected to send the advance publicity material and photos.

Too stubborn to give up and return empty-handed to St. Louis or Oklahoma, Will pounded the pavement from booking office to vaudeville theater. Upon overhearing the house manager at the Cleveland Theatre trying to find a replacement act over the telephone, Will interrupted and said he had an act and could get it together as quick as he could get back to his hotel room and return with his rope. "Well, in five minutes I was opening his show. I dident have time to get scared," wrote Will.

He played the Cleveland Theatre the rest of the week and finished up just before his twenty-fifth birthday. During one show, a dog from a trained animal act broke loose and scooted across the stage. Instinctively, Will lassoed the dog to the utter delight of the audience. From that experience Will concluded that people wanted him to rope something instead of just performing rope tricks. In time, that fortunate incident led to the development of Will's act with his famous show horse, Teddy (named after President Theodore Roosevelt), and partner Buck McKee.

Will rejoined Zach Mulhall in April 1905 when Mulhall's Wild West Show traveled to New York City to take part in the National Horse Show at Madison Square Garden. Mulhall had been convicted and sentenced to three years in jail for the shooting in St. Louis but was acquitted on appeal. On the way there, Rogers and the Mulhall show participated in an exhibition on the grounds of the White House for President Roosevelt's (a friend of Mulhall's) family.

On April 23, 1905, Will made his New York debut at Madison Square Garden while earning the grand sum of $20 per week as the show's featured roper. Will quickly gained attention in the New York press. One reporter wrote, "Will Rogers, a lariat expert from the Indian Territory, distinguished himself by throwing a rope around the neck of a horse and another rope about the neck of the rider at the same time."

Four days later, Will wrangled even greater press coverage when a steer from a roping act ran wild, leaped over the arena railing and plunged into the spectator stands. As the panicked audience scrambled to get out of the path of the 1,000-pound steer and its 5-foot horns, a flurry of cowboys pursued the steer up the stairs toward the balcony. Will headed the steer off on the other side, coiled his lariat and let it fly, landing it over the steer's horns. The story appeared in the *New York Times* and the *New York Herald*.

Will later recounted the story in vaudeville's *Keith News*, "[T]he steer broke loose, leaped the rail separating the arena from the audience and threw the spectators into a wild panic. A couple of — well, they *said* they were — cowboys tried to lasso the steer, but couldn't do so and it made my blood boil to see their helplessness. I leaped over the rail, snatched a rope. Lassoed the plunging beast and led him back to the arena. Didn't mean to attract so much attention but the next day the papers were full of it."

Several days later, the *New York Times* carried a story of another Mulhall family member involved in a shooting. A local horse dealer received powder burns from a blank cartridge when his groom grabbed one of Zach Mulhall's son's guns from his holster and tried performing some fancy gun-twirling tricks. The six-shooter discharged and caught the horse dealer in the face.

When the show closed its Madison Square Garden run, Will and Zach Mulhall parted company. Will stayed on in New York, determined to make his name on the vaudeville circuit. His little bit of success on stage in Chicago gave him confidence, and the new horse act he had been painstakingly practicing for the indoor stage promised to please the crowds.

Betty Blake

When I roped Betty, that was the star performance of my life.

While Will was beginning his lifelong travels, paying his dues and setting the stage to make his mark on the world, another important set of events in his life also began to

Will Rogers' family at Santa Monica Ranch. *Left to right*: Jimmy, Will, Jr., Mary, Will, and Betty (courtesy Will Rogers Memorial).

take shape. Will had first encountered Betty Blake of Rogers, Arkansas, in the fall of 1900 when she came to Oologah to visit her sister, the wife of the Missouri Pacific Railway station master. While Betty recovered from a severe attack of typhoid fever, her hair had been cut as short as a boy's. One cold evening, as Betty sat in the depot's bay window and watched the train pull in from Kansas City, a young man swung down the steps before the train ground to a complete stop. Betty related their first meeting several years after Will's death in her book, *Will Rogers: His Wife's Story*:

> I think I must have known that it was Will Rogers. He walked briskly into the waiting room and up to the ticket window. My brother-in-law was outside taking care of the baggage, so I hopped down from the telegraph table and stepped to the window to see what the boy wanted. I looked at him and he looked at me, and before I could even ask his business, he turned on his heel and was gone without so much as saying a word.
>
> A moment or so later, my brother-in-law came in with the express packages. One was a banjo addressed to Will Rogers. I knew then that he had come to get it, but had been too shy to ask. I hoped that he would come back, but he didn't. He spent the night at the hotel across the road.
>
> Very early next morning, even before our lamp-lighted breakfast, I heard

> the sound of horse's hoofs on the frozen ground outside. Perhaps I was still thinking about Will Rogers. Anyway, I jumped up from my couch in the sitting room and ran to the window in my nightgown. It was the same boy I had seen the night before. He was on a little dun pony, his overcoat collar turned up against the cold, reins in one hand, a valise in the other, and, absurdly enough a derby hat high on his head.
>
> I watched him ride down the deep-rutted road that ran through the town and out into the prairie. I watched him as far as I could see and until he was out of sight. And then I was sorry that he had not spoken to me at the ticket window, and I wondered how he would ever get his banjo.

Several evenings later, Betty and Will were invited by the parents of one of Betty's friends, Mr. and Mrs. Ellis, to the Ellis Hotel for supper. Will Rogers was back in town, and he had brought all of the latest popular songs from Kansas City. Will was awkward and very quiet during supper but later in the sitting room he took on a new persona. With a roll of music in his lap, Will sang all of the songs he had heard on the stage in Kansas City, including *Hello, My Baby, Hello, My Honey, Hello, My Ragtime Gal.* Over the next few days and weeks, Will and Betty met to sing songs and mingle at social gatherings. "I don't think you would call our meetings there in Oologah incidents in a courtship. We simply became good friends," said Betty.

Betty left Oologah just before Christmas in order to spend the holiday with her family in Rogers, Arkansas. Shortly after the New Year, she received a letter from Will:

> Miss Betty Blake
> Rogers Arkansas
>
> My Dear Friend: No doubt you will be madly surprised on receipt of this epistle but never the less I could not resist the temptation and I hope if you cannot do me the great favor of dropping me a few lines you will at least excuse me for this for I can't help it.
>
> Well I know you are having a great time after being out among the "wild tribes" for so long. Well I have had a great time this Christmas myself. Have not been at home three nights in a month; taken in every Ball in the Territory and everything else I hear of. I was in Ft. Gibson last week to a Masked Ball. I had a time. The Ball came near being a failure, it was managed by Sidney Haygood which accounts for it.
>
> Say you folks never did come out as you said you would and see us "wooly cowboys" rope a steer. I have some pictures of it I think and if you want them I will send them to you if you send me some of those kodak pictures you had up here of yourself and all those girls. Now isn't (?) that a "mammoth inducement for you" to have your picture in a lonely "Indian Wigwam."
>
> I never have had that Swell Ball that we talked of when you were here. But if you had staid we would of had it but you would not stay long enough for us to show you a hot time we were just getting acquainted when you left. If you will only come back up here we will endeavor to do all that we can to make you have a time.
>
> Well, I guess you have an ample sufficiency of nonsense so I will stop. Hoping you will take pity on this poor heart broken Cow pealer and having him rejoicing over these bald prairies on receipt of a few words from you I remain your True Friend and Injun Cowboy.
>
> W. P. Rogers
> Oologah, I. T.

Will had immediately fallen head over heels in love with Betty. While his first letter could be classified as an icebreaker for the shy young man, Will's second letter, dated March 14, 1900, could more properly be called a love letter, Will Rogers–style.

> My Dear Betty,
>
> For me to express my delight for your sweet letter would be utterly impossible so will just put it mildly and say I was *very very* much pleased. I was also surprised for I thought you had forgotten your Cowboy (for I am yours as far as I am concerned).... I ought not to have gotten so broke up over you. But I could not help it so if you do not see fit to answer this please do not say a word about it to anyone for the sake of a broken hearted Cherokee Cowboy....
>
> I am going to Fort Smith sometime soon and, if you will permit, I can probably come up, but I know it would be a slam on your society career to have it known that you ever knew an ignorant Indian cowboy. I still have lots of pretty ponies here and if you will come out I will let you pick the herd. Now, Bettie, please burn this up for my sake. Hoping you will consider what I have told you in my undignified way, and if not, please never say anything about it and burn this up.
>
> I am yours with love.
>
> Will Rogers

Betty and Will met several times over the next few months, but his travels on business for his father, various roping contests and running the ranch kept him busy until he took off for South America with Dick Parris in March 1902. Betty next saw Will in St. Louis at the World's Fair in 1904.

Betty recalled:

> I had come up from my home in Arkansas to visit a sister who lived in St. Louis and to take in the fair. Though I had heard vaguely that Will had returned, I had received no word from him and had no inkling of where he was or what he might be doing. Wandering aimlessly through the Oklahoma State Building at the exposition I heard someone near me mention the name of Will Rogers. An Indian girl was telling her companion that she had seen Will Rogers perform that afternoon at the Cummins Wild West Show on the Pike in the fairgrounds.
>
> I sent Will a note at once. An answer came back almost immediately, inviting me and my sister to a matinee performance of his show the next day, and to dinner afterward.... Finally Will entered the arena for his roping act. To my horror, he was decked out in a very tight-fitting red velvet suit, bespattered with gold braid. He looked so funny, and I was so embarrassed when my sister and Mary [a friend] gave me sidelong glances and smiled at the costume, that I didn't hear the applause or find much joy in Will's expertness with the rope.

Will later told Betty that the gaudy velvet suit was not his regular roping costume. Since Mexican cowboys had invented the first lasso tricks, Will decided to wear the red velvet suit especially in her honor. The suit had been handmade for Will by Mrs. George Wirth of the Wirth Brothers Circus when he performed in Australia under the billing "The Mexican Rope Artist." Will always treasured that suit, but he never wore it again.

Betty and Will saw each other a few more times before Will went to New York with Zach Mulhall to play at the National Horse Show. He sent Betty clippings of his heroic capture of the runaway steer in the stands of Madison Square Garden that led to his vaudeville career.

Breaking into Vaudeville

Swinging a rope isn't so bad, as long as your neck's not in it.

Will Rogers with lariat on the vaudeville circuit (courtesy Will Rogers Memorial).

"I tried about everything to make a living, outside of work. All kinds of writing and play acting, and trying to appear foolish and trying to appear smart."

Armed with the Madison Square Garden steer-roping story, Will set out to convince theater managers to book his horse-roping act. At first, the booking agents and theater managers were incredulous that Will wanted to rope a horse on stage. They insisted that there was not enough room to perform such an act but Will pressed on for nearly a month until he finally got booked for a "supper show" on the Keith Vaudeville Circuit. His New York vaudeville debut took place on June 11, 1905, at Keith's Union Square Theatre. Rogers was booked for a single act, but the audience liked his novel act so well he finished out the week at a salary of $75. Will originally teamed up with Jim Minnick riding the horse while Will roped. Minnick eventually returned to his Texas ranch, and Buck McKee took over the riding duties.

Will broke into Hammerstein's

Teddy, Buck McKee and Will Rogers in vaudeville (courtesy Will Rogers Memorial).

Paradise Roof Garden, one of New York's leading vaudeville houses, following the Keith performances. He received sixth billing out of eleven acts and a large salary raise to $140 per week. Will and Teddy rode the elevator to reach the roof.

When the curtain rose, the audience found Will sitting on his horse dressed in chaps, a colored shirt and a small hat. He started out with some simple rope tricks, leading into lassoing Teddy by all four feet, and closed his act to roaring applause with perfect execution of the Big Crinoline, the same trick roping that had won him the job with Texas Jack in South Africa.

At first, Will kept his "dumb act" simple. He gradually improved it while he honed his showmanship. He added his own musical score of western tunes, purchased a beautiful dark blue blanket for Teddy with a gold border framing "Will Rogers" in gold lettering and inserted new roping tricks into his act after hours of practice.

However, the major addition to Will's act (and the key to his future success) came about accidentally. During one of these early vaudeville appearances, another performer suggested to Will that he announce his difficult catches prior to beginning them. He took the advice and the rest, as they say, is history. When Will started to speak with his halting, southwestern drawl, the crowd broke up laughing. At first, Will felt hurt at being laughed at since he didn't think he had said anything funny. "It's one thing to have your jokes laughed at but another to be laughed at yourself," reasoned Will.

Fortunately, he was convinced to keep his homespun monologue in the act. He later explained his success: "We were pretty good, and I didn't know enough to act and the people sorter liked it." Here are some examples of Will's musings that delighted audiences:

"Ladies and gentlemen, I want to call your sho nuff attention to this next little stunt I am going to pull on you, as I am going to throw about two o' these ropes at once, catching the horse with one and the rider with the other. I don't have any idea I'll get it, but here goes."

Will Rogers spinning the Big Crinoline in vaudeville (courtesy Will Rogers Memorial).

"Out West where I come from, they won't let me play with this rope, afraid I might hurt myself."

"That's one thing I must say for this ferocious animal. He was never much for sticking his neck into things."

"Now this is much easier to do on a blind horse … those dont see the rope coming."

"Well, I got all my feet through … but one."

"They may call me a rube, but I'd a lot rather be the man who bought the Brooklyn Bridge than the one who sold it."

"I am just an old country boy in a big town trying to get along. I have been eating pretty regular and the reason I have been is because I have stayed an old country boy."

Will had broken through. He was promptly booked for stints in Boston, Cleveland, Detroit, Newark, Philadelphia, Rochester, Toledo and Washington, D.C. He signed contracts with a variety of vaudeville circuits and theaters, including Chase's, B. F. Hyde & Behman, the Grand Opera House, Keith's, the Maryland Theatre, B. A. Myers, Moore, William Morris, the Palace Theatre, F. F. Proctor, the Trent Theatre and Percy Williams.

In October 1905, he wrote to his sisters from Toledo, Ohio, "I am the headliner on the main squeeze here this week." At Chase's in Washington, D.C., the program listed Will's act as "King of the Lariat on Plains and Cattle Trail, assisted by Buck McKee, ex-sheriff of Pawnee Co., Oklahoma and favorite bronco, in a marvelous exhibition of skill and dexterity." By the time he reached Keith's Theatre in Providence, Rhode Island, in late November, Will commanded a salary of $250 per week. The November 20, 1905, Providence *Keith News* wrote:

> Perhaps the most interesting entertainer we anticipate presenting this season is Will Rogers, known as "The Lariat King." Rogers is at once a character compelling admiration by his skill with the lasso and mirth by his quaint humor.… Will Rogers … is now drawing a big salary at the leading vaudeville houses and is admittedly the most popular novelty of the season.… From the time he was two years old, Rogers says he used to "rope" his mother's turkeys out on the ranch, and prairie dogs and other things not meant to be lassoed.… His feats of rope throwing are truly extraordinary, especially the throwing of two lassoes at the same time — one with each hand — but the young man's unique individuality is no small feature of his success.

During this time on the road, Will formed his wariness of talking to reporters. "They ask you a few questions and then put it down to suit themselves.… I have observed that any time a reporter takes down notes, it's just to show how different they can write a thing in the article from what you told them."

Will plied the vaudeville circuit but looked with envy at the New Amsterdam Theatre in New York City, where Florenz Ziegfeld regularly turned the theatrical world on end with his lavish productions. One night, as Will and a friend walked along the street, the friend predicted, "One of these days your name will be up on that marquee in lights of 100-candle power each."

To which Will replied, "Quit kiddin. There's ten letters in my name and that would take 1,000-candle power. There ain't that much candle power in the whole doggone State of Oklahoma."

The successful domestic tour drew considerable interest abroad, and Will boarded the SS *Philadelphia* on March 17, 1906, for a four-week engagement at the Winter Garden in Berlin, Europe's premier vaudeville theater, for a fee of $3,700. Teddy and Buck McKee had already departed on an earlier boat.

Will recounted a humorous incident that occurred while he was on stage in Berlin: "In the theatres in Germany there's a fireman stands right in the wings on duty, and you have to climb over him to get on or off the stage. So one night I thought it would be a big laugh if I roped him and pulled him on stage. So I did. Say, there was 'most a panic! I had interfered with his dignified position. They liked to have called out the whole army. They were going to invade me like they did Belgium. The manager had to come out and tell 'em that my rope slipped. In America I have done that stunt, and it's a yell. But in Germany they have cultivated everything they got but their humor."

After the Berlin stint, they played vaudeville houses in London and Paris. While in London, the Ranelagh Club invited them out for a special performance with King Edward VII in attendance. The club presented Will with a beautiful silver cup for his lassoing feats and his splendid exhibition of trick riding. In the span of a little more than a year, Will went from pounding the pavement to secure vaudeville bookings to playing before European royalty.

Will returned to the United States via Austria and Italy, landing in New York City on July 4, 1906, and making his way to Oklahoma a few days later with the intention of renewing his acquaintance with Betty Blake.

Betty recalled their awkward reunion:

> His theatrical success hadn't changed him a bit. He was still bashful ... he had come up to Vinita on an early-morning train to meet me, it happened that the chair next to mine was occupied. Will reached over, shook hands and then found a seat for himself far ahead in the crowded coach. And that was the way we finished the journey.... Will was very elusive during the busy days Maude and Sallie [Will's sisters] had planned for us. We took horseback rides around the country. Parties and dinners were given. But half of the time Will wouldn't go, and if he did, he never looked in my direction or singled me out.... He never came around where I was unless we were playing and singing at the piano. I just could not understand him.... So far as Will was concerned, I was a baffled young lady when I left for home. But I had not been home more than a week, I believe, when he came by on his way to New York, with the idea that we should get married at once.
>
> Will had a good season booked for the fall and winter, and was proud of his success in the theater. He had no intention of giving up his stage career and settling down at home. But from my point of view, show business was not a very stable occupation.... And I simply could not see a life of trouping the country in vaudeville. Will could not understand my attitude. Our parting was a sad one, but we promised to write.

Will returned to the vaudeville circuit and continued to fine-tune his act. He added new rope tricks and inserted some monologue material about the acts that preceded him and his rope tricks.

In April 1907, Will returned to Europe with a Wild West act he had put together. The troupe consisted of Will, Buck McKee, two other cowboys, Teddy and three ponies. They played the Palace Theatre in London and other engagements in England, but the act proved a big disappointment. Will and McKee had to resort to performing their regular roping act around the provinces in order to pay the return passage for the performers and horses. Disappointed but not yet ready to give up on his entertainment career, Will once again returned to the American vaudeville circuit, playing most of the major vaudeville houses across the nation.

His June 1907 contract with the William Morris Agency specified, "It is understood that during this engagement the cost of railroad fares from town to town will not average more than five dollars per week for each person. It is also understood that if the party of the second part [Will Rogers] plays west of Chicago during this engagement, the fares from Chicago and back to Chicago are to be paid by the party of the first part [William Morris Agency]."

That same year also marked Will's debut on the stage in the musical *The Girl Rangers*. The George W. Lederer production sported a western theme, and the producers hired Will to appear between scenes and perform his roping specialty. *The Girl Rangers* opened in Chicago on September 1, 1907, and played there four weeks before moving to Philadelphia's Walnut Street Theatre in October. Will left the show during the third week of October and returned to the vaudeville circuit.

All during this time, Will relentlessly pursued Betty Blake through his letters and occasional visits back to Oklahoma. On one visit, Will confided to Betty that "the same old show afternoon and night was growing monotonous, and that trouping around the country was losing its interest."

The financial panic of 1907 was also settling in and hit the vaudeville business hard. From Philadelphia, Will wrote, "I am headlined ... this week.... I have not got a cent of that $1,275 yet and don't think I will."

Despite the periodic financial problems and discouraging times from being on the road so long, Will had to be buoyed by the favorable critical reviews and packed audiences, proving that audiences and critics alike considered Will a hit.

Dateline: Philadelphia: "Will Rogers and his company ... proved the feature of this week's bill."

Dateline: Newark: "Business has been on the increase for the past several weeks.... Will Rogers, with his lariat throwing, a pleasing novelty."

Dateline: Baltimore: "Will Rogers is the extra attraction and helps to pack the house."

Dateline: New York City: "Will Rogers always contributes fifteen minutes of real enjoyment. His rope work is well done and liked. The audience took to Mr. Rogers just as quickly as they did to his lassoing.... Rogers' incidental remarks are fresh and breezy as can be and the act runs along entertainly. Rogers affects not to take himself seriously, and therein lies the novelty of his attitude."

Dateline: Toronto: "Large audiences were pleased with the excellent bill offered during the week.... A special feature was Will Rogers with his lariat and pony."

Will had to abruptly leave his March 1908 engagement in New Haven, Connecticut, after receiving a telegram notifying him of his father's serious illness. The Five Cliftons were substituted on the bill. Clem Rogers eventually recovered, and Will returned to his remaining vaudeville engagements. His act was getting so popular his agent was able to book one vaudeville engagement after another. His only breaks between bookings occurred due to miscommunications or changes in the vaudeville houses themselves. In

May 1908, Will wrote, "I do believe I will have to lay off … there is a hitch some place 'cause Scranton, Pa. where I was booked is to change for the summer and play stock instead of vaudeville.... If I should lay off I will be in N.Y. … my address will be care of White Rats Club."

For once Will's agent booked him for a vaudeville tour west of Chicago. He made a wide-ranging trip from late May through the end of August 1908 that included performances at Winnipeg, Duluth, Butte, Spokane, Seattle, Tacoma, Portland, Sacramento, San Francisco and Oakland before jumping back on the Keith Vaudeville Circuit once again on September 7 in Detroit.

During the western tour, Will stopped for a visit at Yellowstone before showing up two days late for his appearance in Butte, Montana. From Yellowstone he wrote to Betty Blake, "[S]tayed at the Big Canyon Hotel, the first and only guest.... I had the whole hotel to myself. They even had the orchestra to play while I was in a dining room."

Several days later he wrote about Butte, "[T]hey just throw the keys to all the places away and never close up … this is the dirtiest—gamblingest corrupt town on earth … in the last town I played [Butte], where I missed two days on account of going by the Park, the Manager on Fri. when I left paid me in full and did not take out a cent."

Will turned twenty-nine on November 4, 1908, and headed for Rogers, Arkansas, to continue his pursuit of Betty Blake. His letters to her had grown more frequent and were often accompanied by gifts of books, gloves and hosiery.

Betty recounted his arrival:

> Then one day early in November, 1908, he arrived in Rogers without any forewarning to announce flatly that he was going to take me back to New York with him.... Will had to play a few weeks' engagements in the East, and then, in early spring he was booked for a tour on the Orpheum Circuit. This would be our honeymoon, he said. I had never been East, and Will wanted me to see New York. And the prospect, afterward, of a tour of the Pacific Coast sounded very nice indeed. As for my scruples about show business, there was a most definite promise that, once this tour was finished, we would settle down in the house his father had given him in Claremore. In two weeks we were married. The ceremony was performed at my mother's home, November 25, 1908 … performed by Doctor Bailey, a close friend of ours and pastor of the little Congregational Church.... We drove down the muddy, deep-rutted street in a carriage and found the whole town gathered on the station platform to bid us goodbye with rice and cheers.

En route to New York, Will and Betty stopped off in St. Louis to watch the Carlisle Indians defeat St. Louis University 17–0. After Thanksgiving dinner in the Planters Hotel, where Betty sipped her first champagne, they went to see Maude Adams appearing in *What Every Woman Knows* at the Olympic Theatre. Before the curtain rose, Betty began to feel strange. Will led her out of the theater and walked her back to the hotel.

"I didn't understand until afterward, when Will explained that he had wondered during dinner just what sort of a girl he had married. From the way I drank champagne … he had decided champagne-drinking must be an old Arkansas custom," said Betty.

Will and Betty were made for each other. Although Betty didn't relish all of the traveling and staying in cheap hotels, she and Will enjoyed touring all of the sights along the way. One of Betty's great thrills was seeing Enrico Caruso perform in New York City.

Years later, Will described his first opera experience at a dinner speaking engagement:

> Well, the wife said I had to put on my wedding suit, that spoiled it even if it had been a good show. I had to crawl into that Montgomery Ward. We were living just across the street from the Met, at the Albany Hotel, but she said everyone went in a cab to the opera so we got a cab and crossed the street. My wife was right about the cab, we should of kept it till we found our seats. I dident know a seat could be so far away and still be in the same theatre, we could just see the drummer, my wife was worried about how we could tell Caruso and I told her he would be the fellow that sings, my lord thats all all of them did. My wife wanted to know who was in the boxes, I dident know but they all looked about as miserable as we did. Well, we stuck it out till intermission and then I went up to Hammersteins to see the three Keatons and a good show.

Near the end of the tour, Will and Betty began to make plans for their home in Claremore. However, as the tour wound up, an offer came to play the Percy Williams' vaudeville houses in the East at a much higher salary than Will had previously been paid. After much soul searching, Betty agreed that the offer should be accepted and their return to Claremore postponed — forever. Betty realized that this was to be her life with Will and accepted it in stride.

Will aptly summed up his marriage to Betty, "When I roped Betty, that was the star performance of my life."

Ever the experimenter, Will hired Goldie St. Clair, who had just won the woman's bucking-horse championship at the Cheyenne Frontier Days Rodeo, and several other female roping and riding performers. According to Betty, this is when Will really started to speak in his act, keeping up a continual patter about the women and the feats they were performing. Ironically, at the same time, one of the theater managers told Betty, "Why does Will carry all those horses and people around with him? I would rather have Will Rogers alone than that whole bunch put together."

That settled the matter for Will. Performing as a single would eliminate the need to work out new routines, purchase elaborate costumes, take care of and transport horses and have others on his payroll. Within months, Will went back to the original act with which he had started, just his rope and himself, but this time he talked during his routine. Quips such as, "I've got enough jokes for one miss. I've either got to practice roping or learn more jokes," "It's a pretty good trick when I do it good" and "I got it good the other night. You should have been here then" endeared Will to the audience. But even more than the gag, it was Will's way of speaking, his delivery, unique mannerisms and innate sense of timing that proved to be the real key to his success.

About this time, Will's trademark chewing gum joined the act. Will had picked up the chewing habit from his days of playing baseball (a common pastime of vaudeville performers) in between acts. One day he inadvertently walked on stage with a big wad of gum still in his mouth. Seeing the cowboy chewing away, the crowd broke into laughter. Embarrassed, Will removed the gum from his mouth and stuck it onto the proscenium arch, making the crowd roar even more. Will was a quick learner. Laughs did not have to happen twice before he figured out the reason why and kept a certain piece in his act. From then on, he often used chewing gum as a prop. Missing a rope trick on purpose, he would ceremoniously park the gum somewhere on stage and then perform the trick perfectly before retrieving his gum and popping it back into his mouth.

He even used chewing gum to good advantage to promote his brand of humor. "If it wasn't for chewing gum, Americans would wear their teeth off just hitting them against each other. Every scientist has been figuring out who the different races descend from. I don't know about the other tribes, but I do know that the American race descended from the cow. And Wrigley was smart enough to furnish the cud. He made the whole world chew for democracy.... I have chewed more gum than any living man. My act on the stage depended on the grade of gum I chewed. Lots of my readers have seen me and perhaps noted the poor quality of my jokes on that particular night. Now I was not personally responsible for that. I just happened to hit on a poor piece of gum.... Chewing gum is the only ingredient of our national life of which no one knows of what it is made.... Maybe it's better that way."

Another change to Will's act grew out of the lifelong friendship he and Fred Stone had struck up during the early vaudeville years. Whenever the two happened to be playing in the same city, they would meet for breakfast. Will taught Fred many new rope tricks, and Fred returned the favor by teaching Will dance steps. As a result, Will incorporated an imitation of Fred's rope dance from *The Old Town* into his act, using Fred's music, *I Am a Cowboy with Gun and Lariat. Variety* hailed Will's new talent: "Rogers is a surprise when he starts dancing, and gets away with it big."

Will explained his longtime friendship with Fred Stone in one of his weekly columns. "Fred Stone ... got as far as the Fourth Reader, while I only reached the Third. So that is why I think we always hit it off together so well, neither was liable to use a word which the other couldn't understand."

Although Betty and Will kept to themselves while working and traveling the vaudeville circuit, Will established some strong friendships with fellow performers. Besides Fred Stone, Will became good friends with Eddie Cantor, Mike Donlon, Louise Dresser, Chick Sale and a man billed as "The Greatest of Tramp Jugglers on Earth," W. C. Fields.

The June 24, 1911, issue of *Variety* reported that Will Rogers earned the honor of being only the second act in history that had been held over for another week's run at the Majestic Theatre in Chicago. "Will Rogers, whom the management thought worthy of a two weeks engagement, went better than he did last week. Rogers is a relief from the conventional comedy single. His talk is made doubly valuable through his peculiar delivery, and it never fails to bring the desired laugh."

When Will decided to introduce new material he broke it in this way. "I've been getting away with this junk for so long that I thought you would get wise to me sooner or later, so I went and dug up a little new stuff with which to bunk you for a few more years."

Will's success finally won over his father. Once, Clem brought his daughters, Maude and Sallie, to Washington for a week to see Will perform. Clem attended every performance and stood out front after the show to listen in on what people were saying about Will's act. If they questioned whether or not Will was a real cowboy, Clem would step up and say, "Sure he's a real cowboy and from Oklahoma, too." Then he would introduce himself as Will's father and offer to introduce the people to Will. When Will emerged from the stage door he inevitably found Clem surrounded by a crowd waiting to meet him.

Will knew that he was an embarrassment to his father in his younger years and liked to tell the story that one of Clem's cohorts had once visited New York and had seen Will's act in vaudeville. When the old-timer returned to Claremore, the rest of Clem's friends asked what young Willie was doing, to which he replied, "Oh, just acting the fool like he used to do around here."

On October 20, 1911, Betty gave birth to their first son, William Vann Rogers (Will, Jr.). Proud grandfather Clem sent three pairs of black wool baby stockings and a tiny pair of beaded Indian moccasins. Moments after they opened the package, a telegram arrived informing Betty and Will of Clem's death on October 29.

The following spring marked Will's first appearance in a Broadway production, a musical called *The Wall Stree*t *Girl*, featuring Blanche Ring. Just as in his 1907 tour with *The Girl Rangers*, Will's role consisted of standing on stage during the scenery change and performing his act. His self-consciousness showed through when he spoke of his act and the difference charged for theater versus vaudeville tickets: "I knew it was all right at fifty cents, but I was a little afraid of it at two dollars." Despite Will's reservations, he won rave reviews.

The Wall Street Girl opened on April 1, 1912, at George M. Cohan's Theatre in New York City. The *New York Times* reported, "There were two high spots ... Blanche Ring ... and the other was that extraordinary lariat performer Will Rogers, who did his regular vaudeville act, but who undoubtedly scored the success of the evening, doing things with ropes and conversing in his quaint way with the audience ... ending with his imitation of Eddie Foy." Acton Davies of the *Evening Sun* wrote, "There was a poet with his lariat who had come out of the West and inserted himself right in the middle of the play who was worth his weight in gold to the management. His specialty, to which Miss Ring wisely gave plenty of rope, was really one of the cleverest exhibitions of lariat throwing which this town has seen."

The June 1912 issue of *Munsey Magazine* also praised Will's performance in *The Wall Street Girl:* "Will Rogers was recruited to the cast from vaudeville, as Lariat Bill, and he appears in the Reno scene without one dissenting voice to protest his breaking up the plot. What he does with a rope you wouldn't believe unless you saw it for yourself, so there is no use in my telling you about it. I can imagine his making good even without his rope, for his slow, drawling way of throwing in his humorous comments on his work, on the show itself, and on politics, gives a unique character to his act. He possesses the same offhand, perfectly-at-home-on-the-stage air as Miss Ring herself."

The opening night of *The Wall Street Girl* was accompanied by tragedy. A murmur went through the theater and people abruptly got up to leave. Will came on stage and, interrupting the regular action of the play, announced that the *Titanic* had sunk. The next week Will, Blanche Ring, George M. Cohan, Fannie Brice and Eddie Foy were among the performers on the program for the Titanic Relief Benefit. Despite the tragic opening, *The Wall Street Girl* experienced a good New York run.

After a summer break, the show went on a seven-month national tour. By this time, Will had top billing, after Blanche Ring, along with a speaking part and two musical numbers in the production. The tour ended in April, and Betty gave birth to their second child, Mary Amelia Rogers, on May 18, 1913. Will reported, "I got the wire and went on stage for my matinee and told 'em about you."

Left to right: Will Rogers, Jr., Betty Rogers, Will Rogers, Mary Rogers, Jimmy Rogers (courtesy Will Rogers Memorial).

In May 1914, Will and Betty traveled to Europe aboard the luxurious German liner *Vaterland,* making its return trip to Europe after its maiden voyage. The vacation, booked to be strictly pleasurable, changed upon the Rogerses' arrival in London. Sir Alfred Butt convinced Will to perform at his Empire Theater in the revue *The Merry-Go-Round.* Will tried to beg off because the converted music hall's layout was not conducive to Will's talking act. He reluctantly agreed to do one show but would not accept a salary unless the show went over well. To Will's surprise, the show was a success and ran for a month while Betty toured Europe with a friend. Sir Alfred wanted Will to extend his engagement even longer, but the rumors of war convinced Will that he and Betty should set sail for America. By the time they docked in New York aboard another German liner, the *Imperator,* newspapers carried reports of the hostilities in Europe already under way.

Will and Betty settled in Amityville, New York, across the road from Fred Stone, while Will worked the vaudeville circuit. Their third child, James Blake Rogers, arrived on July 25, 1915. That summer, Will suffered an accident while diving with Rex Beach. Will hit his head on the bottom of the ocean and for weeks could not rope with his right arm. In order to protect his theater bookings, Will painstakingly learned how to perform roping feats with his left arm. After his right arm healed, Will delighted audiences by spinning lariats with both hands.

The Ziegfeld Frolic/*Ziegfeld* Follies

Ziegfeld took Michaelangelo's statues, took some of the fat off them with a diet of lamb chops and pineapples, and he and a Confederate named Ben Ali Hagen brought the statues to life, only with better figures, and the only marble about them was from the ears north.

Will interspersed his 1915 vaudeville engagements with appearances in two Broadway productions, Shubert's *Hands Up* and Ned Wayburn's *Town Topics.* The crowds enthusiastically greeted Will, but both productions proved short-lived. However, Will attracted the attention of Florenz Ziegfeld, Jr.'s right-hand man, Gene Buck, during the run of *Hands Up.* Buck strongly believed that Will's considerable roping talent and cowboy humor would play well with the affluent businessmen and members of the cabaret society who frequented the *Frolic.*

Since 1907, the flamboyant Ziegfeld had developed the reputation of "The Great Glorifier," staging elaborate productions featuring a wealth of discreetly semi-clothed, beautiful, hometown American girls. Ziegfeld's *Midnight Frolic* specialized in providing late-night entertainment filled with delicious food, glamorous showgirls, variety acts and a live orchestra. The *Frolic* represented the most lavish, popular nightclub scene in New York City.

Over Ziegfeld's better judgment, Buck convinced him to hire the cowboy for Ziegfeld's *Midnight Frolic* at the aerial gardens on the roof of the New Amsterdam Theatre. Will debuted as part of the *Frolic*'s revue, *Just Girls,* on August 23, 1915. After Ziegfeld observed Rogers' *Frolic* performance and the crowd's less-than-enthusiastic response, he ordered Buck, "That damn cowboy has to go."

Ziegfeld left town for several weeks, and Buck let Rogers convince him that inserting new material into his act would capture the attention of the repeaters. Betty gets credit for suggesting to Will that he develop new material for his act from the papers he devoured every day. Will's country charm and wit proved to be perfect for the sophisticated audience and luxurious setting. By September 1915, the *New York Times* wrote about the rooftop New Amsterdam *Frolic*, "Will Rogers is the chief source of entertainment."

Will's shaky 1915 beginning with Ziegfeld began a professional relationship and personal friendship that would last for many years and change Will Rogers' life forever. At age 36, Will Rogers finally broke into the big time, ending years of being pigeonholed as a supporting vaudeville act. The year also marked another fateful event: Will took his first airplane flight at Atlantic City, New Jersey, and began his lifelong fascination with flying.

Will's use of the news allowed him to show off his wit, hitting upon topics and concerns of the day. Likewise, the *Frolic* itself and its audience were fair game to be targets of Will's barbs. He would find out the names of prominent public figures sitting in the audience and pry any and all information about the person from anyone he could find in and around the theater, from other performers to the doormen and taxi drivers. During his monologue he would slyly slip in bits of information about the person and then highlight the person either by a spotlight or by lassoing him from the stage. It never failed to cause an uproar of laughter from the rest of the crowd. It got to the point that you weren't "somebody" unless Will singled you out during one of his performances. At times, he would put the spotlight on someone of distinction in the audience, pause, and then go on without saying a word about the person, to the utter delight of everyone else.

In an interview reported in the October 3, 1915, issue of the *New York Times*, Will modestly described his act: "I don't know how I get by. I often think it's because they take pity on me. Each year I think they'll get next to me, and when they don't I am surprised. Until they do I'll keep at it, and when they've had enough I'll go back to my little ranch in Oklahoma."

When asked if he wrote his own material, Will responded, "It ain't written. I just get out there and trust to luck, after figuring out something I think will go. But half the time I don't know what I'm going to say or what I'm saying. Sometimes I get twisted and then again I spring something that makes 'em laugh and I remember it and use it again. But mostly I trust to luck and figure that something will happen."

Will did reveal the sources of some of his material: "Most people and actors appearing on the stage have some writer to write their material but Congress is good enough for me.... Why, I just watch Congress and report the facts.... They are the professional joke makers. I could study all my life and not think up half the amount of funny things they can think of in one session of Congress.... Compared to them I'm an amateur.... My little jokes don't hurt nobody, but when Congress makes a joke, it's a law. When they make a law, it's a joke....

"The papers write it, all I do is get all the papers I can carry, and then read all that is going on. I have found that the more up-to-date a subject is, the more credit you get for talking on it. The remarks you make must be found on facts. You can exaggerate and

Will with Ziegfeld *Follies* girl Annette Bade (courtesy Will Rogers Memorial).

make it ridiculous, but it must have the plain facts in it. Then you will hear the audience say: 'Well that's pretty near right.'" When complimented on his previous night's performance, Will demurred, "You caught me right. I went big last night, better than I knew how, but I don't mind telling you it ain't like that every night."

In reality, Will worked very hard in preparing for his act. He was a natural at reading the news and realizing what would hit home with the audience. Behind his opening line, "All I know is what I read in the newspapers," were hours and hours of reading and analysis. Will Rogers was the ultimate showman.

The following example illustrates his ingenuity. He used to arrive at the vaudeville houses carrying a number of cases containing musical instruments. He would walk on stage and place his banjo and other musical instruments on a table in full view of the audience and then proceed to perform his rope tricks. At the end of his act he would gather up the instruments and walk off stage—leaving the audience in fits.

Will simply said, "That was why I carried them."

Of the Ziegfeld *Midnight Frolic* dancers, Will wrote, "We had the most beautiful girls that Ziegfeld ever put on, for the beautiful ones wouldent work in the *Follies;* they wouldent work at a matinee, for they never got up that early. We used to have a time getting 'em up for the midnight show. I dident mean I did. I dident have to go round waking any of 'em up, but somebody did.... You know this fellow knows just how to drape 'em so you don't know just whether they have or have not."

Rogers frequently mixed political and topical conversation into his act. When Henry Ford initiated a pacifist movement and sent the Peace Ship to try to stop the World War, Will quipped, "If Mr. Ford had taken this bunch of girls in this show, and let 'em wear the same costumes they wear here, and marched them down between the trenches, believe me, the boys would have been out before Christmas!"

Will's appearance at the *Frolic* created a stir among New York City vaudeville house managers, and they banned him "forever and ever" from performing in their vaudeville houses for his desertion to the ranks of cabaret-style, swank nightclubs. Within a week, the theater managers dropped the ban, but by then Will was on his way to greater show business challenges. The March 1, 1916, issue of the *New York Times* carried an article about Will under the headline, "The Laughable Mr. Rogers: He of the Rope Is Welcomed Back to Vaudeville." The article went on to say, "Equipped with his rope, his chewing gum, his grin, and his sense of humor, the inimitable Will Rogers has returned to vaudeville. When, by making a little appearance on the side ... he incurred the displeasure of vaudeville he was banished therefrom for ever and ever, but his stock has been rising steadily ever since, and the two-a-day quickly forgives any one it covets."

In the spring of 1916, Will gave one of his most nerve-wracking performances. As part of an all-star show put on by the Friars Club, Will performed in front of the president of the United States, Woodrow Wilson. Upon President Wilson's death years later, Will wrote in his column about his nervousness before the performance because he had never heard of a president personally being the brunt of jokes in a public theater. Will was also honestly concerned about the weight of the problems on President Wilson's shoulders with the war in Europe and other national troubles. However, Will's nervousness vanished when he saw the typically reserved president laughing along with everyone else at his jokes:

"There is some talk of our getting a machine gun … if we can borrow one."

"We're going to have an army of 250,000 men. Mister Ford makes 300,000 cars a year. I think, Mr. President, we ought to have a man in every car."

"I see the President made another speech the other day. Suppose some guy will come along now and misunderstand him. It must be awful hard for a smart man like the President to make a speech in such a way that the bonehead and highbrow will both get what he means."

"I see where they have captured Villa. Yes, they got him in the morning editions and then the afternoon ones let him get away.... Villa raided Columbus, New Mexico. We had a guard that night at the post. But to show you how crooked this Villa was, he sneaked up on the opposite side.... We chased him over the line five miles, but run into a lot of government red tape and had to come back."

Despite his jokes, Will took the war seriously and in March and April 1916 presided over two benefits for War Aid that raised $20,000 at the Hippodrome in New York City. He also appeared in a benefit performance to raise money for the Permanent Blind Relief War Fund. Will further exhibited his generosity when he pledged ten percent of his salary to the Red Cross until the end of the war.

After months of Will's successful performances at the *Frolic,* Ziegfeld cunningly decided to capitalize on Will's growing popularity and asked Will to join the *Follies.* However, Will and Betty felt the pay was too low and did not like the prospect of hitting the road once again when the *Follies* went on tour.

Betty and Will attended the opening night of the *Ziegfeld Follies of 1916.* After one top-heavy number after another failed to liven up the audience, Will began to regret his and Betty's decision not to join the production. He knew he could have helped pick up the pace. Throughout the night, Will murmured to Betty, "See Blake, what did I tell you.... This was my big chance.... Boy, I wish I could have got my crack at it." By the time Will and Betty reached home that evening, they were feeling down in the dumps at the missed opportunity.

A few days later, Ziegfeld called Will and asked him to come down to the theater. They arranged that Will would come to the show that night and walk on stage without any announcement whatsoever. At the time, no mention was made of salary. When Ziegfeld came to Will's dressing room to discuss salary, he offered $600 a week for the first year and $750 for the second year, doubling Will's salary over that time frame. Will and Betty had expected to be paid $500 a week.

When Ziegfeld suggested that Will come to his office the next day to sign the contract, Will countered with, "I don't like contracts.... My word is good and the other feller's ought to be, too." For all the years that Will worked for Ziegfeld that informal gentlemen's agreement stood without the need for a signed contract.

The *New York Times* commented, "That cowboy wag, Will Rogers, has tiptoed into the cast since the opening night and entrenched himself firmly." Will had moved from the status of star performer to being a celebrity in his own right before his thirty-seventh birthday. Will played the *Follies* in New York and on tour through 1916, 1917 and 1918 as well as appearing in the *Frolic* when he was in New York City.

The *New York Times* ran a big spread on Will on July 1, 1917:

> Will Rogers has reached the goal of the imitated, and now almost every impersonator's equipment includes a few yards of rope and chewing gum as surely as it does a Cohan cane and derby.... Mr. Rogers is nothing if not individual. He is also American to the grass roots, the most American of comedians, in fact, since through his veins courses Cherokee Indian blood.... It is because Mr. Rogers is these things and highly intelligent besides, that he occupies the unique position of being the world's only cowboy comedian.... Mr. Rogers is not an actor; when he slouches out on the stage, grinning, savagely chewing gum, and giving his nose a furtive rub with the back of his hand he is not acting, but merely being himself. And the things he says are not the jokes of some author retained to supply him with fresh material but his own observations on the human comedy.

Will broke into the journalism world with an article he wrote titled, "The Extemporaneous Line," which appeared in the July 1917 issue of *Theatre* magazine. Like his act, the article was filled with plenty of Rogerisms:

> How did you get on the stage? Say, anybody can get on the stage. Its keeping them off that's hard. A fellow can be the champion soup eater and if he can locate a manager that will set him up behind a bowl, and tell him to go to it—if he can keep the audience amused—why he's on the stage.... I start in on a subject and if it is no good then I have to switch quick and lots of times when I come off of the stage I have done an entirely different act from what I intended when I went on. Sometimes an audience is not so good and my stuff that night may not be very good, so it is then you see the old ropes commence to do something. It gets their mind off the bum stuff I am telling them and as I often say to the folks in the show, I reach away back in my hip pocket and dig up a sure fire gag, as I always try to save some of my best gags—just like a prohibition State man will his last drink.

The October 1917 issue of *Everybody's Magazine* described Will Rogers as the "unique personality on Broadway." Discussing his route to a successful Broadway career, Rogers said, "Well, I was born, of course: you've got to be born; that's about the only thing you have to do to get on the stage.... I was born the year after all the cattle had died from the blizzard in our country, and any old longhorn out there can tell you when that was.... I knew my grammar was not big league stuff; but I'd always figured out that just as long as I dident try to spell the words I used, I'd get by.... Mr. Ziegfeld once told me I was getting to be too much of a socialist—'all talk and no work'—that night there was more of the rope.... If I can keep on my friendly relations with the audience and not have them suffer, I will stick to my job on what is in the newspaper, and not try to put over any outside propaganda."

Ziegfeld had a knack for attracting the best entertainment talent and the most beautiful women around. With talented choreographer Ned Wayburn, he put together dazzling shows that featured the likes of Billie Burke (Ziegfeld's second wife), Ina Claire, Marion Davies, Anna Held (brought over from London), Billie Dove, Ruth Etting, Marilyn Miller, Ann Pennington and Mae Murray; many of whom went on to spectacular movie careers. Many a talented comedian also earned their spurs on the *Follies* stage. Along with Will Rogers, Fanny Brice, Eddie Cantor, Leon Errol, W. C. Fields, Frank Tinney, Bert Williams and Ed Wynn all delighted audiences and developed a national following during their years with the *Follies.*

Will Rogers with *Follies* girls (courtesy Will Rogers Memorial).

Ziegfeld spared no expense in putting on his extravaganzas. He spent large sums of money on intricate set designs, lighting effects, stunning costumes, elaborate choreography and rousing chorus numbers. He hired the nation's best songwriters, including Irving Berlin, Jerome Kern and Victor Herbert, to capture the perfect *Follies* mood. *Shine On, Harvest Moon* and *Second Hand Rose* are just two of many *Follies* songs that grew into national favorites. Will Rogers, the shy cowboy, provided the perfect counterpoint for the flashy showgirls and elaborate production numbers. Song sheets from the 1919, 1920 and 1921 *Follies* hint at the elaborate costumes and "glorification of the American girl" that Ziegfeld successfully attained.

Will spent his time at the *Follies* roping chorus girls and honing his delivery of well-crafted comments on topics of the day:

"Our soldiers can win wars faster than our diplomats can talk us into them."

"I have a girl acquaintance who has sent five sweethearts to France, and is still recruiting."

"The reason we could get troops over there and get them trained so quickly was that we don't teach our troups to retreat, and when you only have to teach an army to go one way you can do it in half the time."

Here and on facing page, these front and back covers of sheet music from the 1921 Ziegfeld *Follies* hint at the elaborate costumes and "glorification of the American girl" that characterized a Ziegfeld production (authors' collection).

201

President Wilson liked this last quip so well that he used it himself, properly attributing it to Will Rogers. When the president's appropriation of his joke was reported to Will, he responded, "Now, up to the time President Wilson quoted me as being a humorist I had only been an ordinary rope tangler. But it is pretty tough when the President steals your act."

And further: "President Wilson is gettin' along fine now to what he was a few months ago. Do you realize, people, that at one time in our negotiations with Germany he was five notes behind."

And also: "Every war has been preceded by a peace conference. That's what always starts the next war."

About the *Follies* showgirls, Will quipped, "We had a hard time keeping our girls together. Every time we get to a new town some of them marry millionaires, but in a few weeks they catch up with the show again."

"Everyone flocks to the opening of the *Follies* and brings his present wife to observe how his old one acts and see where the alimony goes."

"I have threatened to write a book called 'My Years with the *Follies,* or Prominent Men I've Met at the Stage Door.'"

In his autobiography, *W. C. Fields: By Himself,* Fields recalled the time Will Rogers, Eddie Cantor and Bert Williams performed in a *Follies* blackface skit: "Poor Will didn't know whether to use a Southern dialect or a Yiddish accent like Cantor or Jessel."

Fields' fondness for Rogers did not prevent him from throwing his characteristic digs at a fellow comedian. Once when someone commented that they just loved Will's way of speaking, Fields responded with this retort: "The son of a bitch is a fake. I'll bet a hundred dollars he talks just like everybody else when he gets home."

Will often traveled with Fields and Cantor when the *Follies* went on tour, driving Fields' car between the towns. One night in late March 1917, en route from Washington, D.C., back to New York, Fields lost control of his automobile and careened into a ditch. The car turned over and pitched out its occupants, and Will Rogers injured his leg. Despite barely being able to walk, Will went on with the show the next night.

Theatre magazine featured Will in an August 1918 article titled, "The Cowboy That Conquered New York." Under a photo captioned, "Me and the Missus and the kids," the author captures Will Rogers perfectly:

> Will Rogers is the man who lassoed and hobbled Broadway. A tanned cowboy from Oklahoma has done what thousands of pale students, and bright-eyed beauties have failed to do. He has captured the most captious street in the world. He has conquered Broadway.... Is the lean brown-faced man with the shrewd glance and the nimble tongue grateful to the thespian gods for his victory? Not particularly. Is he awed by the heights he has attained? No. Are his prairie-filled eyes dazzled by the white lights? They can see as far and as clearly as when they stared across the plains seeking a nomad yearling. Do the gauds and the glitter of the shining street claim him? You wouldn't think so if you saw him after the curtain falls on the Ziegfeld *Follies,* "streaking" for the Long Island station to catch the train for his home at Amityville.... Will Rogers has the rare gift of enormous common sense. That quality which is simply the power of seeing things in proportion has been his since birth. He sees far and clear. He perceives that the number of essentials is small and the number of non-essentials great. He cancels the non-essentials.

When Ziegfeld traveled away from New York he had the annoying habit of firing off lengthy telegrams to his staff and performers. While others rushed around trying to fulfill Ziegfeld's commands, Rogers paid them no heed. During one of these barrages of longer and hotter telegrams, Will finally telegraphed Ziegfeld a response: "Keep this up. Am on my way to buy more Western Union stock."

Will summed up his Ziegfeld training ground: "We spent our literary apprenticeship in the same school of knocks, Mr. Ziegfeld's *Follies.* We eked out a bare existence among nothing but bare backs. There was diamond necklaces to the right of us and Rolls Royces to the left of us, and costumes of powder completely surrounding us.... Those were hardship days, but great training for our journalistic future."

Will kept in good shape playing baseball on the vaudeville circuit and later as a polo player. After one polo match a fellow player commented to Will, "You've sure got a great pair of legs on you." Will did not miss a beat. With his trademark twinkling eyes and boyish grin he came back with, "Why do you think Mr. Ziegfeld kept me in the *Follies* all those years?"

The Celluloid Lure

I've been hearing a lot about how good it was but I notice nobody is making me any of those big offers to do another one. So I guess that's the tip-off.

Will regarded his Ziegfeld *Follies* years fondly and greatly appreciated the opportunity that Ziegfeld had provided him to showcase his considerable talents, but fate would soon lead him in another direction. A Polish immigrant to the United States launched Will's movie career. "Will does not have to play the lead character, he is the character," said Rex Beach. At the urging of Beach (Fred Stone's brother-in-law) and his wife, fledgling producer Samuel Goldfish (Americanized from Schmuel Geldfisz and later changed to Samuel Goldwyn) took in one of Will's performances at the *Follies* in early 1918.

Will was not convinced that he would make an effective screen actor but agreed to give it a try as long as he could remain in New York and continue to work the *Follies.* Will felt comfortable in New York, and Betty had just given birth to their fourth child, Fred Stone Rogers, on July 15, 1918.

By August, Will had arrived at Goldfish's Fort Lee, New Jersey, movie studios to begin filming Rex Beach's book *Laughing Bill Hyde,* an adventure set in the Klondike goldfields. When Ziegfeld got wind of Will's intentions to make motion pictures, he let it be known that he had "exclusive control of the professional services of every member of the *Follies* cast." However, Will had fulfilled his commitment to Ziegfeld, and without a written contract prohibiting Will from entertaining new artistic adventures, Ziegfeld could not prevent Will from making pictures.

When asked how the filming was going, Will characteristically exclaimed, "It's another mule." He immediately took a dislike to using makeup, saying, "That makeup stuff just can't disguise this old, homely pan of mine."

Laughing Bill Hyde opened in New York City at the Rivoli Theatre in late September 1918, achieving critical and commercial success. While Will's strengths, his manner of speaking and witticisms, could not be captured to their best advantage in the movie titles, the reviews treated Will kindly.

Goldfish caught up with Will in December 1918 in Cleveland, where he was performing with the *Follies* on tour. He offered Will a contract paying $2,250 a week for the first year, with an option to renew for $3,000 a week for the second year. Goldfish stipulated that in order for the contract to be accepted, Will and Betty would have to move to California. It did not take long to decide. Will's current salary stood at $1,000 a week, and Betty had long desired to settle down and call one place home. On March 2, 1919, Samuel Goldwyn announced, "Will Rogers will give up the stage and devote all of his time to the screen when his present season in the *Follies* ends."

Will started for the West Coast on June 5 and reported to the Goldwyn Studios. He later said, "When Goldwyn decided to make fewer and worse pictures, he sent for me."

"The first movie I ever made was in '18, an Alaskan story by Rex Beach called *Laughing Bill Hyde*. I played by request of Mrs. Rex Beach.... The part was rather that of a crook, who received money under false pretenses. Mrs. Beach had seen my little act in the *Follies,* so she decided that I was the one to do naturally ... this crook who obtained money under false pretenses."

Fledgling Author

Everybody is writing something nowadays. It used to be just the Literary or Newspaper men who were supposed to know what they were writing about that did all the writing. But nowadays all a man goes into office for is so he can try to find out something and then write about it when he comes out.

Rex Beach also played an instrumental role in getting Will's writing and publishing career launched. Before leaving for California, Will inked a contract with Harper & Brothers Publishers, which decided to produce two books based on collections of Rogerisms from his *Follies* comments. Upon returning copies of the signed contracts to Will, William Briggs of Harper & Brothers wrote, "The more I think about it the more tickled I am about undertaking these books [*The Cowboy Philosopher on the Peace Conference* and *The Cowboy Philosopher on Prohibition*]. There is going to be real joy in publishing them, and we want to start the first one off with bells.... I certainly want to thank Rex Beach for his happy thought in heading you in this direction. I hope that some time you will have a chance to mill with the Harper crowd."

The *Cowboy Philosopher* books were a natural extension of Will's appeal to the general public and his ability to get to the heart of topics of the day. These small volumes were the first of six books to eventually carry Will Rogers' byline and record the flavor of Will's quips:

"I made this book short so you could finish it before the next war."

"The peace treaty would have been signed earlier but the German generals whom they sent out there to sign it had never been to the front and dident know where it was.... The Kaiser was on the verge at one time of visiting the Western front when he said, 'No, I will just wait a few days until it comes to me.'"

"You won't find the country any drier than this book."

"Statistics have proved that listening to prohibition lectures has driven more people to drink than any other cause."

"[Prohibition has been] the cause of more road improvement between dry and wet towns than any other thing.... Bad roads have broke more bottles of booze than any other thing."

The book contracts were a nice bonus, but Will was concentrating on his move to Hollywood.

Chapter 2

Hollywood Beckons

The Goldwyn Silents

It's the grandest show business I know anything about, and the only place where an actor can act and at the same time sit down in the front and clap for himself.

Will carried over his special style of humor into his interviews with the Hollywood reporters. In an early interview he chided Goldwyn for his low salary despite making many times more than he ever made on stage:

> About this picture game, I have signed a contract with Samuel Goldwyn for a year, with an option for two more years. I have taken a bungalow in California close to the Culver City studios, and so far spent most of my salary sending out West the pet collection of ponies, dogs and cats belonging to four children. Say, I am the only picture star in captivity who is working for less than $10,000 a week. My salary is so much smaller than $10,000 I would be ashamed to tell you the dismal truth. Also behold the one actor who has never in all his stage career had a mash note. Honestly, I am so blame homely, no girl excepting my wife ever fell for me. I bet I am the homeliest moving picture star on the screen. That's why sometimes I am afraid the Goldwyn company is going to think they have a bad bargain.... When I saw myself in *Laughing Bill Hyde* I was depressed and unhappy for several weeks. I thought, my lands, no man ought to be so homely and live. And do you know I never had any idea I was so homely until I went into the projection room and saw myself. I knew I was no Apollo Belvidere, but I did not know I was so blamed ugly. Ever since that time I have been suspicious when I see people staring at me. I know it is because they are trying to get a closer view of my ugly face.

Will summed up his critical review of his performance in *Laughing Bill Hyde:* "It wasn't much shucks.... I am the world's worst actor. Leave the acting business to them that can act.... All I know to do is to throw a lariat and crack jokes."

During the filming of *Laughing Bill Hyde,* the director inquired whether Will had ever had any camera experience. Will responded, "Only with a little Brownie No. 2."

In *Laughing Bill Hyde,* Will Rogers played the role of a convict, Bill Hyde, who escapes from a western jail. During the picture, Will gets to display a few of his rope tricks.

"It's sorta like the old days because I can throw a rope without having a crowd in front waiting to see me miss. You have to hand it to the movies for that. If you don't do a thing right the first time the director will make you do it again, and nobody will be wise to the fact that you gummed up the job several times before you put it over," said Will.

"We are providing [Will] with the surest-fire role that a player could have for his screen debut.... I felt ... that there was just one actor on earth that I wanted to see the hero of my story, and that actor is Will Rogers. I believe, as does Samuel Goldfish, that he is going to be a huge success on the screen," said Rex Beach in an interview for *Moving Picture World.*

Advertisements for *Laughing Bill Hyde* described the movie as a "Tremendous drama of redemption ... a romance of loyalty and money-hunger ... a story of strong men fight-

Will Rogers as Bill Hyde and Dan Mason as Danny Dorgan, escaped convicts in *Laughing Bill Hyde* (1918) (courtesy Will Rogers Memorial).

Anna Lehr as Ponotah and Will Rogers as Bill Hyde in *Laughing Bill Hyde* (courtesy Will Rogers Memorial).

ing Nature and each other.... Will Rogers is the most *human* player who ever faced a camera. With his abashed, real smile and the tears welling up in his eyes he will hold audiences as few actors are ever able to do."

During one scene in the picture, Bill Hyde (Rogers) leads a pack donkey over a hill; the action takes less than ten seconds. After viewing the movie with his three-year-old son, Will asked him how he liked the movie. "It was all right, Pop ... but they didn't show enough of the donkey."

The critics were another story: They wanted to see more of Will Rogers, the movie star. The *New York Times* proclaimed, "Those inclined to believe that all of the magnetic Rogers personality is in his conversation will realize their mistake if they see this picture. The real Will Rogers is on the reels. Whether Rogers can act or whether he can do anything before the camera except be himself, is not the question. He is 75 percent himself in *Laughing Bill Hyde* and that much of Will Rogers is thoroughly enjoyable. The story ... affords Rogers all of the opportunity he needs to grin in his own contagious way and go through his other expressions of face and body to the delight of the spectators."

"A new star to filmdom is necessarily a matter of importance to the trade and it should be stated early Rogers is a success," wrote *Variety*. "He registers humor and pathos as incisively as his monologues are punctuated with humor."

Wid's Daily proclaimed, "Director Hobart Henley jumped funny old Bill Rogers right up into the big league his first time out."

Motion Picture Magazine followed with, "Taking everything into consideration—direction, action, continuity, titles and acting—this is the very finest film release under the Goldwyn banner. *Laughing Bill Hyde* serves as the debut of Will Rogers, and his performance would have been a credit to any veteran in the business."

With those kind of reviews, it's no wonder that Goldwyn hurried to Cleveland to sign Will Rogers to a movie contract. The December 28, 1918, issue of *Moving Picture World* announced Goldwyn's signing of Rogers: "Goldwyn has been negotiating with Rogers ever since *Laughing Bill Hyde* was released, because his personal success was so instantaneous and unquestionable that there could be no doubt of his future in the cinema. The stories to be provided for Will Rogers will be big, gripping, human dramas."

In March 1919, Goldwyn purchased the screen rights to two stories to be used as vehicles starring Will Rogers: *Alec Lloyd, Cowpuncher* by Eleanor Gates, noted author of *Poor Little Rich Girl* and other stories, and *Overland Red* by H. H. Knibbs, whose stories had appeared in the *Saturday Evening Post* and other national publications. The Gates story resulted in the production of *Cupid, the Cowpuncher,* released in July 1920, but Will did not appear in movies based on Knibbs' stories.

March also marked another film deal for Will. He signed a contract to appear in the *Ford Educational Weekly* feature of Gaumont News Reels, which was scheduled to be shown in 4,000 theaters throughout the United States. Rogers agreed to give a talk featuring his wit and commentary on timely topics for the weekly production.

In June 1919, Goldwyn reported that Will Rogers would begin work on his first movie at the firm's Culver City studios under their new contract. Goldwyn chose a Billy Fortune story written by William Rheem Lighton, *Doubled Stakes,* which the *Saturday Evening Post* featured. The *New York Times* reported, "The originality and wit of Rogers will be sought in the composition of the titles for his pictures." Around the same time, Goldwyn announced that Peggy Wood would be Will Rogers' leading lady in the series of films based on Billy Fortune stories appearing in the *Saturday Evening Post.*

Peggy Wood did appear as the leading lady in Will's next movie. However it was not the *Doubled Stakes* story written by Lighton. Instead, Will's second film under the Goldwyn banner came out in August 1919 under the title *Almost a Husband*, adapted from the novel *Old Ebenezer* written by Opie Percival Read.

Goldwyn placed director Clarence G. Badger in charge of the *Almost a Husband* production. Will and Badger hit it off so well that Will later requested Badger as the director for his remaining films with Goldwyn Pictures. This move so angered Goldwyn that he berated Badger for plotting with Rogers against him before finally giving his approval. Rogers also got Goldwyn's goat by routinely lassoing the "Keep off the Grass" sign while tramping about on Goldwyn's prized lawn.

In *Almost a Husband*, Will showed his versatility and forsook his lariat and western persona, taking on the role of a country schoolteacher who ends up married when a mock marriage turns out to be valid. Will inserted his own brand of humor into the production of *Almost a Husband* by personally writing the humorous titles.

A July 1919 *Photoplay* article showed Will's reluctance to consider himself a "movie star" in the usual vein:

> I can't see any sense in an awkward maverick like me tryin' to look sweet and purty before the camera.... I'm not an actor. I'm a rope-thrower. I can't act. I can't be nothin' but myself.... Movie people are funny! They send me a book to read and ask if I'd like to do it in pictures. I read the book and write back that I would. Then they don't buy it. And if I say I don't like a story they buy it. I don't know much about pictures, though.... I don't want to be a hero. Let Bill Hart and Tom Mix do that. Heroes are right good to look at and we all like to see thrillers but I don't aim to play in those parts. I was never much on killin' people and I'd rather not gallop through my pictures armed like a battleship and linin' a dozen bad men against the Arizona skyline dyin' of fright. I'm friendly by nature, I guess, and in my pictures I'd like to smile a lot and make everyone feel sociable and at home-like. Then, mebbe we could take a weddin' on the end, with love scenes and all, y'know.

An August 23, 1919, a advertisement for the movie in *Motion Picture News* stated, "Will Rogers [is] an actor who never acts, who makes you laugh just to look at him. If human nature is the same as it used to be, then Will Rogers is the one of all comedians before the film public today who will carry off first honors. A plain looking man to be sure, he gets the plain folks by his sympathetic manner and the bigger folks by his dry humor." The *Exhibitor's Trade Review* urged movie theater owners and managers to

Will Rogers on location with *Almost a Husband* filming crew (courtesy Will Rogers Memorial).

Will Rogers as Sam Lyman and Peggy Wood as Eva McElwyn in a tender scene in *Almost a Husband* (1919) (courtesy Will Rogers Memorial).

"Boost the name of the star in all program advertising and billing ... mention the fact that Will Rogers was a success on the legitimate stage and also state that his peculiar characteristics make his part on this production of especial interest."

Again, critics and the general public took to Will's performance with a passion. *Wid's Daily* headlined its review of *Almost a Husband* with "Will Rogers Puts It Over" and went on to say, "The star part is ideally suited to Will Rogers. He is not called upon to act but merely to be his own natural self and he does it to perfection. As an awkward, bashful, country school teacher, he's a bear, and then some." *Motion Pictures News* declared, "Will Rogers Scores in Quaint Comedy."

The *New York Times* reported that "Will Rogers' personality penetrates through lenses and film to the screen. Rogers in motion pictures is not Rogers himself, with his chewing gum, rope and conversation, but there is a thoroughly delightful person in a photoplay called *Almost a Husband*.... Rogers is genuine in everything he does, and genuineness counts for as much on the screen as on the stage, and, furthermore, he is by no means an insignificant actor."

To help promote *Almost a Husband*, Will appeared in person and entertained the audience at Miller's California Theatre. In addition to Will and *Almost a Husband*, the

Will Rogers as Sam Lyman, flanked by Clara Horton as Jane Sheldon and Cullen Landis as Jerry Wilson in *Almost a Husband* (authors' collection).

billing included the California Concert Orchestra and the California Chorus of Voices performing *Southern Fantasie*, two organists performing *Southern Rhapsody*, soprano Constance Balfour singing *Ave Maria* and Pathé Exchange's Harold Lloyd starring in his first two-reel comedy, *Bumping into Broadway.*

The July 20, 1919, issue of the *New York Times* mentioned that noted actress Mabel Normand had agreed to appear as an extra in Will's new movie, *Almost a Husband.* In return, Will promised to appear as an extra in one of her upcoming photoplays. It is possible that Miss Normand did appear in *Almost a Husband,* and Will's name has been linked with the December 1919 release of *Pinto,* a western feature starring Mabel Normand.

Years later, director Clarence Badger reminisced about his relationship with Will Rogers, which lasted through fifteen different film projects, including three pictures Rogers financed himself. Badger echoed the sentiment of many who worked with Will over the years:

> Among the many fond memories of my early film days I have preserved against time, the most treasured is that of my association with Will Rogers.... I had seen him many times at the Ziegfeld *Follies* and had become so

> intrigued by his cleverness with a rope, rare wit and personality.... I would have gladly given my eye teeth to be his director.... My first meeting with Will ... well, I can still see, still feel, Will's follow-up barrage of appraising, analytical glances streaming down at me from under the rim of his Stetson as I hurried up to greet him.... As we shook hands up there on that high landing, he said he hoped I did not mind; it was just that he had been waiting "for you all to show up up here 'cause of an itchin' notion we should get acquainted like." ... I found the association to be most inspiring; and, because of the inimitable humanness of his acting, a pleasure to direct ... our friendship [was] a tie that had grown during our association at Goldwyn's ... to an unbreakable bond of depth, warmth and understanding.... Despite Will's richly deserved fame and popularity which grew to such outstanding proportions through the years, he never forgot or neglected old friends. Time and again where their lives had been dealt with harshly ... he healed their situations with direct personal action, or financial balm.

A Ben Ames Williams story, *Jubilo*, which appeared in the *Saturday Evening Post*, formed the basis for Will's next starring role, a happy-go-lucky tramp. Characteristically, Will explained how he obtained the tramp role and the attraction of the picture:

> After Mr. Goldwyn saw me several times in my street clothes he said there is the fellow to play the tramp.... We have a cast that can act and a star that cannot, an unusual combination in this business.... The directions was very good when you consider the director wore no puttees or riding breeches.... The photography was mostly shot in focus, the camera used was a Brownie No. 2.... Straight on I didn't look so good and even sideways I wasn't so terrific, but a cross between back and a three-quarters view, why, Brother, I was hot. The way my ear stood out from my head was just bordering on perfect. That rear view gave you just the shot needed.

Before the release of the picture, Sam Goldwyn had decided to change the title of the picture from *Jubilo* to *A Poor But Honest Tramp*. In response, Will fired off a telegram to Goldwyn's office in New York City in protest. "Thought I was supposed to be a comedian but when you suggest changing the title of *Jubilo* you are funnier than I ever was." He ended the telegraph with, "What would you have called *The Birth of a Nation*?"

Needless to say, the movie title remained *Jubilo*, and Will scored another success with the critics and movie audiences when the picture was released in December 1919. *Theatre Magazine* featured *Jubilo* as one of the "Worth While Pictures of the Month" and described the movie as "a typical American genre study, tender, humorous and sincere, with the subtitles illuminated by the whimsical philosophy that could come from none other than Will Rogers."

Motion Picture News reviewer Tom Hamlin praised Will: "In one of the most charming photoplays we have seen in a long time Will Rogers thoroughly establishes himself as a screen star of the first magnitude." The *New York Times* chimed in: "The pleasing personality of Will Rogers, enhanced by quite a bit of acting talent, brightens *Jubilo*." *Harrison's Reports* predicted that "picture goers will certainly get their money's worth out of *Jubilo*. It is a human interest story, with thrills and suspense." In the minority view, *Variety* wrote, "The story seems somewhat inconsistent throughout and if Rogers has any ability as a screen actor he is not able to show it here."

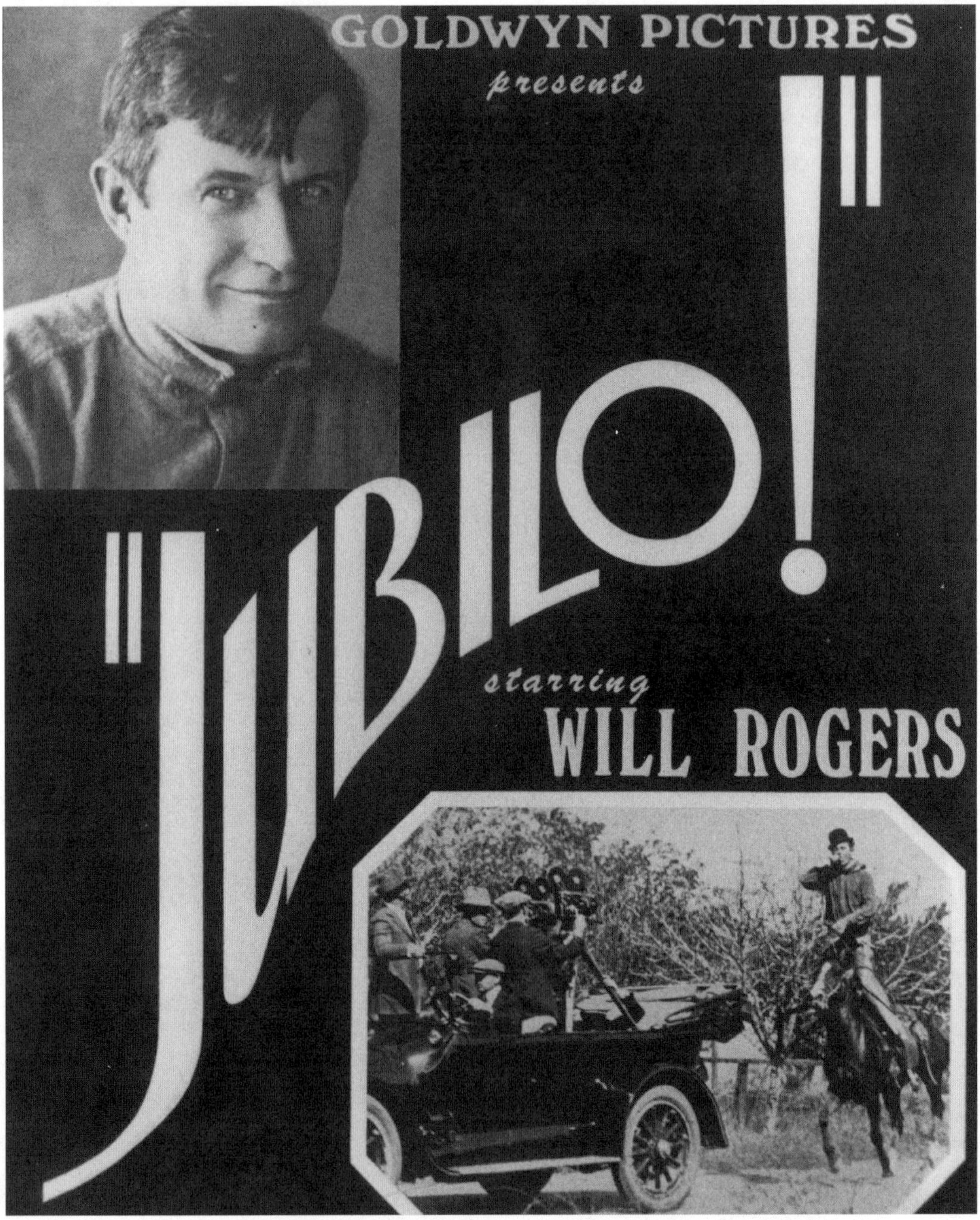

Lobby card for *Jubilo* (1919) (authors' collection).

In addition to acting, Will made a series of weekly shorts for Pathé Exchange titled *The Illiterate Digest* with Will doing humorous takeoffs on the popular *Literary Digest Topics of the Day.* These films intercut brief scenes of Will on stage with titles about current topics in the news. At first considered lost, several of these short subjects have been discovered in the Motion Picture Section of the US Archives in Washington, D.C.

Will's takeoffs were not viewed humorously by Funk and Wagnalls Company, producers of the *Literary Digest Topics of the Day.* Will received a letter from William Beverly Winslow, a lawyer representing Funk and Wagnalls, warning Will to stop using the title *The Illiterate Digest* or face possible action on the charge of "unfair competition" and an "injunction restraining" Will against such use. The letter ended with the stern warning, "Unless I hear favorably from you ... I shall conclude that you are not willing to accede to this suggestion and will take such steps as I may deem advisable."

Instead of resorting to a battle of the lawyers, Will defused the issue by responding with a letter:

> Dear Sir,
>
> Your letter in regard to my competition with the *Literary Digest* received and I never felt so swelled up in my life. And am glad you wrote directly to me instead of communicating with my lawyers, as I have not yet reached that stage of prominence where I was committing unlawful acts and requiring a lawyer. Now if the *Literary Digest* feels that the competition is too keen for them — to show you my good sportsmanship I will withdraw. In fact I had already quit as the gentlemen who put it out were behind in their payments and my humor kinder waned, in fact after a few weeks of no payments I couldn't think of a single joke. And now I want to inform you truly that this is the first that I knew my title of the *Illiterate Digest* was an infringement on yours as they mean the direct opposite. If a magazine was published called *Yes,* and another bird put one out called *No,* I suppose he would be infringing. But you are a lawyer and its your business to change the meaning of words, so I lose from the start.
>
> Now I have not written for these people in months and they haven't put any gags out unless it is some of the old ones still playing. If they are using gags that I wrote on topical things 6 months ago then I must admit that they would be in competition with the ones the *Literary Digest Screen* uses now. I will gladly furnish you with their address, in case you want to enter suit. And as I have no lawyer you can take my case too, and whatever we get out of them, we will split at the usual lawyer rates of 80:20, the client of course getting the 20.
>
> Now you inform your editors at once that their most dangerous rival has withdrawn, and that they can go ahead and resume publication. But you inform your clients that if they ever take up rope throwing, or chewing gum, I will consider it a direct infringement of my rights and will protect it with one of the best lawyers in Oklahoma.
>
> Your letter to me telling me I was in competition with the *Digest* would be just like [President] Harding writing to Cox [Democratic candidate] and telling him he took some of his votes.
>
> So long Beverly, if you ever come to California, come out to Beverly where I live and see me.
>
> Illiterately yours,
>
> Will Rogers

When asked in 1920 to buy space — or as Will put it, "to contribute, at so much a contribution" — in *Wid's Year Book,* Will penned his famous fourteen points of the moving picture industry.

> President Wilson and I each have fourteen points. He took his to Paris where they not only saw his fourteen but raised him twelve more, I brought my

fourteen points to the coast. The first five and principal of mine a wife and four children in itself constitutes a novelty in this business, that is provided you still live with them.

Point Number Six: I heard there was a movement on to revive moving pictures.

Point Number Seven: Producers decided to make fewer and worse pictures. They may make fewer but they will never make worse.

Point Number Eight: I hold the distinction of being the ugliest man in pictures.

Point Number Nine: Caruso and I and Jesse Willard were the last to go in.

Point Number Ten: Goldwyn figured by getting a good cast and a great story, it would about offset the action of the star.

Point Number Eleven: I can't roll a cigarette with one hand and can't whip but one man at a time (and he must be littler than I am).

Point Number Twelve: I made a picture last year and some theatres bought it. So they figured if I made another one they could double the sale on this one. Get two to use it.

Point Number Thirteen: Moving pictures are the only way in the world that you can play and tour and not have to worry about hotels.

Point Number Fourteen: It's the only business where you can sit out front and applaud yourself.

He concluded the piece with "P.S. If I don't last in the business till the next *Year Book* is issued, I take this means now of wishing everybody good luck, as I have certainly met some fine folks out here in the business. I love it, and only hope I am able to string along with you, even if it's in the rear, and Oh! You know what I like, to forget the climate, isn't it dear. Turkey is the only prohibition country in the world besides us. If we enjoyed a few of their privileges it wouldn't be so bad."

Will Rogers as Jubilo (authors' collection).

Will signed a six-month contract in February 1920 with Goldwyn Pictures Corporation to provide "at least fifteen original sayings or comments or witticisms, of the same general character as are now being exhibited at the California Theatre in the City of Los Angeles, California, for every week of the term of this agreement." For this, Will received $750 per week with the first six weeks in advance.

Water, Water Everywhere, released on February 8, 1920, co-starred Will and Irene Rich in the first of many movies they would make together over the next

Top: Will Rogers as Jubilo with Josie Sedgwick as Rose Hardy in ***Jubilo*** (authors' collection). ***Bottom:*** Will Rogers as Jubilo takes a punch on the chin from Charles French as Jim Hardy while Josie Sedgwick as Rose Hardy looks on in ***Jubilo*** (courtesy Will Rogers Memorial).

Will Rogers in *Water, Water Everywhere* (1920) (courtesy Will Rogers Memorial).

decade and a half. *Water, Water Everywhere* marked Will's first appearance in a Billy Fortune role, this one based on William Rheem Lighton and Louis D. Lighton's novel *Billy Fortune and the Hard Proposition.*

Motion Picture News headlined its review, "Will Rogers Makes This Picture Worth While" and followed that up with "*Water, Water Everywhere* is quite an ordinary picture, but the inimitable Will Rogers makes it enjoyable through his magnetic personality and his histrionic talent."

Two Will Rogers movies were released in May 1920, both co-starring Irene Rich. *The Strange Boarder* featured Will as an Arizona rancher who is swindled out of his life's savings when he and his young son visit the big city. Will's four-year-old son Jimmy plays the role of the young boy. Jimmy expanded his movie career by also appearing as Harry Benedict in *Jes' Call Me Jim,* starring his father and Irene Rich.

Harrison's Reports predicted, "You can mark this picture on your book 100%. It is doubtful if a better selection of types could have ever been made. Every one fits the part with perfection. Mr. Rogers, as the innocent farmer, is unexcelled.... Mr. Rogers' little son seems to have taken to acting as a duck to water.... This picture nails one from the very start. The human element in it is powerful and abundant." *Moving Picture World* called *The Strange Boarder* "by far the best picture Rogers has yet produced. It contains all the elements of success. It is a real picture, full of love interest, thrilling action and comedy of the kind which only Rogers knows how to put over.... The star is better than ever, if such a thing is possible, and contributes much to the success of the picture. His

Will Rogers as Billy Fortune flanked by Rowland Lee as Lyman Jennings Jordan and Irene Rich as Hope Beecher in *Water, Water Everywhere* (courtesy Will Rogers Memorial).

son, Jimmy Rogers, lends capable support and arouses much admiration, especially from the fair sex."

In the other May 1920 film, *Jes' Call Me Jim*, Will rescues an inventor from an insane asylum when the lady he loves convinces him that a prominent citizen stole the inventor's patents and incarcerated him to hide his thievery. Production of the movie had to be held up for a time due to Will's son's bout with the measles.

Irene Rich showed a bit of her own rescue talents during the filming of the movie on location. A canoe turned over, and Miss Rich pulled fellow actor Nick Cogley from certain death.

Director Clarence G. Badger recalled a difficult prayer scene in which they were trying to achieve a special ethereal effect with divine shafts of light shining among the giant redwoods. Nature would not cooperate with the desired shafts of light, and time was wasting, so the scene was shot anyway. After the crew finished its work, Will invited everybody to "a fill 'er bacon and eggs" that Betty was frying up. As Badger headed down the slope to join the feast, he froze in his tracks, blinded by the elusive shafts of light—being created from the smoke rising from the sizzling bacon. Badger reorganized the crew, shot the beautiful and touching scene, and then they all returned to chow down on Betty's cooking.

Top: Irene Rich and Will Rogers in ***The Strange Boarder*** (1920) (courtesy Will Rogers Memorial). ***Bottom:*** Doris Pawn, Will Rogers and James Mason in ***The Strange Boarder*** (courtesy Will Rogers Memorial).

The *Photoplay* reviewer wrote, "I say *Jes' Call Me Jim* is Rogers' best picture. And to me it is.... Familiar movie material, you'll say, reading the outline. But see the picture and you'll see how it is possible to take a story that could have been as easily spoiled as any of them and by the employment of intelligence in its adaptation and direction, and by the refreshingly real and wholesome appeal of a man like Rogers, make of it a fine evening's entertainment. In this picture Rogers gives the lie to all those who have been insisting that he is only a rough comedian blessed with a likable personality."

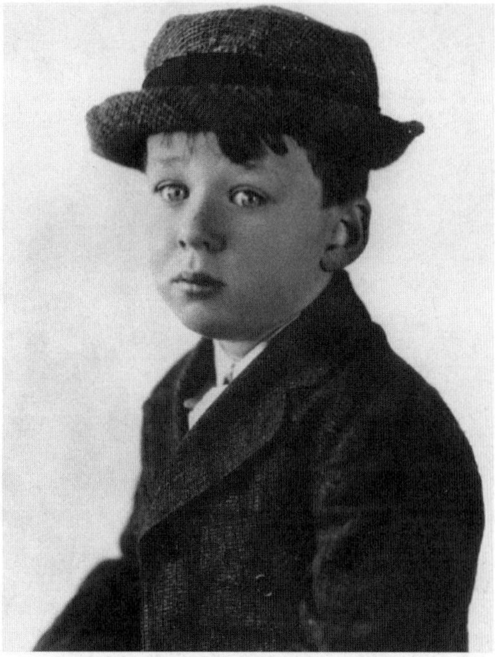

Will's son, Jimmy Rogers, as Harry Benedict in *Jes' Call Me Jim* (1920) (courtesy Will Rogers Memorial).

Variety found favor with Badger's hard-earned scene: "One bit of footage is quite impressive—that of a child praying for the recovery of his father amid a grove of huge redwood trees. The comparison in size between the two-footed youth and the gigantic trees is designed to visualize the respective works of the Almighty. It is a pretty idea." Of the over-all film, *Variety* reported, "Without the personality of Will Rogers, the Goldwyn production of *Jes' Call Me Jim* would be a simple, old-fashioned melodrama ... but the sentiment is sweet and clean and it is unfolded in a delightful comedy way that pleased the Strand audience.... A most felicitous cast has been selected to support the star."

Tragedy marred Will's success in mid-June 1920, when his children were struck by diphtheria. Will drove all night to get some antitoxin, but by the time he arrived back home their youngest child, Fred Stone Rogers, had died. The family took Fred's death hard, moving to a new home in Beverly Hills to help ease the pain. Will dove back into his new career in the movies.

Often the children joined Will on Goldwyn's backlot. Will's son, James Blake Rogers, remembered the early Goldwyn days with fondness: "We had our horses at the Goldwyn lot and we would ride our ponies all day. We didn't pay much attention to the movie stars, instead we hung around with the extras and friends like Guinn 'Big Boy' Williams because they were 'horse people' and a lot more interesting. Watching a movie shoot was like watching paint dry."

Will finished up 1920 with three more Goldwyn productions: *Cupid, the Cowpuncher,* released on July 25, H*onest Hutch,* released on September 19, and *Guile of Women,* released on December 26. Although in *The Rise of the American Film,* Lewis Jacobs stated that Sidney Olcott reappeared as the director of one of Will Rogers' most hilarious comedies, *Scratch My Back*, there is no evidence that Will had anything to do with this movie. A March 13, 1920, article in *Moving Picture World* announcing the production start-up of *Scratch My Back* under the direction of Sidney Olcott boasted of an all-star cast, but Will's name did

Will Rogers and Irene Rich in *Jes' Call Me Jim* (courtesy Will Rogers Memorial).

not appear in the listing. Likewise, the June 1920 reviews of *Scratch My Back* in *Harrison's Reports* and *Variety* failed to mention Will in conjunction with the movie.

Helene Chadwick co-starred with Will in *Cupid, the Cowpuncher*. The movie also marked the first appearance of Guinn "Big Boy" Williams as a member of the recognized supporting cast in one of Will's pictures. Williams had previously appeared as an extra in *Almost a Husband* and *Jubilo*.

Harrison's Reports called *Cupid, the Cowpuncher* "a wholesome farce-comedy, the kind that gives hearty satisfaction.... Lassoing and dare-devil horse riding are among the features." *Variety* commented that "Mr. Rogers is his usual slouching home-spun shirted self and wins his audience to a fair extent.... Miss Chadwick makes a charming heroine." *Wid's Daily* found that "Will Rogers scores again in *Cupid, the Cowpuncher*. Here is comedy superb in every sense, filled to the brim with genuine humor and dominated by that wonderful personality of Will Rogers that has made him one of the most likable stars on the screen."

Guinn Williams and Will Rogers hit it off right from the start. Both started out as honest-to-goodness cowboys, Will in Oklahoma and Guinn in nearby Texas. Both of them had a passion for polo and frequently played as teammates and against each other in the Hollywood polo leagues. To be sure, Will could hold his own on the polo field, but Guinn was widely regarded as Hollywood's number one polo player. At one time, Guinn owned 125 polo ponies.

Will, Jr., Jimmy and Mary Rogers on Goldwyn lot (courtesy Will Rogers Memorial).

While filming *Almost a Husband,* Will took one look at Guinn's six-foot, two-inch, two-hundred-pound frame and tabbed him "Big Boy." The name stuck for life and so did their friendship. "Big Boy" was a regular visitor to Will's ranch. Will teased Guinn, "'Big Boy' fell off a horse once but didn't hurt him none ... he landed on his head."

"Big Boy" went on to make 34 "oaters" and more than 100 films overall. He appeared with John Wayne in *The Alamo*, and his last supporting role took place in the 1962 movie *Comancheros,* also starring Wayne. He made the transition to television, portraying the village blacksmith in the series *My Friend Flicka.*

In early 1935, Williams wrote of his first meeting with Will Rogers:

> The first time I ever saw Will Rogers, he was sitting on "Dopey," his favorite pony. It was between scenes of *Almost a Husband*.... Bill was slouched easily in the saddle of the little black nag. Paying no attention to those around him, he was twirling a rope and tossing it at a nearby fence post. I was a $7.50 extra ... just a cowboy.... My idea of a leading man at that time was a cross between an Arrow Collar ad and an olympic swimming champion.... I took one look at Rogers. I decided that if that guy could be a star, I would be one myself inside of six months.... I knew I was no worse looking than Bill.... Six months later I knew I was all wrong. By that time Will Rogers to me was the handsomest and finest fellow—inside and out—that I ever have known.... Bill took to me and I took to him right away.... Bill was never any shakes at talking sentiment. But, one day after we'd been clowning around together for several months, he came to me and shoved my hand full of money. He said,

"Big, you've been away from home long enough. You take time off between this picture and the next. Go to ... see your maw." I'm telling you that floored me. I went. And, after that I sorta worshipped Bill. But that's only one of the million kind things I've seen him do.

After the fun of the day was over, Bill would join the cowboys.... Bill didn't care about riding with big-shot players and directors. He'd climb into any car with the mob.... He is always twirling a rope.... I saw him rope everything, everywhere, from saddle horns to humans and from goats to fence posts. Undoubtedly, he is the greatest trick roper in the world. The only man that didn't appreciate his art was Marcel Le Picard, a camera man on many of his early pictures. Bill almost drove him crazy, roping him and his camera."

Once "Big Boy" asked Will if he ever got tired of fooling around with his lariat. Will replied, "Nope, a feller's got to keep in shape. You can never tell when Ziegfeld'll put in a call for my services and I've gotta be ready." Of course, Will realized the fickleness of the movie business and that he had better not give up the trade that got him to the movies in the first place. The philosophy proved prophetic.

Theatre Magazine called Will's next effort, *Honest Hutch,*

the best Will Rogers picture we have ever seen, which is perhaps the best thing that could be said of any comedy now on the film market. Indeed, if we were not coy about our superlatives, we would say that it is the most delight-

Guinn "Big Boy" Williams and Will Rogers in *Cupid, the Cowpuncher* (1920) (courtesy Will Rogers Memorial).

Helene Chadwick and Will Rogers in *Cupid, the Cowpuncher* (courtesy Will Rogers Memorial).

> ful picture of this type ever screened. In addition to the study of the laconic loafer, which only Will Rogers can do without pathos and without burlesque, it has a really significant story.... Never was the beloved vagabond of the screen more dearly loved than in *Honest Hutch* recently produced by Goldwyn. Here we have the inimitable Will Rogers as the lovable loafer with the crafty look of aroused ambition in his eyes.

Reviewer Frederick James Smith in *Motion Picture Classic* described Will's performance: "Rogers is Hutch to the life. It is an honest, close to the sail performance, and his best celluloid role thus far." *Exhibitor's Trade Review* declared *Honest Hutch* "Another 'Big Win' for Will Rogers" and advised theater managers to "go strong on advertising this one as the best thing Rogers has done to date, and that's saying something. Play it up as a sweet, human interest story, the delightful comedy. Let it be known that this was the featured attraction at the Capitol, in New York, the world's largest theatre."

In *Guile of Women*, Rogers gets to show his acting range, assuming a very different role, that of a Swedish sailor beguiled by women and buffeted on love's rough seas until he meets a woman worthy of his faith. Mary Warren co-stars as Hulda, the heroine who ultimately wins his heart.

The March 4, 1921, *Variety* review of *Guile of Women* commented, "Will Rogers in

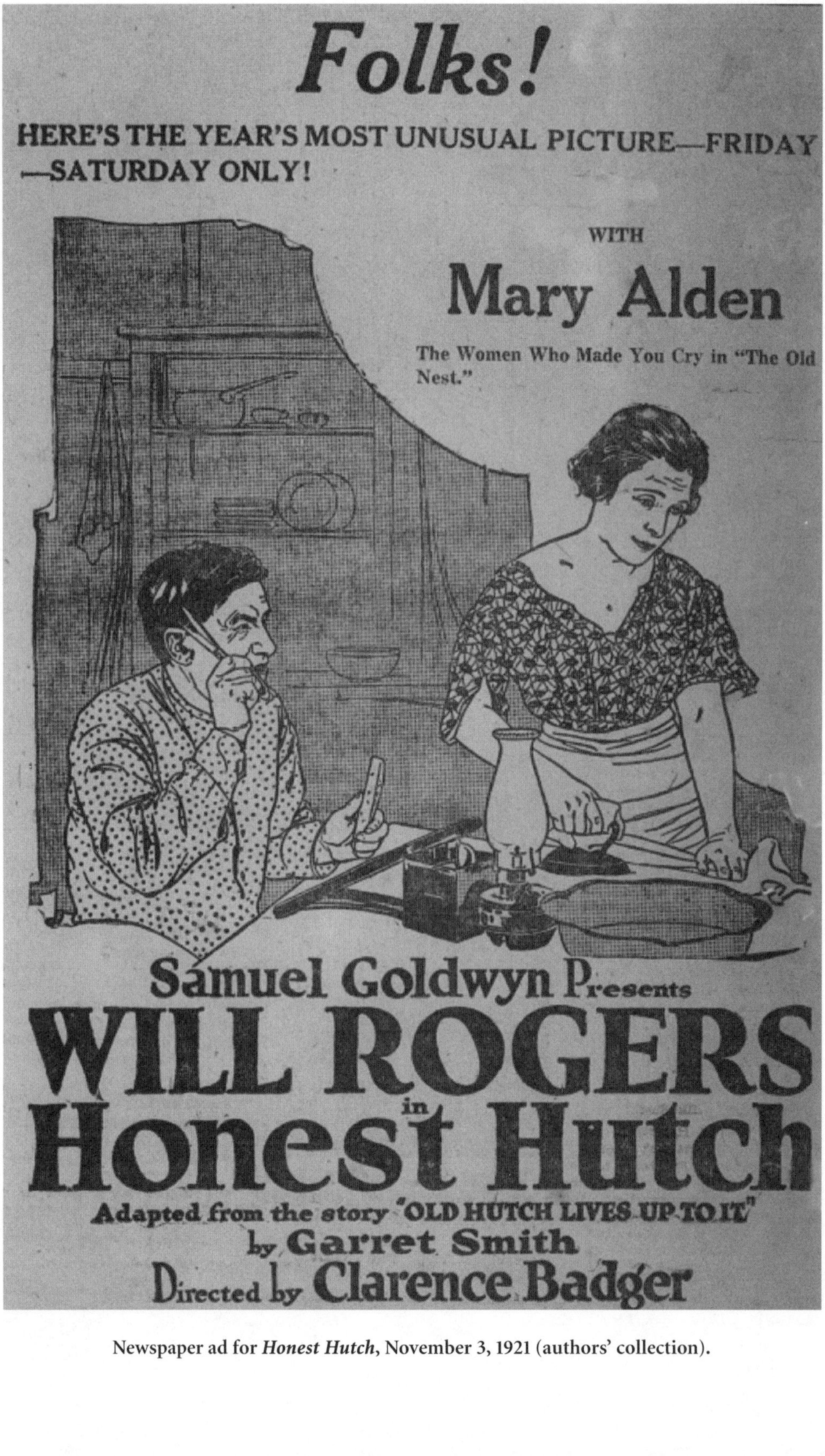

Folks!
HERE'S THE YEAR'S MOST UNUSUAL PICTURE—FRIDAY —SATURDAY ONLY!
WITH
Mary Alden
The Women Who Made You Cry in "The Old Nest."
Samuel Goldwyn Presents
WILL ROGERS
in
Honest Hutch
Adapted from the story "OLD HUTCH LIVES UP TO IT"
by Garret Smith
Directed by Clarence Badger

Newspaper ad for *Honest Hutch*, November 3, 1921 (authors' collection).

Will Rogers in *Honest Hutch* (1920) (courtesy Will Rogers Memorial).

the role of a Swede sailorman is a long leap from the cow range, but he gets away with it in splendid style.... While Rogers is the star of the picture, and all honors are due him, the story actually centers around the heroine and Mary Warren, a beautiful girl and an unusually intelligent actress, all but steals it away from the comedian. This is no reflection on Rogers, because he gets every ounce of value out of his part and is especially effective in the close-ups, where his facial expressions register strongly."

Around this time Charlie Chaplin and Will Rogers were taking some publicity photographs together, imitating each other. Chaplin interrupted one of Will's shots saying, "Try it over, that isn't how I stand." Without missing a beat, Will quipped, "Keep out of this, will yer, you ain't made a comedy in so long nobody knows how you stand."

In January 1921, *Moving Picture World* carried an article heralding Will Rogers' success with the headline, "Will Rogers, Discovered by Rex Beach Proves His Stellar Worth to Goldwyn." The article went on:

> Every year, one or more screen actors and actresses join the company of those favored few whose names frolic in frisking lights above picture theatres. Nineteen hundred and twenty has added the name of Will Rogers to the handful of stars the mention of whose name is sufficient to draw full houses to any theatre. In commercial terms, this means that Will Rogers has become a sure-fire financial investment for the theatre that books his pictures.... His

Will Rogers and Mary Warren in *Guile of Women* (1920) (courtesy Will Rogers Memorial).

> work for Goldwyn this past year has stamped him as a comedian with a method all his own, whose art is so unconsciously finished that nobody really knows whether he is acting or just being himself.
>
> Is Will Rogers a great actor or just a real human being? It is hard to tell from his pictures. I believe the truth is that Mr. Rogers is both.... Will Rogers ... injects into his characterizations that indefinite personal magnetism that has made him one of the best steady box office names the screen knows.

Despite this glowing praise of Will, his popular pictures and box office draw, rumors began to emerge that Goldwyn would not renew Will's contract upon its expiration in June 1921, after completion of the production *A Poor Relation.* A newspaper item in February 1921 indicated the Will would begin producing his own pictures after his obligations with Goldwyn were completed, and an April 1921 article mentioned that Will might align himself with United Artists.

In *Boys Will Be Boys*, Will again teamed up with Irene Rich in an Irvin S. Cobb story from the Judge Priest series. (Will would later star in the 1934 production of *Judge Priest* for Fox Film Corporation.) The *Goldwyn Press Sheet* promised that "Will Rogers has appealing role in picture from Irvin Cobb's Pen.... Noted film star scores success as 'Peep O'Day' in noted author's story."

As indicated by the reviews for *Boys Will Be Boys*, the problem may not have been Will Rogers or his acting but, instead, the production vehicles in which Goldwyn placed him. *Harrison's Report* commented, "It seems that Will Rogers cannot be in a bad pic-

Will Rogers gets instruction from Irene Rich in *Boys Will Be Boys* (1921) (courtesy Will Rogers Memorial).

ture. Even if the plot is weak he is able to pull it through." Reviewer Mary Kelly observed, "The lack of real drama in *Boys Will Be Boys* places it in the class of a rambling, somewhat lazy yarn without any definite thread of interest, but unravelling many mild, inconsequential incidents that follow one another without suspense." The *New York Times*, usually complimentary of Will's pictures, observed, "*Boys Will Be Boys* is padded out with so much labored melodrama, comedy and sentimentality ... as a featured photoplay ... this comedy would be disappointing. Save for the homely grace of Rogers and a number of deft strokes of characterization he is able to get in, it is pretty flat."

Will's next Goldwyn picture, *An Unwilling Hero,* used an O. Henry story, *Whistling Dick's Christmas Stocking,* for its storyline. One of the scenes shot at Goldwyn's Culver City studios called for a roaring fire. A well-meaning passerby noticed a building blazing away and notified the Culver City fire department, which responded promptly. Fortunately, director Clarence Badger convinced the fire crew to hold back on their rescue efforts and prevented them from ruining the planned fire scene. Will and the cast also traveled to New Orleans for a number of on-location shots in that city.

Photoplay observed, "There is a quality in Will Rogers' acting which harmonizes perfectly with O. Henry's stories; and this noted harmony is evident all through *An Unwilling Hero*.... It is a pleasant characterization enabling Rogers to indulge in his quaintly sophisticated wit."

Will Rogers and the boys stealing watermelons in *Boys Will Be Boys* (courtesy Will Rogers Memorial).

Ironically, one of Will's last pictures for Goldwyn turned out to be one of his best. Will garnered rave reviews for his performance in *Doubling for Romeo,* a western satire of William Shakespeare's *Romeo and Juliet. Wid's Daily* concluded, "Rogers' Latest a Big Hit Comedy Number.... His latest is a fine comedy that boasts of three authors — Elmer Rice, Will Rogers and Will Shakespeare — with the added line 'one of these boys is famous.' ... Rice's story is rounded out with plenty of typical Will Rogers humor that gets continual laughs.... Rogers puts over some good comedy in this bit."

Variety applauded the film's novelty: "At last something new in pictures! With *Doubling for Romeo*, a Goldwyn production, Will Rogers has arrived with a satirical burlesque of the screen that is a howl from start to finish. It is a production that has all the more appeal if one knows anything about pictures at all. The more you know, the funnier it is and if you don't know a thing about them, it is funny anyway ... it is far and away the best of the entire series that he has turned out under that [Goldwyn] contract.... The subtitles are a howl. Rogers is given credit for the modern titles and Shakespeare for the ancient ones."

The *New York Times* continued the praise, "*Doubling for Romeo* is about the most hilarious thing Mr. Rogers has ever done ... boisterous fun.... It is the embodiment of merry irreverence for movie romantics." *Harrison's Reports* said, "The reproduction of Shakespeare's Romeo and Juliet, with Mr. Rogers, is actually a scream.... The latest con-

Will Rogers and Molly Malone in *An Unwilling Hero* (1921) (courtesy Will Rogers Memorial).

tribution of Mr. Rogers may be safely classified as entertaining as any in which he has so far appeared. There is good comedy in the situations all the way through. Humor and wit also abound in the subtitles: these have been written by Mr. Rogers himself."

Photoplay heaped praise on Will's young son, Jimmy Rogers, "who is counted upon to sustain the family bankroll when his decrepit old dad retires from the screen — eighty years hence."

Goldwyn exhibited *Doubling for Romeo* and other films at the Goldwyn Sales Convention held at the Culver City studios the week of May 8, 1921.

As Will recalled:

> I like my work in this one a lot, but they had a sales convention at the studio and showed the film to the gang. Although I thought the picture was very funny, the boys seemed to think different and refused to laugh. At the time I was nearly heartbroken. I felt that I was a flop and was about to quit pictures. Gosh it was awful!
>
> Why up to the time I went into pictures I had never annoyed more than one audience at a time. I made one picture, *Doubling for Romeo.* The reason we made it was that we could use the same costumes that Miss Geraldine Farrar and a friend of hers (at the time) had worn in some costume pictures — all these Shakespearean tights and everything. I don't say this egotistically, but I wore Geraldine's.

Top: Sylvia Breamer and Will Rogers in ***Doubling for Romeo*** (1921) (courtesy Will Rogers Memorial). ***Bottom:*** Will Rogers saddling up in ***Doubling for Romeo*** (courtesy Will Rogers Memorial).

Top: **Sylvia Breamer, Will Rogers and Wallace MacDonald in *A Poor Relation* (1921) (courtesy Will Rogers Memorial). *Bottom:* Robert De Vilbiss, Will Rogers, Jeanette Trebaol and Sylvia Breamer in *A Poor Relation* (courtesy Will Rogers Memorial).**

In March 1921, Goldwyn announced that it had purchased the motion picture rights for *A Poor Relation* by Edward E. Kidder. The late noted actor Sol Smith Russell had made it a popular stage success. The script would be used as a starring vehicle for Will Rogers. The May 1, 1921, issue of the *New York Morning Telegraph* reported that Sylvia Breamer liked the Goldwyn lot and working with Will Rogers so well in *Doubling for Romeo* that she signed another contract to appear with Will in his final Goldwyn picture, *A Poor Relation.*

Variety characterized Sylvia Breamer as "An effective ingenue" but concluded that "Will Rogers should be provided with better vehicles."

Several years after Goldwyn parted company with Will Rogers, his affection for the man and the performer showed through as he wrote in his 1923 book *Behind the Screen*:

> I have set aside chronological considerations in order to save for last my recollection of a man whose comedy touches brightened the Goldwyn lot almost as much as they did the Goldwyn screen. ... He used to stand around the Goldwyn lawn and, surrounded by a crowd of cowboys and extras, would amuse himself by throwing the lariat at our "Keep Off the Grass" signs. ... Imagine what a personality like this did for a studio somewhat overcharged with the artist temperament. Temperament itself seemed to find relief in those droll remarks with which Rogers meets almost every issue of the day.... There may be those in the screen world who are overridden by emotions, who are played upon by gusts of alternate personal attraction and repulsion. Not so Rogers.... There is nothing waspish about Rogers' fun-making. Such a quality of humor as his implies, in fact, a true sense of life's values, a very wise and mellow spirit ... his *Jubilo* was one of the best pictures ever produced by the Goldwyn Company."

When Will heard that Goldwyn was writing his memoirs, he wrote Sam, "Now I don't know what you are going to put into this catalogue of yours, but I do hope for the salvation of the Infant Industry you don't tell all — especially not what some of my pictures grossed. But if you've got to say something about me, say this — they were the two happiest years of my life that I spent on the Goldwyn lot. We had some great troops in those days — all of them good fellows."

Will Rogers on His Own

> *I was in pictures in Hollywood way back, when some of these big stars were just learning to get married. You see, pictures have to undergo a poor, or what Will Hays would call a "mediocre" stage before they get to be big. Well, there is the stage that I assisted the great film industry through. The minute they commenced getting better, why, my mission had been fulfilled. In other words, I am what they might call a pioneer. I am all right in anything while it is in its crude state, but the minute it gets to having class, why I am sunk.*

In July 1921, the *New York Times* reported that "Will Rogers has completed his term with the Goldwyn Company ... and will head his own organization for the production of two-reel comedies.... Clarence G. Badger, who has directed the former Rogers pictures, will be associated with him." The *Morning Telegraph* said, "Add Will Rogers' name to the roster of star-producers! He's going to have his own independent production company ... and that's not the half of it, either. Mr. Rogers is not only to have his own company but he is also to launch said company by making two-reel features instead of five-reelers. Imagine it! A headlining star decides he can give an admiring public quite enough of himself and his story in two reels! Leave it to Will Rogers, the inimitable!"

"About all the pictures I have ever seen could be told in two reels, anyway. The only man who can beat me is the fellow who will come along and tell 'em in one reel," said Rogers in *Photoplay.*

The July 30, 1921, issue of *Moving Picture World* reported that Will had associated himself with Pathé Exchange for the production and release of movies from O. Henry–type stories. However, no movies were released through Pathé until late in 1922.

With his contract with Goldwyn completed and not renewed, Will had his chance to test out his own motion picture theories in 1921 and 1922. Earlier he had published his fourteen points for the movie industry and then followed that up with a list of suggestions for improving the industry. Here is some more of Will's sage advice:

"Use your audience for a press agent instead of hiring one."

"Don't tell your audience what your picture cost, they know what they were stung by the price of admission."

"How can you make five movies a year of over four million different pictures each when it took Rembrant five years to make one still?"

"You hear it asked, are movie audiences getting smarter? The answer is no. Ain't more people going to movies than there ever was?"

"There is only one thing that can kill the movies, and that is education."

"What movies need is another name for an All-Star cast."

"What the movie audience needs is endurance."

"What the movie actor needs is better doubles (so they can do better stunts)."

"What the weeping movie heroine needs is glycerine that won't stay in one place, but will run down the face."

"What the entire movie industry needs is a sense of humor."

"If the movies want to advance, all they have to do is not to get new stories but do the old ones over as they were written."

"Producers say pictures have improved, but they haven't. It's only audiences have got used to them."

"You can't spring a new plot on an audience the first time and suspect it to go. It takes a movie audience years to get used to a new plot."

"Moving picture audiences are just like an old gold miner, they will keep on going and going for years hoping against hope to eventually some day strike a picture."

"The finish of the movies will be when they run out of suggestive titles."

"Some say, What is the salvation of the movies? I say run 'em backward. It can't hurt 'em and it's worth a trial."

"Some cinics ask, Is movies really art yet? Yes, selling them is."

"Which one of the arts will it supplant? It must have been literature, as there hasn't been any in a long time (if it hadn't been for my book)."

"The average life of the movie is till it reaches the critic."

"The average life of the movie hero is till he is found out."

Will went to work on a James Cruze production, *One Glorious Day*, for Famous Players–Lasky Corporation. Will's role of psychology professor Ezra Botts was originally scheduled to go to Roscoe "Fatty" Arbuckle but Arbuckle's well-publicized scandal put an end to that scenario. Lila Lee co-starred with Will in a comedy centering around a spirit entering Botts and transforming him into a new man for 24 hours.

Paramount released *One Glorious Day* in January 1922. A Famous Players–Lasky Corporation ad in *Moving Picture World* exalted the new movie as "an absolute knockout in originality, comedy, romance, and box-office pulling power!" *Moving Picture World* wrote, "Not only is the picture a novelty in itself, but it furnishes Will Rogers with a role that is decidedly different from anything he has ever attempted. With it he is eminently successful."

The *New York Telegraph* found *One Glorious Day* to be "one glorious picture. It is more fun than any picture we have ever seen with perhaps one exception. Exquisitely made." *Photoplay* advised moviegoers, "See this. You'll admit it's out of the ordinary ... you'll love Will Rogers more than ever. He is one actor who's good no matter what you

Lila Lee and Will Rogers in *One Glorious Day* (1922) (authors' collection).

Alan Hale, Will Rogers and Lila Lee in *One Glorious Day* (authors' collection).

give him to do. His rare whimsicality, comparable to Chaplin's, was never more apparent."

In October 1921, Will returned to New York, appearing at Shubert's Winter Garden for a salary of $3,000 a week, his first stage appearance since moving to California to star in pictures for Goldwyn. The *New York Times* welcomed Rogers back: "Will Rogers, one of the most likable comedians extant, came back to town yesterday after a desertion to Hollywood that has been prolonged through many seasons. They welcomed him royally at the Winter Garden when he shuffled amiably on to the stage, gum, lariats, sheepishness, jokes and all. Just as of yore, the ropes whirled and danced while he cast off casually his comments on the news of the day."

In November, he triumphantly returned to the Ziegfeld *Midnight Frolic* on the roof of the New Amsterdam and made a number of appearances for Loew Theatres.

The November 15, 1921, issue of the *New York Times* heralded Rogers' return to the *Frolic*: "The topliners are Will Rogers, Leon Errol and Carl Randall. Mr. Rogers, roping and jesting, is back in his old haunt after a considerable absence, as amusing as ever."

Will closed out 1921 with the *Midnight Frolic* in New York and went on tour with the production in early 1922. He reappeared in the Ziegfeld *Follies* with its opening on

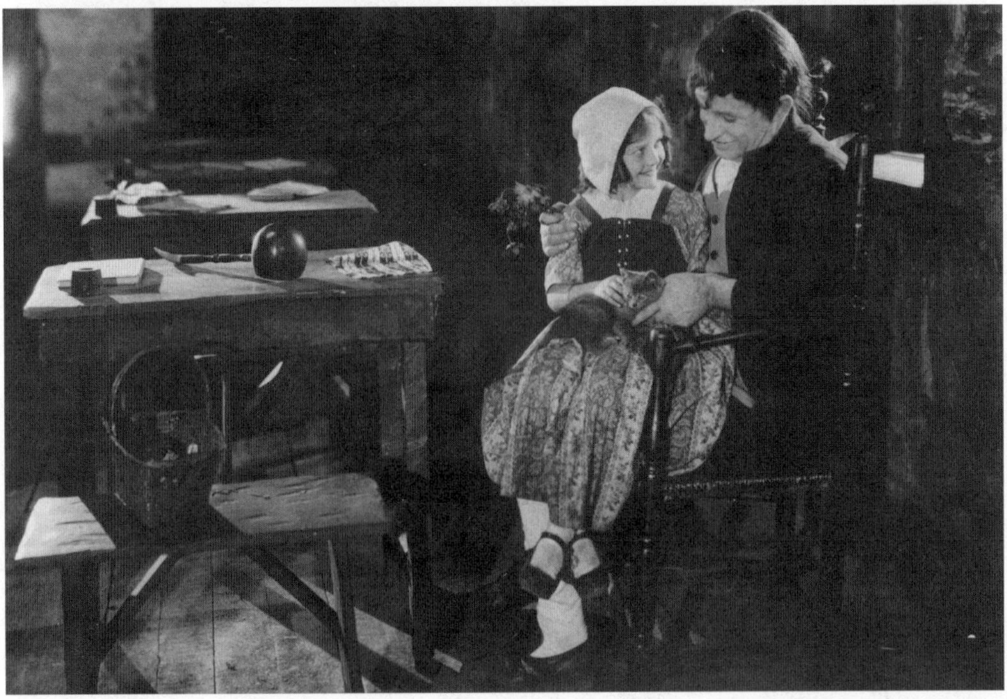

Top: Will Rogers as schoolmaster Ichabod Crane in ***The Headless Horseman*** (1922)(courtesy Will Rogers Memorial). ***Bottom:*** Will Rogers as schoolmaster Ichabod Crane in ***The Headless Horseman*** (courtesy of Will Rogers Memorial).

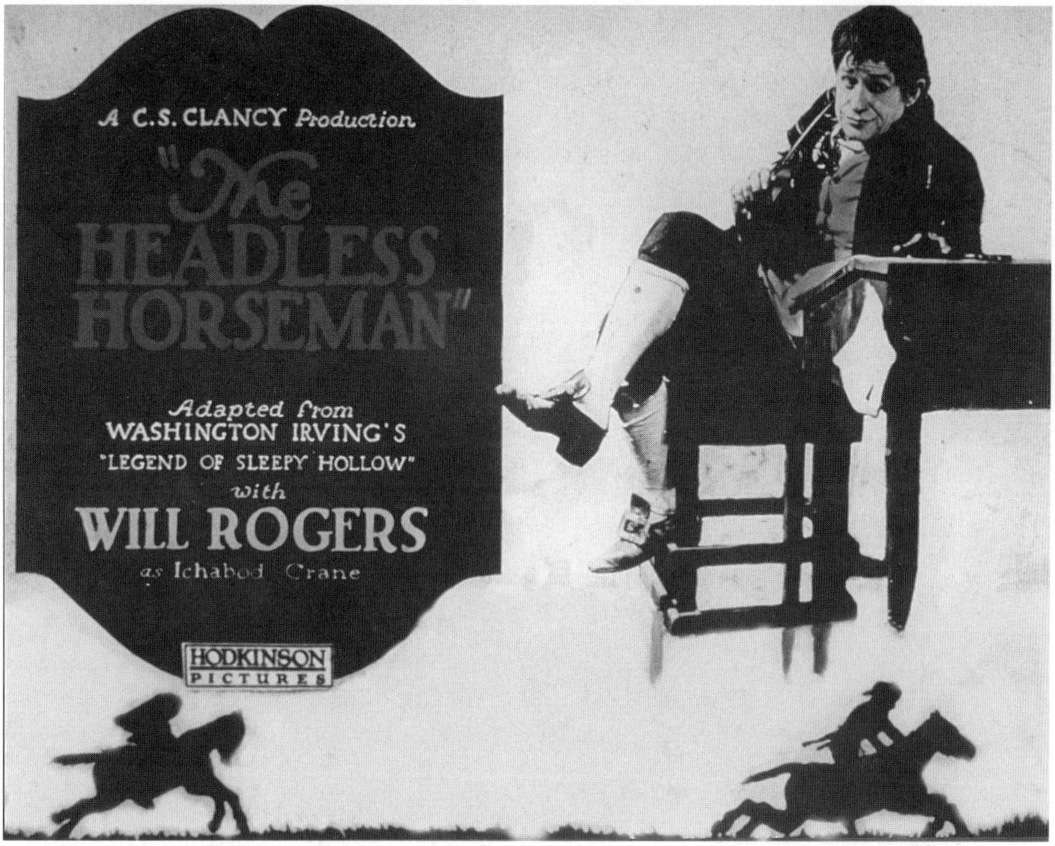

Lobby card for *The Headless Horseman* (authors' collection).

June 5, 1922. When the last *Follies* show of 1922 closed, Will received a gold loving cup from Ziegfeld in appreciation.

Despite being one of the highest paid performers on Broadway, Will had suffered a large salary cut from his movie days. He kept extremely busy. His experience with the movies convinced him to reach out to wider audiences through other forms of mass media. That did not mean, however, that Will had given up on movies. Will still kept his hand in motion pictures, moving ahead with plans to produce his own films.

During the summer of 1922, Will worked on location in Hackensack, New Jersey, filming *The Headless Horseman*, produced by Carl Stearns Clancy for the Sleepy Hollow Corporation. The film was released for distribution by Hodkinson Pictures in November 1922.

When interviewed on location by a *Photoplay* staff writer, Will inquired if it was true that the magazine was made up two months in advance of publication. When he was assured that the publication worked two months ahead he said, "You're takin' an awful chance workin' that far ahead; way things look now, there ain't going to be no film business by that time."

Will's portrayal of Washington Irving's Ichabod Crane rang true with the *New York Times*: "The only thing distinctly cinematographic about the film is the acting of Will Rogers.

He is in truth Ichabod Crane come to life. It is a positive pleasure to watch him." *Exceptional Photoplays* followed suit with "there will be general agreement as to Mr. Rogers having given us a unique and whimsically original character in his figure of the gaunt and comical Yankee schoolmaster of the Irving tale. ...It stamps Rogers as an actor of versatility." Other reviews were not as enthusiastic. *Variety* commented, "Rogers' latest release is picturesque. It reveals splendid photography, but this schoolroom classic lacks the sustaining power on the screen to make it vital." Reviewer Laurence Reid in *Motion Picture News* also found fault: "It is noticeable that the picture is not first class screen material ... it carries no situations, nor incident, but merely presents a series of episodes in the adventures of Crane.... Will Rogers is in character insofar as suggesting a grand conceit, but he fails to catch the real cowardice of the schoolmaster."

Producer Will Rogers

A bad picture is an accident, a good picture is a miracle.

Will once gave his definition of a producer: "That's the fellow that spends a lot of somebody else's money producing pictures somebody else wrote, somebody else directed and a lot of others acted in."

Will took an entirely different tack in his own producing ambitions. For the most part, he wrote, acted in, starred his kids and financed the pictures he produced. Will's dream of becoming a successful movie producer turned into a nightmare and devastated the family's finances. Will had to mortgage their home, borrow against his life insurance and put up his films as collateral for bank financing in order to get all three of his productions completed and ready for distribution.

Will did not intend for *The Ropin' Fool* or any of his other films to be dramatic successes. They were good, wholesome family entertainment with plenty of laughs and comedy situations. He also used his films to poke fun at the "seriousness" of the movie business and his fellow actors.

Will's titles in *The Ropin' Fool* illustrated those points: "There isn't much of a story to the film, but ninety percent of the movies contain no story, but this is the first one to admit it."

"They say Griffith pictures set the movies ahead four years. This one will put them back where they were."

During a lynching scene a sheriff rides by and upon learning that the hanging is just a movie scene says, "Well, as long as it is a movie, go ahead and hang him; I'm in favor of hanging everyone in the movies."

The Ropin' Fool broke new ground with slow motion photography to show Will's skill with the lariat. He performed a number of intricate rope tricks, including the flat loop, wedding ring, Texas skip and a very difficult three-rope catch of horse and rider.

When his films failed to attract audiences in the numbers to make them commer-

Will Rogers romances Irene Rich in *The Ropin' Fool* (1922) (courtesy Will Rogers Memorial).

cially successful, he was hurt. Besides being crippled financially, he was stung by the nastiness of some of his critics. *Variety* called *The Ropin' Fool* "fairly amusing, principally through the titles, but there seems to be just a little too much of the roping stuff ... the picture is short and snappy enough to be interesting ... as a straight picture value in a comedy sense it cannot be said that Rogers classes with either Lloyd or Chaplin as a screen comic, but there seems to be a possibility he will build up into a real two-reel bet."

Moving Picture World properly acknowledged that the movie was "essentially an exhibit of the man's remarkable ability to make a rope tie itself into all sorts of knots by the mere process of being whirled through the air, and to halt the escape of men, horses, geese—all kinds of living things ... no audience can help but marvel as Rogers throws a figure eight around a galloping horse or brings to terms a cat melodiously inclined.... It is to be recommended as a decidedly pleasing novelty in film entertainment, an excellent short subject with which to round out any program anywhere ... in other words, *The Ropin' Fool* made a distinct hit. It marks Rogers' debut as a producer."

Will commented, "I don't know what they call art, but there's 30 years' hard work in this film.... I sweat blood and then some ... especially the part where I snare the rat.

Irene Rich, Will Rogers and Guinn "Big Boy" Williams in *The Ropin' Fool* (courtesy Will Rogers Memorial).

It took me two days to get that rat so it wasn't camera shy and another day to get the hang of twirling a line small enough to noose the rat."

Years later, Will remembered, "I made a picture with my own money once — about the only 100 percent Gentile picture ever made. Never again! Art for art's sake is fine, but I want some business talent. The picture was called *The Ropin' Fool.* Everybody said I wanted too much money for it. I couldn't explain but that there were $10,000 worth of misses cut out of the picture! I was three whole days roping one fool rat — I'm going to train my next rat to jump in a noose and tie himself up!

"Someday I'm going to get me an education and be a critic ... then I'll go out and criticize somethin' I didn't take up."

The Ropin' Fool remains a classic short feature and captures for posterity Will's dexterity with the lariat in over fifty rope tricks. A video copy of this treasure is available from the Will Rogers Memorial in Claremore, Oklahoma.

Will preceded the release of *Fruits of Faith* with the following comments:

> I have made a close study of motion picture audiences. I have discovered, and statistics prove, that the average motion picture audience starts to go to sleep along about the second or third reel. Now I've figured it out that the only way to beat them to it is to make two or three-reel pictures. If they go to sleep on these, I'll make one-reelers.

> A great many so-called wise guys have said, "Isn't it kind of going back to go from five reels to two, or three?" I say, no, not when you tell the same story in two or three reels. I made 14 two-reel pictures which were released in five reels. I'd rather have the credit of making a split reel, if it was any good, than to make the longest picture ever made.
>
> I've been told by some exhibitors that they liked my pictures but that they didn't draw. So I figured it out to make short features to be put in with a full-length feature, and let one of the two get the blame for bringing 'em in or keeping 'em out. All mine's supposed to do is please 'em after they get in.
>
> You want to know what I think about censorship? Well, not much, I ain't worried much about them fellers. You see, one thing about my pictures, we don't even fear the censors. My pictures have been pitied—but never censored.

Motion Picture News predicted, "*Fruits of Faith* is so strong that unless the feature to follow is 'sure fire' the short subject is bound to be the best part of the program. It is a clever blend of comedy and drama, ably directed, artistically photographed, splendidly played and assembled." The *New Evening Mail* said, "*Fruits of Faith* at the Rialto is better [than the feature]. Rogers scores in this with a mingling of pathos and humor."

Even the *New York Times* trumpeted Will's new release: "After you have sat through the featured photoplay, you come to this real feature of the bill. It's only some two or

Lobby card for *Fruits of Faith* (1922) (authors' collection).

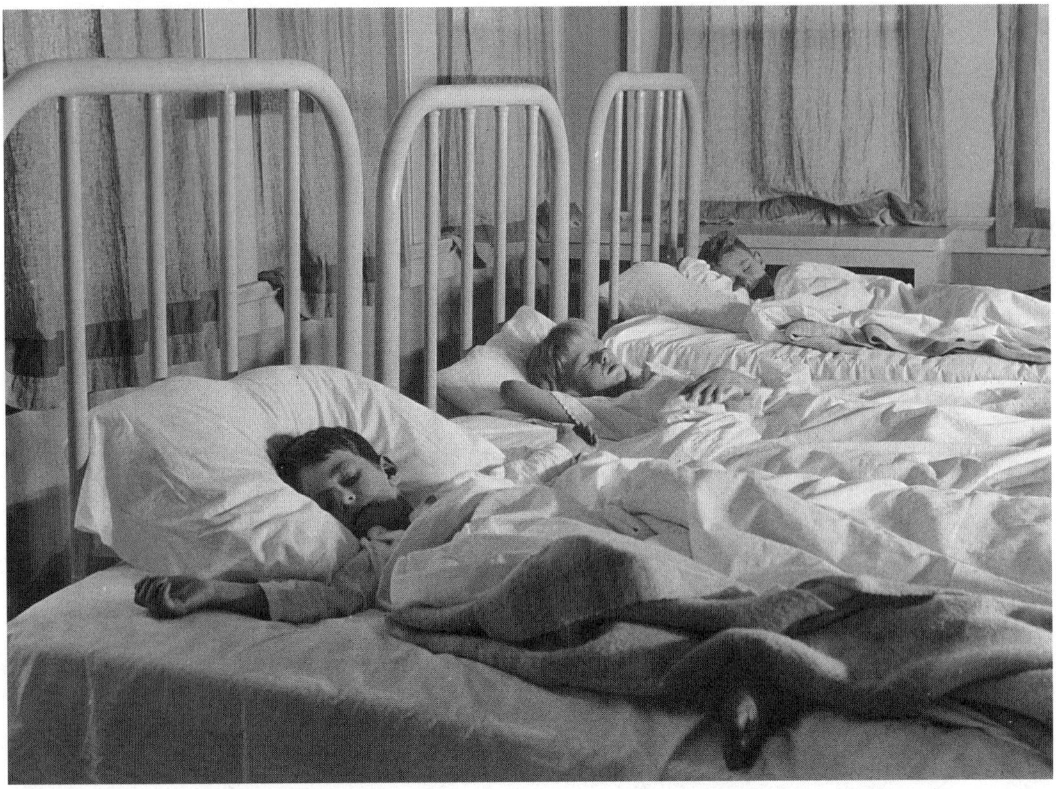

The Rogers kids, Will, Jr., Mary and Jimmy, in *One Day in 365*. "I photograph them asleep because they behave best that way" (1922, never released) (courtesy Will Rogers Memorial).

three reels long and it makes no pretensions as to plot or magnificence of setting.... But there is more genuine entertainment in any hundred feet of it than in all the celluloid miles of agony and adventure that prolongs the heavy hour of the photoplay ... twenty or thirty minutes of slender story made human and humorous by the humanness and humor of Will Rogers."

Unfortunately, both *The Ropin' Fool* and *Fruits of Faith* faced similar disappointing fates at the box office, spelling doom for Will Rogers' short-lived career as a movie producer.

Produced after T*he Ropin' Fool* and *Fruits of Faith, One Day in 365* never made it into distribution. The film featured Will's wife, Betty, and their children and centered around a thin plot of the hazards of living in Beverly Hills, down the road from famous movie stars. The working title for the film was *No Story at All.*

Will returned to Broadway broke, leaving his family behind in California, as he sought to get out of debt. Betty looked back on those disappointing days: "I think he worked as hard this year as he ever did in his life, and without a break or vacation of any kind. He hated to be away from the children, and he missed his favorite ponies: but when he came home the following summer to accept a new movie contract [with Hal Roach], much of his indebtedness had been paid."

Will later wrote about his motion picture–producing experience, "If the loan is made

Will Rogers pointing out Doug Fairbanks' and Mary Pickford's house in *One Day in 365* (courtesy Will Rogers Memorial).

for a moving picture, the president of the bank wants to write the story for you. The directors want to know who the leading lady is, and if they could, they would keep her as collateral."

A Budding Writing Career

When I first started out to write and misspelled a few words, people said I was plain ignorant. But when I got all the words wrong, they declared I was a humorist.

Will's writing career took off in late 1922 with the signing of a contract with the McNaught Syndicate to write a weekly newspaper column. Will's column premiered in the *New York Times* on December 24, 1922, and immediately went into general syndication.

Various *Follies* girls join Will and Betty Rogers for his first radio broadcast (courtesy Will Rogers Memorial).

In typical fashion, Will entered people's homes on a bashful note, "I want to apologize and set the many readers of the *Times* straight as to why I am blossoming out as a weekly infliction on you all."

Will's infliction upon people lasted until his untimely death in Alaska in 1935. During that time, he penned 665 Sunday columns and reached an audience of 40 million readers weekly. People readily took to Will's view of the world and his no-nonsense way of looking at everything from politics to business and from kings to movie stars. He eventually started out his weekly column with a line from his *Follies* act, "All I know is what I read in the papers." Interest in the weekly columns was so great that Will published a collection of his articles in book form as *Illiterate Digest* in 1924. This time no protest letter arrived from Funk and Wagnalls' lawyer.

"The great trouble in writing for the Papers every week is that you are apt to hit on some subject that does not appeal to a certain class of People. For instance, if I write a learned Article on Chewing Gum, I find that I lose my Clientele of Readers who are toothless, because they naturally are not interested in Chewing Gum if they have no teeth. Then when I write on just strictly Politics, I find that the honest People are not interested."

Over the next few years, Will's writing career flourished, as did his propensity for travel. His publishers realized that a daily dose of Will would draw an even greater audience and in 1926 convinced Will to write a series of short articles called *Daily Telegrams*, covering events of the day and topics he came across during his travels. Syndication of *Daily Telegrams* under the "Will Rogers Says" heading reached over 400 newspapers and Will completed 2,817 daily columns over the next nine years. People across the country woke up every morning to get their daily dose of Rogerisms and Will's views of current events.

Also in 1926, Will wrote a series of articles for the *Saturday Evening Post* called "Letters of a Self-Made Diplomat to His President," originating out of his travels in Europe and observations of the international scene. These articles were later published as a book under the same title. Other books that Will authored include *There's Not a Bathing Suit in Russia and Other Bare Facts* and *Ether and Me*, a humorous account of his experience with ether and his gall bladder operation.

In addition to breaking into print on the national scene, Will made an initial step into new technology with his first radio broadcast over Pittsburgh's pioneer radio station KDKA on February 25, 1922. During this first broadcast, Will was surrounded by a number of the *Follies* girls and his wife, Betty. Will first approached radio with a bit of trepidation: "That little microphone is not going to laugh." That first bit of experimentation with radio led to a successful and profitable radio career in the 1930s that reached millions of American listeners.

Will Rogers was well on his way to becoming a star.

Chapter 3

Will Rogers, Star

More Follies

My little act with the lasso was just put into the Ziegfeld Follies *to kill time, while the girls were changing from nothing to nothing.*

In 1923, Will Rogers performed in the Ziegfeld *Follies* skit "Koo Koo Nell." The skit spoofed both the old-time western melodramas and the hit show *Kiki*, starring noted actress Lenore Ulric and playing at the Belasco Theatre on Broadway. Will donned a skirt and played the role of Koo Koo, a San Francisco dance hall girl. The *New York Times* commented, "The most prominent of the additions is 'Koo Koo Nell.' ... The playlet ends happily with the murder of all concerned."

Of course, Will continued with his brand of humor, kidding the girls of the *Follies:* "They are not well up on their Latin and Greek, but, my, how these girls know their Dun's and Bradstreet's!"

In January 1923, Will received an offer from Hal Roach to star in a series of fourteen two-reel comedies for distribution by Pathé Exchange. Before accepting the contract, Will promised Ziegfeld to stay with the *Follies* until its New York engagement closed for the season. When Will finally left the *Follies* in June 1923, Eddie Cantor, who had left the show several years earlier, returned to replace Will.

Will returned to the *Follies* again in 1924, impersonating an Oklahoma senator and getting credit for the first time as an author of the *Follies* script. Will finished out his *Follies* career with Ziegfeld's twentieth anniversary production in 1925 in which Will and W. C. Fields received top billing. The *New York Times* wrote, "The outstanding feature of the new production is W. C. Fields. Not so long ago Fields was known only as a limited specialty comedian — last night he clearly proved his right to be called one of the supreme comedians of our time.... Mr. Rogers, of course, is on hand and to his customary wise and hilarious effect. He, too, has a new contribution, a sketch called 'A Country Store,' in which, as a returned Vermonter, he recounts his experience of a visit to Coolidge. And it all ends, to the great delight of the audience, in Mr. Rogers breaking into song."

Will returned to New York in December 1926 as guest of honor and principal speaker for the laying of the cornerstone and dedication of the New Ziegfeld Theatre at Fifty-fourth Street and Sixth Avenue. The dedication program was broadcast over WGBS.

"In the old days there used to be a saloon on every corner, today we have the theatre. I leave it to you which you like best.... Folks, let me say right here and now, this here new theatre is being dedicated to ART, and—the movies," Will commented.

On the Speaker's Trail

There is only one speech any speech maker in the world can make to a hungry audience, and be heard, and that is "Dinner's ready, come and get it, or we will throw it out."

While performing at the *Follies,* Will fit in a growing number of after-dinner speaking engagements during the early 1920s, commanding $1,000 per night. He spoke to a variety of national organizations, including the Automobile Manufacturers, Corset Manufacturers, Furriers Trade, National Association of Waste Material Dealers, Varnish Salesmen's Association and Wholesale Silk Stocking Manufacturers. In front of the Police Chiefs convention, Will kidded, "Although I had never caught a crook, neither had they."

But perhaps one of Will's most famous statements regarding dinner speaking engagements was not part of his official speech at all. Will had been invited to a dinner party given by a well-known industrialist at his home. After dinner, Will was asked to stand up and say a few remarks, which he did. The next day, Will sent the man a bill for his usual speaking fee. When the man responded that there must have been some mistake, Will had been invited as a guest, Will replied, "Oh, no I wasn't. You got me out as an actor. If I was a guest you'd have invited Mrs. Rogers too!" The man paid the bill.

Will also used his popularity to earn money in other ways. In August 1924, he signed a contract with the American Tobacco Company to write ten pieces of Bull Durham ad copy for $2,500. The contract was extended in September 1924 to encompass the writing of 26 pieces of Bull Durham copy at the rate of $500 each for a total of not more than $13,000.

Will gradually recovered from his devastating plunge into motion picture production. An insurance investigative report listed his 1923 annual income from the *Follies,* speaking engagements and product copy as $500,000 and an additional $150,000 from his earnings from Hal Roach movies. Within five years, his net worth would exceed $3 million with an average annual income in excess of $500,000.

The Hal Roach Comedy Two-Reelers

These two-reelers are going to be funny even if I have to use some Harold Lloyd cut-outs to do it.

Will returned to California in June 1923 with a Hal Roach contract in hand to star in fourteen two-reel comedy shorts for $2,000 per week plus a share of the movies' profits. The lucrative contract made Will Roach's highest paid actor, earning far more than the salaries paid other Roach stars such as Harold Lloyd and Laurel and Hardy.

Will explained his absence from the movie business as follows: "You see, when I left there a year and a half ago, they were cleaning up the morals of Hollywood, and I had to get out. But now that we both have reformed, I am returning."

Before any of the Will Rogers movies produced by Roach were released by Pathé Exchange, Will appeared in the August 1923 Famous Players–Lasky Corporation picture *Hollywood*. Under the direction of James Cruze, a myriad of famous actors, including

Will Rogers (center) in Hal Roach comedy skit (courtesy Will Rogers Memorial).

Will Rogers in Hal Roach comedy skit (courtesy Will Rogers Memorial).

Will Rogers, appeared in cameo roles supporting a story about a young girl trying to break into the big time.

As *Variety* noted, "The girl meets Mary Pickford, to whom she delivers a dress. Mary calls Doug Fairbanks out that the girl may meet him. Other stars appear equally as briefly, but they appear." *Photoplay* commented, "Dozens of the picture stars shown unconventionally to prove they are humans after all. A rattling good picture."

Will started work on *Jus' Passin' Through* in June 1923, and Pathé Exchange released the film in October 1923. The movie teamed Will up with actress Marie Mosquini. "The Big Little Feature" section of *Exhibitors Trade Review* called *Jus' Passin' Through* "excellent" and ranked the picture "high in entertainment value. Don't fail to book it."

The next Rogers/Roach movie out of the chute, *Hustlin' Hank*, put Will on the other side of the lens as a cameraman assigned to help a feminist obtain photographs of wildlife.

Will used the December 1923 release, *Uncensored Movies*, as a vehicle to poke fun at Hollywood, popular movies and other screen stars such as William S. Hart, Tom Mix and Rudolph Valentino. *Moving Picture World* found that "Will Rogers' newest two-reel comedy ... *Uncensored Movies* gives him the opportunity for what is said to be the first time to present a line of entertainment on the screen for which he is famous on the stage. In his own inimitable way he caricatures Bill Hart, Tom Mix and Rudolph Valentino and

Lobby card for ***Hustlin' Hank*** (1923) (authors' collection).

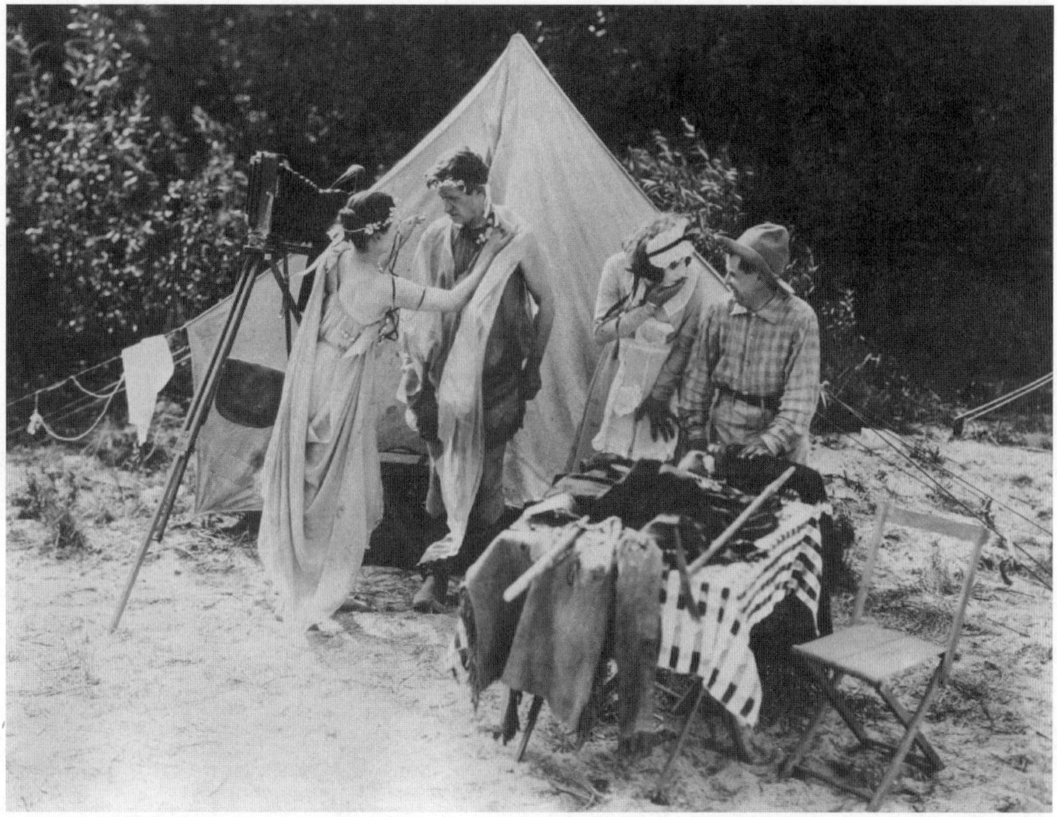

Marie Mosquini, Will Rogers, Vera White and Billy Engle in *Hustlin' Hank* (courtesy Will Rogers Memorial).

makes satirical though inoffensive allusions to De Mille, Griffith and Fairbanks in their respective fields."

Exhibitors Herald proclaimed *Uncensored Movies,* "Will Rogers at his best.... Will Rogers, Marie Mosquini and "Big Boy" Williams put over this clever bit of nonsense in a most satisfactory way. It is an excellent satire on some of our screen idols and the ever-present uplift societies known in Rogers' film as 'Cleaner Screen League.' What could be more delightful than his Bill Hart stuff, where he comes home to his poor, old mother and she accuses him of 'killin' men again' ... as Rudolph Valentino he inspects three beauties of the desert, turns them all down for a fourth in riding habit and orders his slave to drown the other three. A comedy you won't want to miss."

Photoplay took a more negative view of *Uncensored Movies*: "Will Rogers tries, very unsuccessfully to be killingly funny. He impersonates various motion picture stars... and doesn't make any of them worth a great deal. The title writer throws in a word now and then and makes things even worse. Why did Will leave his rope out of the script, anyway? And why is this called a comedy?"

The December 22, 1923, issue of *Exhibitors Trade Review* reported that "Will Rogers has tossed his hat in the ring as a candidate for the King of Shorts.... Polish up the crown, for Will usually finishes everything he starts." A January 1924 full-page advertisement

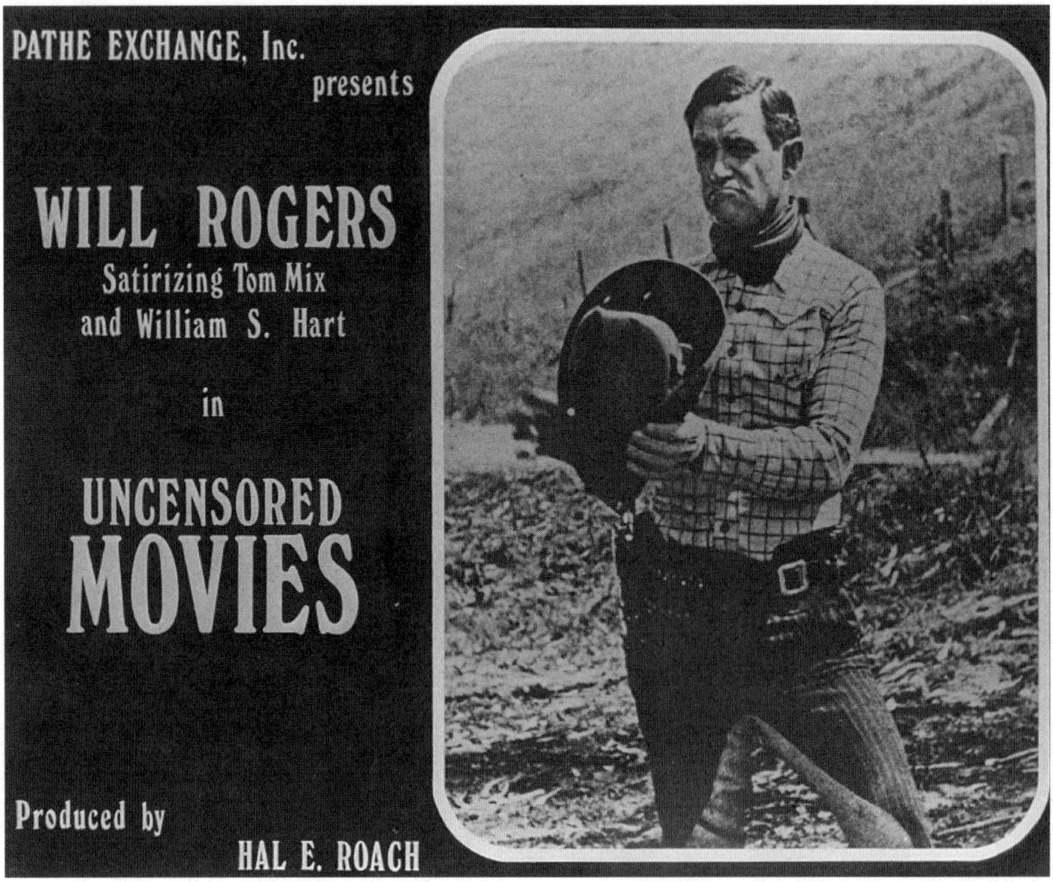
PATHE EXCHANGE, Inc.
presents
WILL ROGERS
Satirizing Tom Mix
and William S. Hart
in
UNCENSORED
MOVIES
Produced by
HAL E. ROACH

Lobby card for *Uncensored Movies* (1923) (authors' collection).

for the Pathé comedy release proclaimed that "Hal Roach presents Will Rogers in two-reel comedies.... The only thing missing is the drawl!"

In February 1924, Will appeared as the master of ceremonies for the western opening of Ernest Lubitsch's *The Marriage Circle*, starring Marie Prevost at Grauman's Rialto Theatre in Los Angeles. Will lassoed audience notables, such as Pola Negri, and praised the movie: "It will be much more popular than 'The Ten Commandments'—some people don't know the ten commandments, but in this picture they know what is going on all the time."

Will next worked on *Gee Whiz, Genevieve*, but production problems postponed the release of that picture until after several others were produced and released. Pathé released *Two Wagons, Both Covered* in January 1924 and followed that with *The Cowboy Sheik* in February 1924.

Will continued his burlesque of prominent actors and movies with *Two Wagons, Both Covered*, a takeoff on an immensely popular epic western film, *The Covered Wagon*, starring J. Warren Kerrigan. The film broke volume-of-bookings records and played an unprecedented two weeks straight at the California Theatre. The *Los Angeles Express* film critic, Charles Goss, wrote that the picture is "so meritorious as to steal first place honors

Will Rogers in *Two Wagons, Both Covered* (1924) (courtesy Will Rogers Memorial).

on the California bill from an excellent feature picture." The *New York Times* called *Two Wagons, Both Covered,* "a splendid burlesque on *The Covered Wagon*.... Will Rogers is the stellar quantity in this laughable parody.... It is as funny as anything we have ever seen on the films, especially when Will Rogers ... is introduced leaning forward on his horse."

This time *Photoplay* joined the chorus of praise: "One of Will Rogers' burlesques and a clever one. Great, if you've seen *The Covered Wagon*.... He gives a good caricature of the part that Ernest Torrence made famous, and in the J. Warren Kerrigan role he is superb."

In the February 1924 release, *The Cowboy Sheik,* Will plays a dim-witted cowpoke, "Two-Straw" Bill, who has to draw straws before deciding anything, giving rise to a number of amusing situations and exciting complications.

On March 10, 1924, the Hal E. Roach Studios notified Will that it was exercising its right and option to extend the term of his employment under the contract for an additional year. Around the same time, Will announced that he was extending the targets of his burlesque to include American politicians. Future films would find Rogers as a congressman and as a visitor to the Court of St. James. Newspapers reported, "Extreme precautions are being taken to avoid any suggestion of political partisanship or bias in the filming of these ... pictures. The political atmosphere merely furnishes the setting for a profusion of scintillating comedy and gentle, inoffensive satire at which Mr. Rogers is so adept."

Will Rogers (hat and beard) with cast and crew on location of *Two Wagons, Both Covered.* Marie Mosquini in wagon, Betty Rogers wearing riding habit in front of wagon (courtesy Will Rogers Memorial).

A full-page Pathé comedy advertisement in *Moving Picture World* proclaimed *The Cake Eater*, starring Will Rogers, as "his best yet.... It may be that it's possible to make a better comedy than this, but it hasn't been made yet."

Exhibitors Trade Review guaranteed "lots of chuckles.... Those who are familiar with Rogers' stage work will revel in the witty titles (written by him) in which he pokes fun at himself in particular and everything in general. A good little plot with some real chuckles that will leave a lasting impression."

The December 6, 1923, issue of the *Tacoma Ledger* stated that "Rogers is proving himself a real mimic ... under direction of Jay A. Howe on a comedy called *Big Moments from Little Pictures*, in which he impersonates Ford Sterling and the Keystone Cops."

Rogers summed up his new slapstick talent, "I stopped my first pie yesterday."

Reviewer Tom Hamlin in *Motion Picture News* remarked, "Will Rogers shows that he is a real travesty artist when he burlesques several big scenes from successful feature pictures.... Mr. Rogers introduces each scene as if he were in the *Follies*, and intersperses his announcements with clever rope jumping. This one should register pleasantly anywhere."

Rob Wagner, the director of many of Will's movies under the Hal Roach banner, reflected on his relationship with Will Rogers:

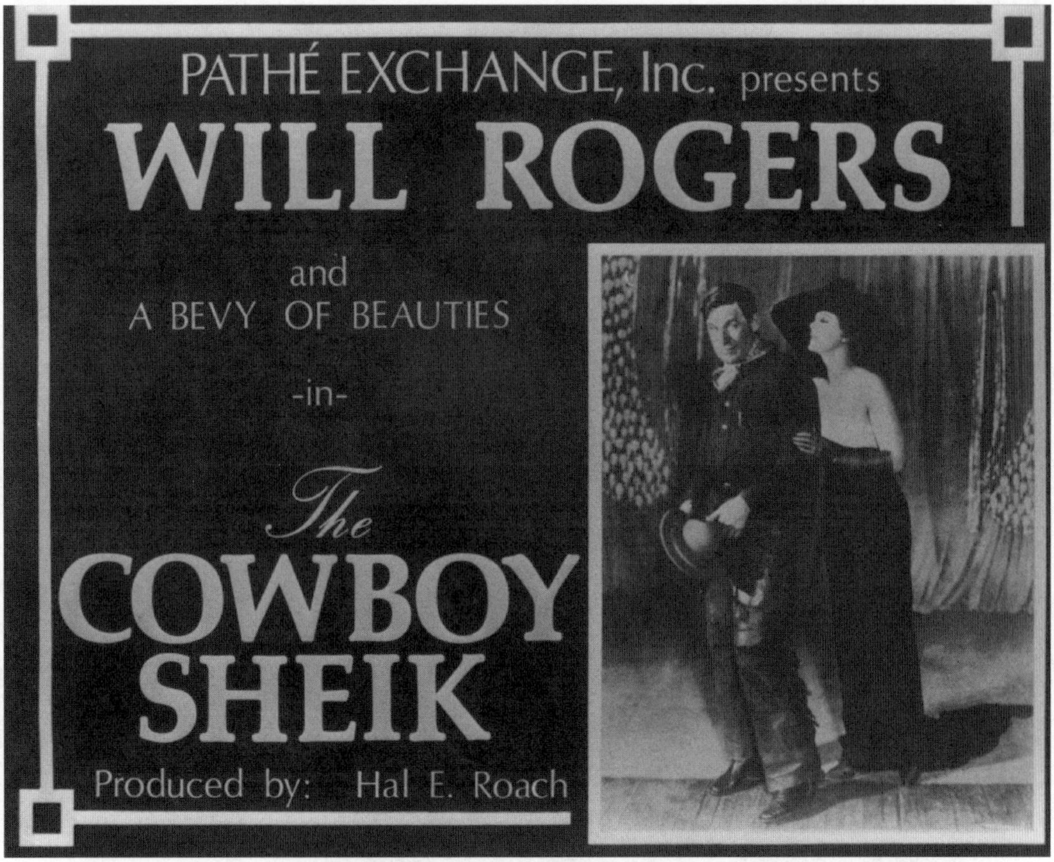

Top: Lobby card for ***The Cowboy Sheik*** (1924) (authors' collection). ***Bottom:*** Will Rogers, Marie Mosquini and Helen Gilmore in ***The Cowboy Sheik*** (courtesy Will Rogers Memorial).

Will Rogers, Marie Mosquini, Earl Mohan and Helen Gilmore in *The Cowboy Sheik* (courtesy Will Rogers Memorial).

> When Will asked me to direct him in a series of short comedies, I was warned, "He's the hardest actor in Hollywood to handle. As stubborn as a little boy." That was true—at first. I tried to explain that while he was responsible for the comedy, I was responsible for the construction. He was bored and irritated. But when I said, "Besides Will, having to argue every point with you hurts my feelings...." With that Will threw his arms around me and shouted: "Rob, I wouldn't hurt your feelings for the world—let's go!" From then on everything was Jake.... We had to provide entertainment for Rogers on location ... entertainment in the form of goats to rope, or else he grew temperamental.... Will was the kindliest fellow I ever knew.

The Wagner/Rogers combination also put together *High Brow Stuff,* an April 1924 release for Roach Studios. In this two-reel comedy short, Will portrays a famous Russian little-theater actor recruited to star in motion pictures. This time Will lampooned a movement running through New York's Greenwich Village with the lofty goal of uplifting the dramatic arts.

Motion Picture News predicted that "*High Brow Stuff* should register with all classes of audiences.... There are plenty of laughs for all in this one." *Exhibitors Trade Review* called the studio scenes "a scream" and concluded, "If you don't laugh at Will Rogers in this one there is something wrong."

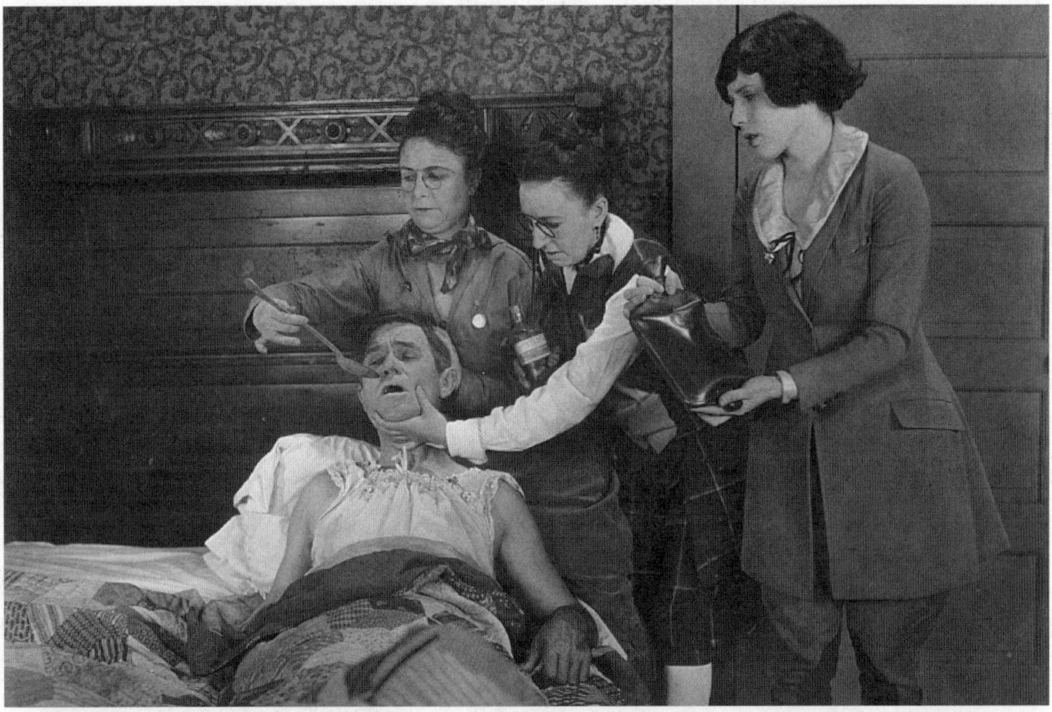

Top: **Patsy O'Byrne feeds Will Rogers with Marie Mosquini (far right) looking on in *The Cake Eater* (1924) (courtesy Will Rogers Memorial). *Bottom:* Will Rogers impersonates Rudolph Valentino in *Big Moments from Little Pictures* (1924) (courtesy Will Rogers Memorial).**

Will Rogers in ***High Brow Stuff*** (1924) (courtesy Will Rogers Memorial).

Will Rogers as movie director in *High Brow Stuff* (courtesy Will Rogers Memorial).

Will began his political satire in the movies with *Going to Congress*, in which he introduces the persona of Alfalfa Doolittle and his political adventures. The popularity of Will Rogers and his political satire is illustrated by the fact that this movie was shown at the Rialto Theatre in New York City during the Democratic National Convention and at the Allen Theatre in Cleveland when the Republican National Convention gathered there in 1924.

Moving Picture World described *Going to Congress* as "a broad satire on how congressmen are picked by the politicians, how they win elections by making impossible promises and how they act after elected.... It is a comedy that will appeal particularly to high-class audiences, but almost everybody will smile, even if they do not laugh aloud, at the good-natured slaps at some of our politicians and lawmakers."

Will Rogers takes on the frustrations of traffic congestion in a number of humorous situations comprising the basis for *Don't Park There*. "This is one of Rogers' best comedies. It hits home and everyone will appreciate the many incidents that happen in the life of every motorist.... The subtitles are especially humorous and bring many good laughs," said *Exhibitors Trade Review*.

Will Rogers once again appears in the role of Jubilo, injecting a bit of human interest in the "Our Gang" fare. *Photoplay* gave *Jubilo, Jr.* a thumbs up in June 1924: "If you

Top: Will Rogers as Alfalfa Doolittle in ***Going to Congress*** (1924) (courtesy Will Rogers Memorial). ***Bottom:*** Will Rogers in ***Jubilo, Jr.*** (1924) (courtesy Will Rogers Memorial).

Will Rogers in *Don't Park There* (1924) (courtesy Will Rogers Memorial).

were ever a kid you will like this picture. Will Rogers and The Gang combine for a lot of fun ... the combination is one of the cleverest things seen on the screen."

Congressman Alfalfa Doolittle (Rogers) settles into Washington and further adventures evolve in the July 1924 continuation of his political satire, *Our Congressman.* "There are a number of amusing situations most of them dealing with Rogers' social errors due to his ignorance of etiquette and to the kidding of the newspaper people who make him believe he is a great man," said *Moving Picture World.* Reviewer Tom Hamlin of *Motion Picture News* concluded, "Every Will Rogers fan will thoroughly enjoy this picture and it should register most strongly in those theatres whose audiences appreciate satire and subtle comedy."

Will finished out his trilogy of political satire and the misadventures of Congressman Doolittle with *A Truthful Liar*. The tale recounts the congressman's humorous experiences as an ambassador. *Moving Picture World* commented, "Because of its extreme burlesque qualities this Will Rogers number should be classed as one of his greatest mirth providers."

The final Will Rogers two-reel comedy film for Hal Roach Studios, *Gee Whiz, Genevieve*, finally went into distribution in September 1924. *Motion Picture News* took a negative view of *Gee Whiz, Genevieve*: "We would be advising Mr. Rogers to place thirteen [it was actually picture fourteen] on his list of pet superstitions. The result of all the

Top: Will Rogers suffers from etiquette ignorance in ***Our Congressman*** (1924) (courtesy Will Rogers Memorial). ***Bottom:*** Will Rogers in ***A Truthful Liar*** (1924) (courtesy Will Rogers Memorial).

Lobby card for *Gee Whiz, Genevieve* (1924) with Marie Mosquini and Will Rogers (courtesy Will Rogers Memorial).

work by scenarist, director and star has not been crowned by any conspicuous luck, and the spectator must be content with Will Rogers, alone, unaided, if not hampered by the poverty of the plot and the lack of spirit, or life, or whatever you will, in the staging of the piece."

Exhibitors Trade Review was more positive: "Will Rogers is a true artist when it comes to comedy. In the part of the tramp, Jubilo, he brings to the screen a real knowledge of what will make the public laugh. There is no sham or near-comedy, but the old fashioned laugh-provoking ability so seldom found today on the screen.... Many exhibitors would doubtless like to see another group following this — for these last were nearly successful everywhere."

On Tour

No nation ever had two better friends than we have. You know who they are. The Atlantic and Pacific oceans.

Despite the *Exhibitors Trade Review*'s prediction that exhibitors would like to see some more Will Rogers comedy shorts, Hal Roach failed to invoke the option to produce any more Will Rogers movies. Will finished out 1924 playing the Ziegfeld *Follies*. In November 1924, *Liberty Magazine* ran a three-page spread on Will and his humor entitled "Will Rogers: The World Laughs with Him." Characteristic of the jokes that caught the public's fancy:

"We can't have another war, we haven't got a slogan."

When asked to help solve New York's traffic problem, Will suggested that "cars move East on Monday and West on Thursday."

When one reporter wanted to know the bright things his kids said, he replied, "They ain't never said anything bright.... They're just normal children."

A 1925 movie, *Pretty Ladies*, has been tied to Will Rogers, but Will did not appear in the MGM production. The confusion lies in the fact that one of the actors, Lew Harvey, portrays Will in a brief scene.

Will did not let his lack of a movie contract keep him out of circulation. He put in another and final shift with the Ziegfeld *Follies* in 1925 and signed a contract with Charles L. Wagner for a lecture tour guaranteeing sixty performances during 1925 and 1926 for $60,000. Will was billed as "America's Greatest Humorist and Prince of Entertainers" and traveled with the De Reszke Singers. During this tour, Will lectured over 150 nights. The next season he lectured at even more stops.

Wagner asked Will to write an introduction for the program. Will titled the piece "A Warning" and went on to say, "Now in the first place, it was a surprise to me to know that we would have a programme. There are only two of us Acts, the Quartette and myself, and I didn't think the audience would be very apt to confuse one with the other. The Quartette is the one where there is four in it, that's in case they all show up, (which is rare) and I am the single individual, the man who will come out and enthrall you with his command of the English Language, with his unmatched dignity, with an oratorial delivery that is second only to Ben Turpin."

Will Rogers in *Tip Toes* (1927) (courtesy Will Rogers Memorial).

Will teamed up again with the De Reszke Singers for a benefit performance at Carnegie Hall on December 8, 1926. The Carnegie Hall program listed Will's act as "Will Rogers — Who is liable to talk about anything or anybody."

Will took off in mid–1926 for a tour of Europe with his family. While in London, he appeared in the Cochran *Revue* of 1926 at the London Pavilion. At the end of the run, which enjoyed sellout audiences for four weeks, Charles Cochran presented Will with a blank check since they had not agreed upon a fee in advance. Rogers tore up the check with the statement that Cochran had proved himself such a great sport and had given Rogers enormous publicity. Will had enjoyed the engagement to such an extent that he felt the producer owed him nothing.

During his London stay, Will signed a contract with British National Pictures Ltd. to appear in the upcoming film *Tip Toes.* The movie was filmed in London during the summer of 1926 and released in June 1927. Will joined fellow American actor Dorothy Gish in a story about the adventures of American vaudevillians stranded in London.

"Every time you finish a scene they bring you a cup of tea," said Will, "and what makes me sore at myself is, I am beginning to like the stuff."

Will's European travels paid off in another way. Carl Stearns Clancy, who earlier had produced *The Headless Horseman*, produced a series of travelogues with Will Rogers as "Our Unofficial Ambassador Abroad." Pathé Exchange distributed the films covering Will's jaunts through and observations of Europe with catchy titles such as *Roaming the Emerald Isle with Will Rogers* and *Hunting for Germans in Berlin with Will Rogers.* The travel films were released over a twelve-month period from early 1927 through early 1928. The December 14, 1926, issue of the *Toledo Blade* reported that Will Rogers

> is going to prove to all America that his famous trip abroad really happened, and that the foreign experiences which he detailed in pungent and uproarious magazine articles and on the lecture platform were not fiction. The cowboy humorist had a motion picture camera and a crack Hollywood cameraman along on his overseas excursion.... Rogers' pictures detail his experiences with royalty, with dictators, with peasants, with airplanes, railroad trains, strange languages, strange foods, all photographed and described with that mingled sense and nonsense, kindly exaggeration and caustic wit for which he is famous.

The *Tulsa Daily World* wrote, "Not since Mark Twain chronicled his immortal tours abroad has any private citizen of Yankeeland described so remarkable a trip as did Rogers in his recent series of articles on the adventures of a 'self-made diplomat to his President,' and the cowboy humorist had the advantage over Clemens, in that he had a motion picture camera."

Pathé Exchange publicized Will's travelogue series with multi-page advertisements in *Motion Picture News* and *Motion Picture Herald,* proclaiming $50 million in publicity behind the "Best Known Man in the World," who had 25 million people reading his words every day: "Here is a new Rogers. Now for the first time you may see the *real* man, with the quaint keen-witted personality that has made him the most talked of man in the world.... Rogers talks to you in the sub-titles. Every one is food for a laugh. Many of them for an uproar.... Yes, it's true. Big features in just one reel!"

A novel bit of advertising in *Motion Picture Herald* appeared in the form of a full-page letter to exhibitors from Will.

> Dear Exhibitors,
>
> Now I haven't bothered you in a long time. I layed off you and let you all get rich and prosperous. When I used to play you were all in little hay barns in the winter and out on vacant lots with a fence around it in the summer. You didn't have a thing to worry about or bother about till every once in awhile a Will Rogers picture would hit you like a rainy night. Now I got out and let you go ahead and accumulate big houses and Mortgages and worry

and high taxes and everything. They told me it was things like me that was retarding the business.

Now this little mess I got here now that these fellows are trying to sell you wont hurt you much. They will just about give you time to go out and get a smoke while they are on. As Pictures are all so good nowadays I thought just as a contrast there ought to be some old has been come along and have something pretty ordinary and it would show off the modern things more.

The Character I am playing here is one I tried out before. I first tried it about forty some years ago and it turned out good and bad, but in the long run it kept me out of the casting line looking for an extra day. I dont know what they are, they aint exactly travelogues. They aint comedies cause comedies are Gags the people are used to laughing at.

The plots are a little too clean for dramas.

Well to be honest they are just about nine hundred feet of celluloid and take up about the same amount of time that a couple of close ups in a love picture would take up. They aint good and they aint bad, they just take up about fifteen minutes of a class of peoples time that time dont mean a thing in the world too.

The *Saturday Evening Post* has already payed for the trip, talking all over the country has made me more than I ever could have made in Pictures even if I had been a real star. The book of the trip has brought enough to pay for another trip, the Vitaphone staggered me to tell about it before their double barrell contraption, and this is just another By product. I wanted the reels to keep myself to show at home in my old days, and I just had them make another extra print. The radio is another by product I just thought of that has already paid for them too. I was raised on a ranch but I never knew before there was so many ways of skinning a calf. I like to forgot Bull Durham paying me to tell also about the same trip.

And oh yes my old friend Sam Goldwyn wants the dramatic right to the book. I sold Keystone the still pictures, the syndicated strip cartoon rights are being negotiated for now.

Your old friend

Will Rogers

Will and his family returned to the United States aboard the *Leviathan* in September 1926. Will resumed his lecture tours, then met Betty and the children in New York for the return trip home to Beverly Hills for the holidays. As they disembarked the train in Beverly Hills, they were met by a surprise delegation gathered to induct Will Rogers as honorary mayor of Beverly Hills. The welcoming party included Doug Fairbanks, William S. Hart, Rob Wagner and Chief of Police Blair heading his motorcycle police.

The Los Angeles Fire Department Band played while Fred Niblo acted as the master of ceremonies and Doug Fairbanks introduced the "man who needs no introduction." Will took his oath as mayor of Beverly Hills to the tune of *The Old Gray Mare*. Billy Dove presented Will with the key to the city. Will considered the honor bestowed on him and muttered, "What, no pay? Only the dignity of the position?"

Fairbanks sternly demanded that the new city executive "provide for the poor of Beverly Hills, and engineer a movement for private swimming pools, bridle paths and golf courses to be cared for out of public funds."

In response, Mayor Rogers responded that his first official act would be "to enlarge the suburban jail." And he would be "the only Mayor who is purposely funny.... I'm for the common people and, as Beverly Hills has no common people, I'll be sure to make

Poster of Will Rogers as "Our Unofficial Ambassador Abroad" (courtesy Will Rogers Memorial).

good.... I won't say that my administration will be exactly honest, but I'll agree to split 50-50 with you and give the town an even break."

After the ceremonies, Will inspected the police and fire department ranks and then mounted a street sweeper, determined to "clean up" Hollywood. When the folks back in Will's home town of Claremore, Oklahoma, got word of his induction as mayor of Beverly Hills, they charged him with treason and issued a warrant for his arrest.

Within weeks, Mayor Rogers was hard at work. In one of his January 1927 columns, Will named Charlie Spencer Chaplin as his lieutenant mayor. "Chaplin ... is temporarily out of a wife, and can therefore devote all his humor to the office." In another column he decried the number of divorces clogging up his office. Will wrote, "Have to get rid of some of them before we can have any new marriages."

In February 1927, the *New York Times* reported that there was a slight insurrection with an "indignation" meeting of film stars demanding the recall of Beverly Hills Mayor Rogers on the ground that he was head of an invisible government—invisible because he had been absent from his desk almost since the day of his inauguration. Cries of "Get out a search warrant for Rogers!" were expressed. Eddie Cantor declared, "Rogers must be recalled either from his ramblings across the continent or from his position as Mayor."

Will responded, "Haven't paid too much attention to that talk out in Beverly Hills about trying to recall the mayor. I am not afraid of that. They can't let me out. I know too much. Why, I will rock the very foundation of the social strata of screen, oil and realtor business."

When Will was laid up in the hospital after his gall bladder operation in August 1927, he was notified by the "sad news committee" that he had been ousted from office due to a law that cited that a city of the sixth class must have an elected mayor.

When Will learned of his ouster he took it hard: "I bet it's a frame-up ... just what a man could expect that had to lay defenseless on his back for a month." However, upon discovering that he had been elevated to mayor emeritus, he brightened up: "By golly, it don't sound as bad as that ... Will Rogers, Mayor Emeritus of Beverly Hills. If you put enough emphasis on the *e* it ain't bad at all."

When Mayor G. A. Rogers of Claremore, Oklahoma, got wind that Will had lost his job as Beverly Hills mayor, he sent a telegram to Will and offered to resign his position immediately in favor of the great humorist. In reply, Will sent a return telegram: "Thanks, Granville, but I got a better offer from Oolagah. I am going to quit the Mayor business and turn honest. Wish I could get to your rodeo but I cannot make it. Would rather see one there than any other place. Best regards to everybody.—Will Rogers."

Will had the final say in his newspaper column: "Tonight in Kansas City I am to be made President of a large body of men, the Ex-Mayors Association, an earnest bunch of men trying to come back, all placed where they are by the honesty of the ballot. What this country needs is more ex–Mayors. Yours, President of the Ex-Mayors Association—Will Rogers."

In another of his columns, Will listed the great accomplishments that occurred during his tenure as mayor of Beverly Hills: "Gloria Swanson had left Paris where she made her mark and was coming home to live under my administration, Lon Chaney had worn some of his most fiendish makeups right under your little Willie's Mayorship and Real Estate men sold lots that they had never been able to pan off on anyone before."

Doug Fairbanks proclaims Will Rogers to be mayor of Beverly Hills. *Left to right*: Doug Fairbanks, Billie Dove, Betty Rogers, Jimmy Rogers, Will Rogers and William S. Hart (courtesy Will Rogers Memorial).

With a parting shot, Will got the entire matter off his chest: "There is only one thing that makes me sore about the whole thing and that is this. This law applies to Cities of the Sixth Class only. My Lord, if I had known that I was ruling in a city of the SIXTH class I would never have taken the thing in the first place, I should sue them for lowering my standing. Sixth Class! Why that's the lowest class there is I reckon, Mayor of a SIXTH class city, why I will be years living that down.... If I had stayed in I could of at least got some ammunition and brought its standing up on a level with Chicago."

In addition to *Tip Toes* and his European travelogue series, Will made one final silent movie in the 1920s, *A Texas Steer*. The March 30, 1927, issue of the *New York Times* reported that Will would receive $100,000 for starring in the movie. Filming took place on location in Texas and Washington, D.C., and centered around the story of a cattle rancher elected to office as a congressman and his escapades rounding up the bad guys in Washington. Will wrote many of the film's subtitles, and the scenario provided plenty of opportunity for Will to humorously portray Washington and politicians. Taking a gander at the names of the characters in the movie, it's a safe bet that Will had his hand in these as well: Fairleigh Bright, Brassy Gall, Dixie Style, Knott Innitt, Bragg and Blow.

A newsboy surveys Maverick Brander (Rogers) in an old frock coat and ten-gallon hat and asks the newly arrived congressman, "Where's the circus?"

Will's character points to the Capitol and says, "Right over there, the biggest circus in the world, and I've just joined it."

During one scene, Will's character dashes down Pennsylvania Avenue on horseback. The scene was performed by a stand-in due to Will's recent operation, a fact that did not sit well with Will: "I may be a bum rider, but I figure that I'm still man enough to lope down the avenue in my ripe old age."

During the filming in Washington, D.C., many government officials came over to watch the day's work. On location one day, Will looked up and saw a distinguished-looking gentleman and said, "How're you, Senator?" When Will found out that the man he addressed as senator was in actuality an extra working for another movie company filming in the area, he said, "I'm sorry I called you Senator, you ain't sore are you?"

The *New York Times* praised Will: "Mr. Rogers is splendid in his part. One must assume that the wild passages were not outlined by him and that he, at the behest of the director, had to go through them. However, in the milder bits, Mr. Rogers is genuinely funny as the Cowboy Representative, who is bossed by a plump wife with social aspirations."

The editors of the January 1928 issue of *Photoplay* extended its list of top films of the month: "In justice to Will Rogers' opus, *A Texas Steer*, it should be noted that only the exigencies of a printing plant operating schedule kept it from the list of the best new pictures viewed in the past four weeks.... There is many a laugh in the screen version ...

Mayor Will Rogers "cleans up" Beverly Hills (courtesy Will Rogers Memorial).

Will Rogers and crew of *A Texas Steer* (1927) (courtesy Will Rogers Memorial).

in which Mr. Rogers wrote the titles and maybe he might even tour the country with the film to sell exhibitors. But the titles he wrote do get laughs."

Will commented about *A Texas Steer*, "That was a smart movie, a comedy special they called it, with real actors helping me out, and all I had to do was act the big comedy part of being a congressman. That's a cinch. Any day in the week any congressman I've known can give me a big laugh acting natural."

Douglas Fairbanks, Jr., played the juvenile lead of Fairleigh Bright in *A Texas Steer*. Seventy years later, Fairbanks offered this observation: "Will Rogers was very pleasant to work with and a very conscientious worker. While his humorous style appeared very relaxed, he worked very hard at his humor. He was very professional.

"He had a great tolerance of others and possessed a great sense of fairness. He was a kindly man. In his humor, he never made fun of or criticized other people. More often than not, he made light of himself."

Will's Observations on Hollywood

Out here in Hollywood, they say you're not a success unless you owe $50,000 to somebody, have five cars, can develop temperament without notice or reason at all, and been mixed up in four divorce cases and two breach of promise suits. Well, as a success in Hollywood, I'm a rank failure and I guess I'm too old to teach new tricks and besides I'm pretty well off domestically speaking *and ain't yearning for a change. I own one car and for recreation spend a great deal of my time enjoying the company of my polo ponies and goats. There's nothing like the companionship of a horse or goat. They can't laugh at you and they never gossip. Anyhow, mine don't.*

Will returned to Hollywood for good in the late 1920s to star in a number of pictures for Fox Film Corporation. Unlike many other movie actors that never made the transition to "talkies," Will Rogers was born to perform in the new medium. While many of Will's silent movies were humorous and several are considered film classics, they never truly captured Will and his humor as his live acts and talking pictures did.

Hollywood represented a ripe target for Will's humor. Many of his movies were successful lampoons of Hollywood, its popular movies and its biggest stars. Likewise, Will often targeted Hollywood and Hollywood goings-on in his lectures and newspaper columns. The following represent samples of Will's Hollywood observations that retain their humor today. Like much of his humor, he only needs to stretch the facts to make his point.

"I'm an ex–*Follies* graduate and if Barrymore had my legs he could still be on the stage."

"Beverly Hills is dead while Hollywood is flourishing, the reason being that Hollywood has received due publicity from scandal. But never mind, I live right between Pola Negri and Gloria Swanson; just give us a year and something may be doing in Beverly

Will Rogers on Capitol steps in *A Texas Steer* (authors' collection).

Hills. If any of you folks are doing anything shady, let the Chamber of Commerce get the advantage of it. Don't do it on the sly for then they miss the publicity."

"Poor Valentino. They won't even let him alone after he is dead. They got him conversing with women in spirit that he wouldn't even speak to in life."

"Up here attending the beautiful Santa Barbara fiesta, showing the life in California before Fords, movies, stars and realtors in knee-breeches made a Coney Island out of the State."

"Doug Fairbanks stated yesterday in an interview that there are more brains on the screen than on the stage. After viewing some of the productions put on lately by both screen and stage, I think most people will agree that in the matter of brains displayed it's an absolute tie between the two."

"Just been over visiting Charlie Chaplin at his studio, and watching him work. I wanted to see how a man acted that had just been separated from a million. That would be the supreme test of a comedian. He is funnier than ever. He showed me the new picture. If the next wife settles for a cent less than two and a half million, she is a chump."

"An awful lot of divorces going on now in the Movies—getting ready for next season's marriages."

"I get a bundle of invitations every day to attend the weddings, but I would always rather wait a few weeks and take in the divorce."

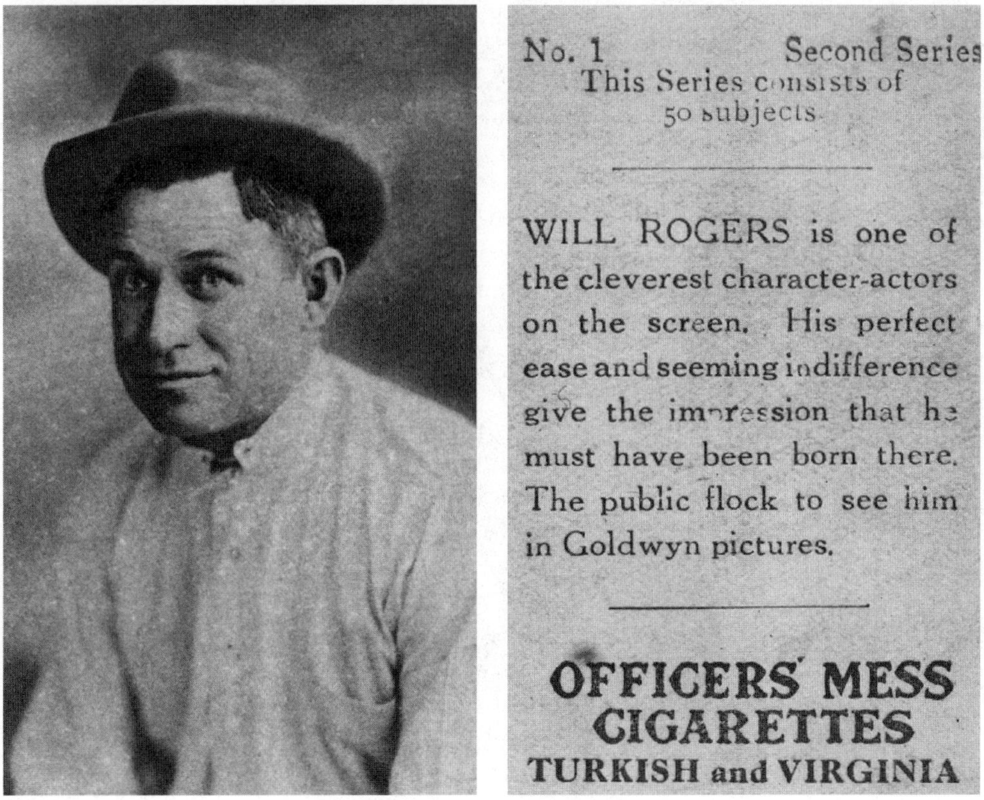
No. 1 Second Series
This Series consists of
50 subjects
WILL ROGERS is one of the cleverest character-actors on the screen. His perfect ease and seeming indifference give the impression that he must have been born there. The public flock to see him in Goldwyn pictures.
OFFICERS' MESS CIGARETTES
TURKISH and VIRGINIA

1920s Will Rogers tobacco card (authors' collection).

"Somebody is always quoting figures to prove that the country is prosperous, and it takes a lot of quoting; but the only real bona fide indication of it was in the paper today: 'Divorces in Reno have increased over 105 percent in the last year.' Now, that's prosperity, for you can't be broke and get a divorce. That's why the poor have to live with each other. There is nothing that denotes prosperity quicker than to hear that 'So and so and his wife ain't getting along.'"

"Another notorious case out here of a young girl and a rich man, assisted, as usual, by the fond mother."

"Old Hollywood is just like a desert water hole in Africa. Hang around long enough and every kind of animal in the world will drift in for refreshments."

"If you missed anybody around their old haunts in the East and have no idea where they are, they are right here in Beverly Hills trying to get into the talkies, and the ones that were in 'em are trying to learn to talk. I haven't had a chance to say a word since I got home for people just practicing on me to show me they talk. In the old days everybody was practicing to make signs. Now they are practicing noises."

"You will see a great improvement in the title. Those beautiful sounding phrases may read all right when they are on there in print alone, but when some live moving Character really says them they sound funny. We never thought before that Real Human beings wouldent use such words.... But now the Titles that the Actors speak have got to be something that the man would really say under those circumstances, and not something that reads good when the Title Writer 'copped' it out of some book. It's going to make pictures about twice as human."

"Us poor film folks do have our troubles lately. We no more than adapt ourselves to some new invention than another knocks us in the creek. Talking pictures hit us at a time when we was as dumb as a rabbit, color photography showed up our red noses and gray hair, and to sink us entirely some guy in Washington yesterday got a patent on an apparatus that will register 'Smell in the movies.' Now we not only got to look colorful, act good, talk good, but our personal odor has got to be above suspicion."

"They was opening my first talking picture tonight in Los Angeles and charging those poor people five dollars, and I just couldn't stand by and be a party to such brigandage. First-night audiences pay their money to look at each other, so if they get stuck tomorrow night, they can't blame me. It will be because they don't look good to each other."

"Einstein left New York flat and is headed for Hollywood. If he's got a theory that nobody knows what it is, or what it's all about, why there is a half dozen companies here that will buy it and produce it along with these enigmas of our own that we put out."

"You know, after all, anybody can open a theatre. It's keeping it open that is the hard thing."

"Say, we have a discoverer out here in California ... who has invented a serum ... a thing that when injected into you will make you tell the truth, at least for a little while anyway.... They tried it on a male movie star in Hollywood and he told his right salary and his press agent quit him. They then tried it on a female movie staress and she recalled things back as far as her first husband's name, and remembered her real maiden name.... Their only failure to date has been a Los Angeles real estate agent. They broke three needles trying to administer the stuff to him and it turned black the minute it touched him, so they had to give him up."

"Compared to Hollywood, Sodom and Gomorrah were a couple of babes in the woods.... In Hollywood you will see things at night that are fast enough to be in the Olympics in the day time.... One good thing about Hollywood is you can find anything there, good or bad."

"In the early days we had no churches. Now we have a lot of churches and no congregation."

"Secretary of Labor Davis was out to the studio here yesterday. He told me he can't find any classification of labor to put the movies in. Put 'em with politics and they still won't be in any classification."

"What you say we have a little chat on the Movies? Havent dished out any Movie scandal to you in a long time. Well, I have been out here for about six weeks, and its just kinder the off season. Spring marrying is about over, and summer divorces havent quite got going good."

"I can't write about the movies for I don't know anything about them and I don't think anybody else knows anything about them. It's the only business in the world nobody knows anything about. Being in them don't give any more of an inkling about them than being out of them.... Call them 'arts and sciences' but do so with your tongue in your cheek. Everything that makes money and gives pleasure is not art. If it was, bootlegging would be the highest form of artistic endeavor. So let's everybody connected with them, and everybody that loves to go see them, as we go to our beds at night, pray to our Supreme Being, that he don't allow it to be found out what is the matter with the movies, for if he ever does, we will all be out of a job."

"Personal income tax is about the only thing that can hold this business back."

"My advice to aspiring movie struck folk is to buy a good twelve-foot rope, practice with it and then if you don't succeed, why you can always stretch it over a nearby tree with one end around your neck."

Broadway Star

When I sing I feel that is as far as any man has ever gone for a friend.

In September 1928, Will showed the boundlessness of his friendship with Fred Stone. Will heard that his friend had broken his legs when the airplane he was piloting crashed near Groton, Connecticut. Stone had been in the process of launching a lavish new Broadway musical comedy with producer Charles Dillingham, *Three Cheers*, starring himself and his daughter, Dorothy.

Will telegrammed Stone, "If you don't want Dorothy to wait until you are entirely recovered I will go in the show with her, just to sort of plug it along till you are able to rejoin, and I will do the best I can with your part. Dorothy can keep telling me how you would have played it. Dorothy would of course be the star, and I don't want any billing. Anything you, Dorothy and Dillingham say goes with me."

Will canceled his previously scheduled lecture tour and would give up thousands of dollars in speaking engagements over a period of many months as the show played Broadway and then went on tour beginning in April 1929. All in all, Will would appear in 210 performances of *Three Cheers* while Fred Stone recuperated. Each week, producer Charles Dillingham presented Will with a blank check for him to fill in the amount for his week's performances. The amount Will accepted as payment in no way repaid him for his lost earnings from his canceled engagements.

Will's unselfishness drew much praise. Burns Mantle of the *Daily News* wrote, "And so Rogers emerges again as a big man in show business and in fact. An impulsive, generous, clean-souled sentimentalist. Let those who will grow mushy over the incident. Fred and Will know what it means and what it stands for. They do that sort of thing, make that kind of sacrifice, in the western ranch country from which these boys come every day in the week and never think anything about it. There is never any question of money involved, nor any mention of it."

Billie Burke wired to Will on opening night, "You are certainly going to break our hearts for being such a darling, but we are certainly proud of belonging to the theatre tonight."

"We will never be able to repay or thank Bill for his kindness. Bill can fill my place, but I can never do his turn," said Stone.

Will rehearsed with the *Three Cheers* cast a mere two weeks before opening in Springfield, Massachusetts, on October 1, 1928. The musical comedy made its Broadway debut on October 15, 1928, at the Globe Theatre.

Will told Betty, "Think of it! Twenty-three years on the stage and never rehearsed before. Its all Greek to me. I feel like a kid at his first school entertainment."

In actuality, Will did not learn his lines very well and carried the script around in his pocket while he was on stage, referring to it whenever necessary. Will tried to follow Fred Stone's part to the letter, but he stopped short of even attempting one of Stone's noted acrobatic dance numbers. He explained it to the audience, "At this juncture, you miss something. Fred was going to make a crazy leap onto that stage boat before it sails. But in order to insure my appearance in the second act I am obligated to omit that feature."

Despite, or because of, Will's improvisations, *Three Cheers* proved to be a tremendous success. One reviewer wrote, "I am afraid Will Rogers disorganized the show but so far as I am concerned, he can continue to disorganize shows for the rest of his and my life."

J. Brooks Atkinson, reviewer for the *New York Times*, commented, "Will Rogers was making it merry at the Globe Theatre, where he was pinch-hitting for his old crony, Fred Stone, at the opening of *Three Cheers*. For, as Will declared in the opening scene, 'I don't know one thing Fred does that I can do.' Plastering his chewing gum up on the wall, this homespun sage thereupon paid as little attention to the book as decency permitted.... Dorothy Stone, who is the star of *Three Cheers*, made the evening legitimately her own by the modest, and at times almost touching, perfection of her dancing, singing and light footing.... There is the glamour of spirited youth in her style.... *Three Cheers* seems to warrant the enthusiasm of its moniker."

Reviewer Robert Littell followed suit with, "*Three Cheers?* Well, a million would be

Will Rogers and Dorothy Stone in *Three Cheers*, which ran in New York from October 1928 through mid–April 1929 before going on tour (courtesy Will Rogers Memorial).

Andy Tombes, Will Rogers, Dorothy Stone, Fred Stone and Mrs. Stone on stage of *Three Cheers* (courtesy Will Rogers Memorial).

more like it. This is one of those rare and wonderful shows that we who saw it last night and all the others who will go to see it for the next couple of years will still be chuckling over in 1968. It's like some marvelous family party from which every one goes home happy and exhausted and aching with laughter. Will Rogers, who at his funniest is funnier than anybody else, was never funnier. And he could not have a better partner than Dorothy Stone.... Never was a musical comedy plot more thoroughly buried under delirious fun-making, excellent dancing, good music and a whole raft of pretty girls; several of whom were raving, tearing peaches."

The December 1928 issue of *Theatre Magazine* wrote:

> *Three Cheers* is nine-tenths Will Rogers, and despite anything the program says it is a rally around that natural comedian and nationally famous wisecracker. When he is on stage he not only stops the show, but so completely upsets the equilibrium of the audience that they sit in dull indifference until the drawling wit from Oklahoma and Hollywood again makes his appearance.... During the first weeks of its performance at the Globe Theatre [Will Rogers], has sent the crowds clamoring to the box office, and registered for *Three Cheers* one of the season's biggest hits.... The result of all this go-as-

> you-please hilarity is an evening of solid fun and a memory of the one comedian who can be called upon (if he will respond) to turn any second-rate musical production into a hit.

Even curmudgeon W. C. Fields cabled his approval: "After careful analyzing and quietly ruminating I still contend that you are giving the best comic performance and the most entertaining I have seen in my life. Miss Stone was also wonderful and Andy Tombes is giving a great performance. God how we enjoyed it all. May we never meet in combat. As always. Bill Fields."

Three Cheers finished up its New York engagement on April 13, 1929, and went on tour. Will finished up his tour with the production in Pittsburgh on May 31, 1929. He returned to California in time to jump-start his movie career by joining Fox Film Corporation in the production of his first talkie, *They Had to See Paris.*

The Fox Talkies

> *The Talkies has made a new style of titles possible. The old titles were always subject to change. The film would be taken out and tried on an audience and if a laugh wasn't forthcoming a new set of wisecracks was prepared. Often as not they would have no relation to the action. In the talkies, conversation is adapted to the actor's personality and the lines stay as spoken. You don't see one picture in the projection room and another in the theater.*

Over an eighteen-month period, ending in March 1929, Fox Film Corporation invested $15 million in the construction of new studios, purchase of machinery and technical experimentation to ready the company for full production of talking pictures. The company dropped many silent film stars who did not measure up to the vocal requirements of movietone tests and contracted with over 200 performers with Broadway "talking" experience. Will Rogers garnered a two-year contract with Fox to star in four films for which he would be paid $600,000. He completed his first Fox production, *They Had to See Paris,* in late August 1929.

As usual, Will played down his newfound star status: "I'm not smart enough to act. If they can find a part that sorta fits me, I'm all right. Otherwise, I'm punk.... I have talked more than any living man so why shouldn't I welcome another chance to talk."

By the time Fox signed Will to a contract, he and his family had moved out to the Santa Monica Ranch house they had built on land purchased back in 1924. Will 'fessed up that the property really wasn't a full-scale ranch: "We call it that. It sounds big and don't really do any harm."

The property stayed in the Rogers family until Betty Rogers' death in 1944 when her will left it to the state of California with the provision that it remain open to the public. Known today as the Will Rogers State Park, the property remains virtually as Will and his family left it, right down to the home's furnishings, Will's battered polo helmet and one of his well-worn typewriters.

Will, Will, Jr., Mary, Jimmy Rogers at the Santa Monica Ranch (courtesy Will Rogers Memorial).

Will started out his association at Fox Film with a big hit. His talkie debut, *They Had to See Paris,* earned a profit of three-quarters of a million dollars in 1929. Adapted from the novel by Homer Croy, the story centers around a family that strikes it rich when oil gushes from their Oklahoma property. The family travels to Paris to engage culture, and numerous humorous situations evolve. Fox imported Fifi Dorsey to add some spice to the Will Rogers/Irene Rich vehicle.

Director Frank Borzage captured the essence of the Croy story and Will Rogers at his best. *They Had to See Paris* set the tone and pattern for many Rogers movies to follow and remains one of Will's most popular productions from the talkie era. Director Borzage later recounted that Will had the ability to make audiences forget that he was a comedian and get them involved in the emotions that flow from the human condition.

"We had many amusing experiences while making the picture. It was really more of a vacation, for working with Mr. Rogers is a refreshing adventure.... When we were shooting the picture he would change the lines to conform with what he thought they should be, and his version was usually better than the original script. I really never enjoyed making a picture as much before as I did this last one with Rogers," said Borzage.

During one of the takes of a scene with Marguerite Churchill, Will had forgotten his line. Not missing a beat, he responded, "I'll answer that just as soon as I think of something to say."

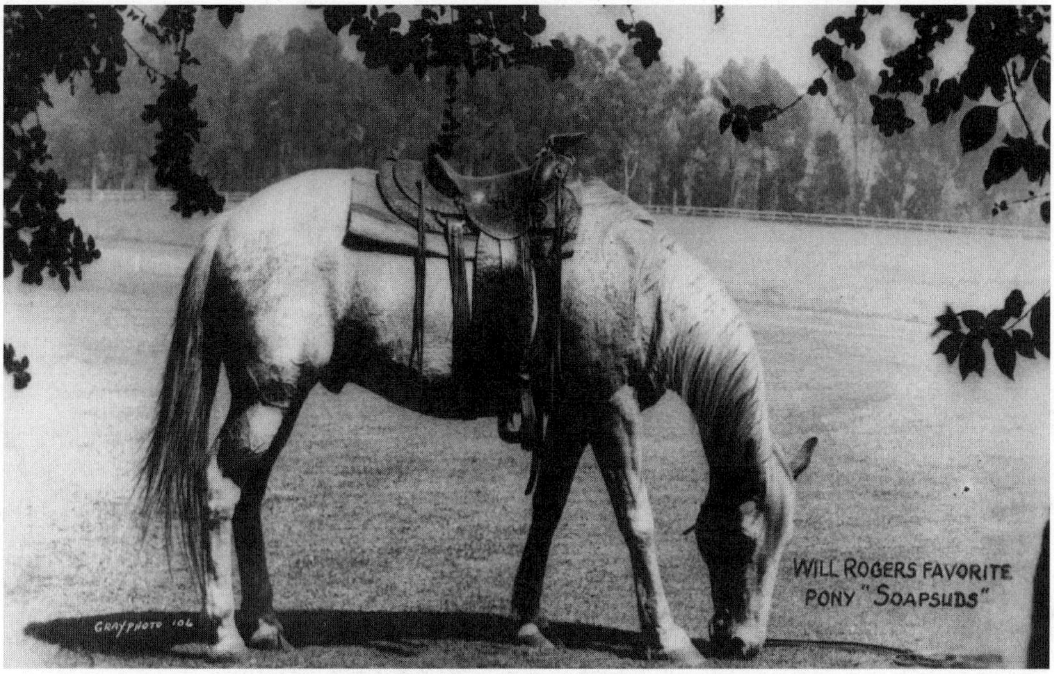

Will Rogers' favorite pony, "Soapsuds" (authors' collection).

Several Rogers firsts took place in this film. He teamed up with vivacious Fifi D'Orsay to croon his first song, *I Could Do It for You*, and Will blushed as Irene Rich planted his first film kiss.

"I don't quite think that face on the screen looks like me. The others appear natural enough, but not mine. And the voice is not mine. It can't be. Not that voice," said Will.

Fox took out a full-page ad in the November 1929 issue of *Photoplay* describing Will and the movie as "America's favorite comedian and most natural talking picture actor is a riot in this hilarious comedy of a newly rich American family who tried to crash Parisian society.... Pike Peters saw everything that Paris had to show—and that's an eyeful. At the Folies-Bergere he shouted, 'Pike's peek or bust.' He paixed and paixed at the Café de la Paix. Ooo-la-la-la."

Will never missed an opportunity to boost his home state of Oklahoma. He insisted that the opening scenes be shot in Claremore, Oklahoma, instead of on a Hollywood set. The movie opens with a shot of Third Street, looking east, and the Claremore Frisco service station. Later in the movie, Will is shown reading the *Claremore Progress.* He also tells other characters in the movie about the famous Claremore Radium Water.

"There's many a good laugh in *They Had to See Paris,* Will Rogers' first talking picture.... Mr. Rogers is capital. His voice is reproduced naturally," wrote the *New York Times. Photoplay* remarked, "This is big entertainment, with Will Rogers giving some of our first rate emotional actors a run for their Saturday night remittance.... The comedy is comedy and the emotional moments are sincere.... Scrap all your John Gilberts, give John Boles back to the Indians and Gary Cooper to anyone who wants him—and let me have Will Rogers." *Photoplay* also ranked *They Had to See Paris* as one of the Best Pic-

Fifi D'Orsay and Will Rogers in *They Had to See Paris* (1929) (courtesy Will Rogers Memorial).

tures of the Month and gave Will Rogers and Irene Rich thumbs up as two of the Best Performances of the Month in the December 1929 issue. *Variety* accurately predicted, "His first talking picture is a certain money maker."

Fox backed Will up with an exceptionally talented cast of Irene Rich, Fifi D'Orsay, Marguerite Churchill, Owen Davis, Jr., Rex Bell and other well-seasoned supporting actors. Rogers had met D'Orsay, originally from Montreal, in vaudeville and recommended her to Fox for the picture. The fiery Fifi D'Orsay engaged in a running battle with Fox Film. In February 1930, *Photoplay* reported that she was complaining about her pictures on the Fox lot. "My first one is *They Had to See Paris.* Then I do *Hot for Paris.* I hope the next one is *Let's Get the Hell Out of Paris,*" said Fifi. In 1931, she pulled a fake publicity stunt, claiming she had been shanghaied on a liner bound for the Canal Zone. Fox took umbrage to the publicity ploy and removed Fifi's name from all advertising copy for her release, *Mr. Lemon of Orange*, and idled her as additional punishment. In 1932, Fifi finally walked out on her contract after Fox lent her out to other studios, paying her only $400 a week.

They Had to See Paris gave Will plenty of opportunity to display his sense of humor and get across some of his homespun philosophy. Some gems from this film include:

Newspaper ad for *They Had to See Paris* (authors' collection).

"A horse doctor is the smartest kind of doctor. He cant ask the horse where it hurts; he's got to know."

"I became a success by hard work, perseverance, and taking advantage of my opportunities—I struck oil."

"When you ain't used to this culture, it kind of gets you."

After his wife hires a valet, he says, "I ain't got a thing in the world to do and you go and hire an able-bodied guy to help me do it."

His view of eating caviar: "It's a good thing those are fashionable cause they ain't

Director Frank Borzage, visitor Ethel Barrymore and Will Rogers on set of *They Had to See Paris* (courtesy Will Rogers Memorial).

nothing else ... listen, when you want to eat eggs you can't improve on the old hen, do you know that?"

To Grand Duke Makiall, "If my wife sent for you, you better go. You don't know my wife. The worst thing that ever happened to you was the revolution."

"You know, marriage is just kind of a poker game and you just got to play your own hand."

"Let's be original. Let's keep our common sense."

"If parents just keep their children out of jail, they've fulfilled their obligation."

Will is credited for supplying the story idea for the musical revue *Fox Movietone Follies,* released in 1929. The annual revue was modeled after the Ziegfeld *Follies*. A full-page ad for *Fox Movietone Follies* in the May 1929 *Photoplay* promised, "Broadway's Dazzle Brought to You ... Broadway's greatest song and dance entertainment, dazzling with beautiful girls, comes to the screen of your nearest Theatre."

The December 1929 issue of *Photoplay* announced that Will Rogers' next film for Fox would be a Ben Ames Williams story, *By the Way Bill,* based on Will Rogers' life, to be directed by William Howard. The *New York Times* reported that work had begun on the *By the Way Bill* production on the Fox lot in early December 1929. No other mention has been found regarding the production of this film. Will's name was also linked to two

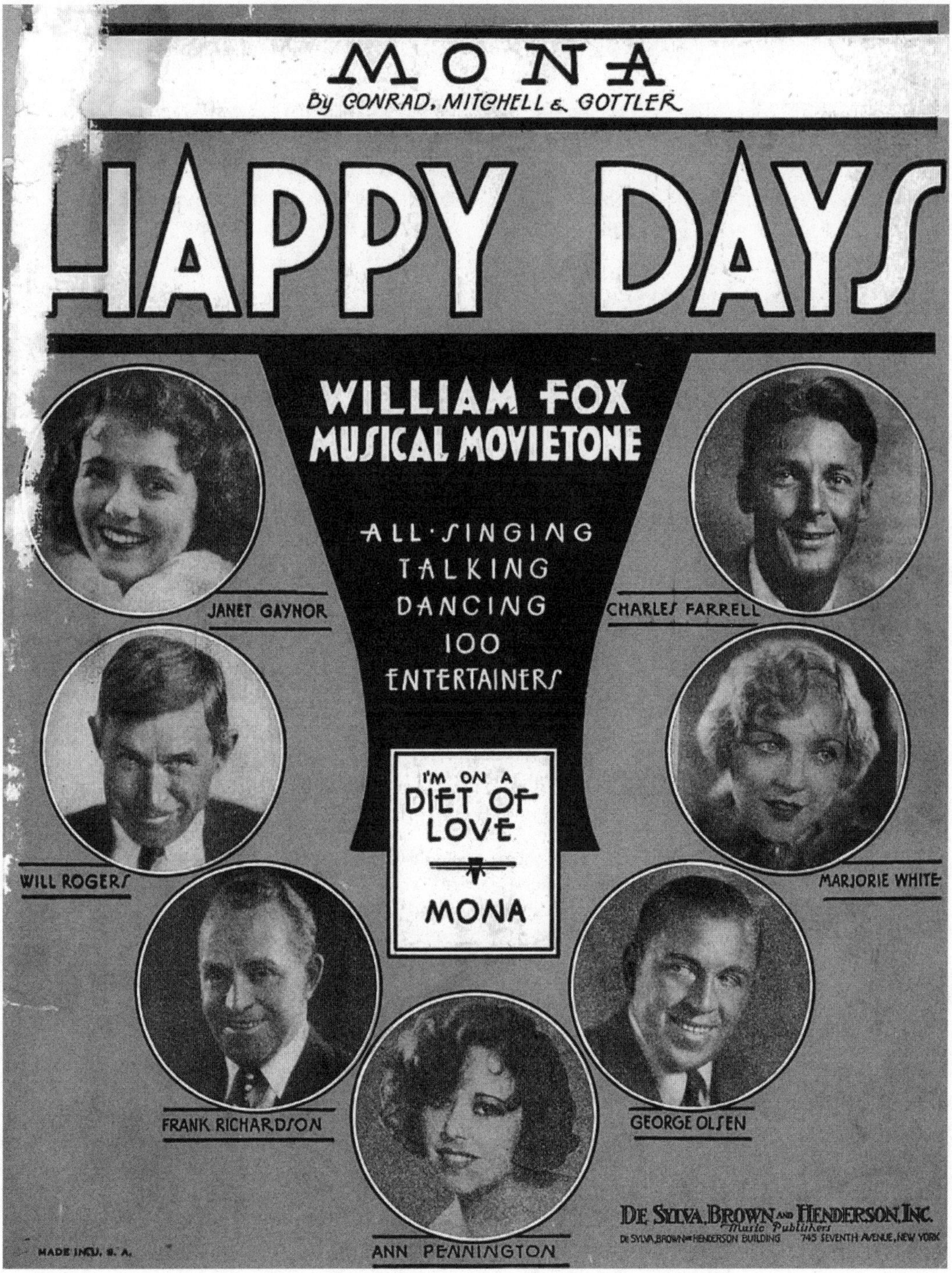

Sheet music for a number from *Happy Days* (1930) (authors' collection).

other film projects that never materialized, *A Lift Home* and *See America First*. A Louella O. Parsons column appearing in February 1930 mentioned that English actress Gilliam Sande was in Hollywood and would star as Will Rogers' leading lady in *A Lift Home*. The *New York Times* followed that up with Sande being picked from a contest involving over 600 women to play opposite Will in *So This Is London*. However, Sande does not appear in any of the cast listings. Later in 1930, the *New York Times* reported that Will Rogers would be appearing in *See America First*. No other mention of this film can be found.

Will did appear, however, in the February 1930 Fox release *Happy Days*. Unfortunately, Will's role consisted of a brief cameo shot with George Jessel and William Collier, Sr. The film featured a thin storyline that served mainly to allow Fox to display its line of star talent in a musical revue setting.

Photoplay ranked *Happy Days* as one of the six best pictures of the month in its May 1930 issue: "*Happy Days* is Fox's latest in the big parade of photoplay revues. It wears a minstrel suit and carries a big red banner.... A bunch of entertainers band to help an old showman save his troupe. And what an entertainment!"

Will did get in one humorous line: "I'm not much of a man for telling jokes, but the invitation goes and I've got two airplanes to take you down in but you have to furnish your own pastrami."

When the hotel page searches for Will she asks a gentleman, "Which one is Mr. Rogers?" The man responds, "The one chewing gum."

In February 1930, Claremore returned the publicity favors Will had given the town over the years, dedicating the new $250,000 Will Rogers Hotel. Will responded to the honor in his February 17, 1930, newspaper column:

> I sure used to envy General Grant and Jesse James when they had smokeless cigars named after 'em, but here I am sitting in the brand new, most up-to-date hotel in the Southwest, the Will Rogers Hotel in Claremore. It's six stories high. That's higher than any hotel in London, and it's got more baths in one room than Buckingham Palace, where the King lives, has all put together. Got more elevators than the Rice Hotel in Houston had during the Democratic convention, and these run cracked ice and White Rock in each room. That's standard equipment. Here is the town that you take those wonderful baths that cure you of everything but being a Democrat. I know now how proud Christopher Columbus must have felt when he heard they had named Columbus, Ohio, after him.

Will began shooting his next feature film for Fox, *So This Is London*, on February 20, 1930. The storyline was based on the stageplay by George M. Cohan. Cottonmill-owner Hiram Draper (Rogers) hates the English but travels to London on business. The fun begins when Draper and his wife (Irene Rich) apply for passports and continues with Will getting seasick on an ocean liner and through a number of humorous adventures in London. Fox again supported Will with an able group of actors, including Rich, Maureen O'Sullivan, Lamsden Hare and Frank Albertson.

The Oklahoma University debating team visited the Fox set with Will, and he later took them on a tour around Hollywood, including a visit to his Santa Monica Ranch. The movie premiered at the Fox Carthay Theatre in Los Angeles on June 19, 1930. Will Rogers, Jr., shared the master of ceremonies duties with *So This Is London* actor Frank Albertson.

Will Rogers Hotel brochure (authors' collection).

Screenland named *So This Is London* as one of the six most important films for the month of September 1930: "Will Rogers! When you've said that you've said everything about this picture. You'll take it whether you happen to be addicted to Will or not, if you prize an evening's entertainment of the good, old, simple school.... [It] only proves that Will Rogers is deservedly the People's Comedy Choice.... I think you will find his new movietone refreshingly sincere and human."

The *New Yorker* called *So This Is London* "a delightful adaptation of the George M. Cohan farce for Will Rogers. It takes advantage of the possibilities offered by a cinematic version to wander all over shipboard and the countryside, and the slow, rich comedy of Mr. Rogers has rarely, if ever, been better displayed."

The *Film Daily* regarded the film as a "sure fire box office bet, with Will Rogers in

Will Rogers Hotel postcard (authors' collection).

fine form. Full of pungent humor. First-rate cast." Mordaunt Hall, reviewer for the *New York Times*, commented, "Will Rogers rings the bell again in *So This Is London*.... It is a film in which Mr. Rogers' dry humor is wonderfully successful. His facial expressions are also extremely amusing. The final scene is splendid, for Draper and Lord Worthing (Hare) sing the same tune, one in bass and the other in falsetto, to different words—'My Country 'Tis of Thee' and 'God Save the King.' It caused the spectators to greet this ending with a hurricane of laughter."

Variety regarded Will's performance as follows: "His comical stuff is 100% up to the minute and the puns on current topics are all sharp, comprehensive and amusing." *Photoplay* found favor with Will's new film: "The droll Will is at his funniest as the American who unhappily gets mixed up with a flock of anti–American Britons.... Rogers fans will be mad about this mad picture.... An amusing follow-up for *They Had to See Paris*."

When the passport examiner asks for proof of Will's birth he responds, "I gather from you that you doubt I was born. 'Course out in our country if you walk up and appear before anybody in person why we take it as fairly positive proof that you must have been born. We just kinda trust in that way. We might wonder why you were born but would never question the fact that you were born."

After going through the hassle of getting their passports and photos, Will says, "If it's as hard to get into this country as it is to get out, we'll never get back."

Abroad ship, Will suffers from seasickness and laments, "Lindbergh had the right dope on how to cross this ocean.... I hope I feel good enough to get off of this thing."

Speaking of the English, "They think we are people with nothing but bad manners and good money.... Say listen. What's the matter with the United States? The best thing we raise over there is girls."

Irene Rich and Will Rogers in *So This Is London* (1930) (courtesy Will Rogers Memorial).

Upon entering a country estate, Will comments, "I had no idea there's anything like this in England. I bet it's one of those old places they moved over here from Long Island."

"My plan worked fine. My whole scheme. It played out wonderful. There's only one little thing wrong with it. It might have been the wrong plan."

"I'm a very cultured gentleman when I'm going good.... I'm a temperance man but the situation calls for a slight libation."

Will personally picked *Lightnin'*, a successful Broadway stageplay, for his next Fox picture. Will and the cast started filming *Lightnin'* on location in the Lake Tahoe, Nevada, and Camp Richardson, California, region beginning in August 1930. The story centers around the exploits of Will and his wife, who run the Cal/Nevada Hotel, catering to the divorce trade. The divorce case between Lightnin' and Mrs. Jones was shot in the Reno Divorce Court.

"We got a funny situation here. We brought up about a dozen girls to play the 'divorcees' in the hotel scene in *Lightnin'* and here every day watching us shoot is a hundred real 'divorcees' from Reno."

Will wryly commented on the competition for the divorce trade:

> The biggest thing in legislation nowadays is the different States' race for the divorce business. Arkansas guarantees a divorce in three months including room and board. Nevada heard about it and called a special session of their

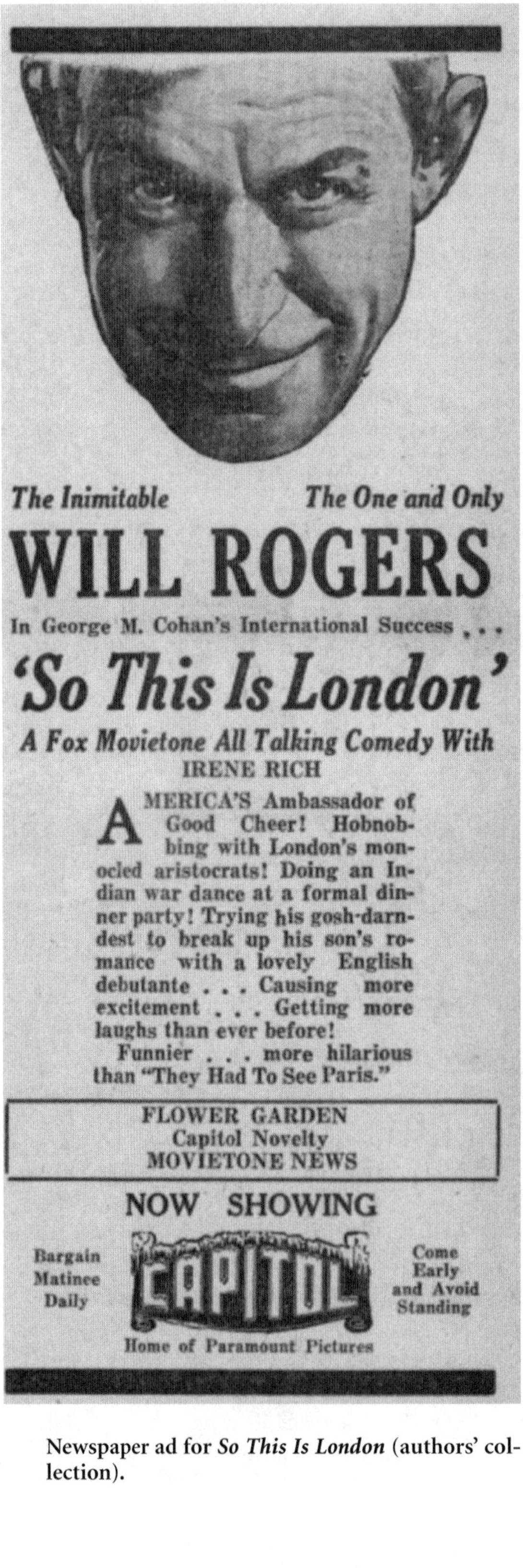

The Inimitable
The One and Only
WILL ROGERS
In George M. Cohan's International Success . . .
'So This Is London'
A Fox Movietone All Talking Comedy With
IRENE RICH
AMERICA'S Ambassador of Good Cheer! Hobnobbing with London's monocled aristocrats! Doing an Indian war dance at a formal dinner party! Trying his gosh-darndest to break up his son's romance with a lovely English debutante . . . Causing more excitement . . . Getting more laughs than ever before!
Funnier . . . more hilarious than "They Had To See Paris."
FLOWER GARDEN
Capitol Novelty
MOVIETONE NEWS
NOW SHOWING
Bargain Matinee Daily
CAPITOL
Come Early and Avoid Standing
Home of Paramount Pictures

Newspaper ad for *So This Is London* (authors' collection).

> Legislature and says: "We will give you one in six weeks, and if any other State goes under that time, we will give you a divorce, marriage and another divorce all for the same time. In other words, that's our business. We have built it up to what it is today. If there had been no Reno, you would still have been living with the same old gal. So, remember, we are the State that will divorce you, even if we have to do it by telegraph."

Will also peppered the movie with a number of other funny lines such as:

"We're in California right now. The horse is in Nevada…most of him."

During one scene, Will rolls a cigarette, telling Joel McCrea he learned it from the movies. When McCrea asks, "You don't try everything they do in the movies do you?" Will responds, "Not at my age."

"There will never be divorce in our family. She would never find another man like me."

After studying his pension check, Will muses, "It has all these big names on it. The President and Secretary of the Treasury and it aint no good unless I sign it."

During the court scene, Will insinuates that the rival lawyer is less than honest. The lawyer protests, "I absolutely refuse to be made to look like a criminal." Will replies, "Well, you look natural."

Lightnin' proved to be a smash hit. *Photoplay* called it one of the Best Pictures of January 1931 and one of the Forty Best Films of 1931 while the *New York Times* ranked the film fourth in its list of Top Ten Films of the year. In addition, *Photoplay* credited both Will and Louise Dresser with Best Performances of the Month.

Will Rogers and Luke Cosgrave transporting divorcées-to-be in *Lightnin'* (1931) (courtesy Will Rogers Memorial).

"Here's willrogersing at its best. And what more do you need to know?… Of course this role is a 'natural' for Will Rogers. As the shiftless, whimsical, truth-embroidering Bill Jones, he's a nine-reel scream. Call it the best role of his screen career, and you'll not be far wrong…. If you have something else to do, postpone it and see *Lightnin'* anyway. You'll feel better about everything…. Don't miss this, for it's Will Rogers at his best," gushed *Photoplay.*

The *Film Daily* said, "Young and old of all denominations will get a big batch of thorough satisfaction out of the talker version of this famous stage play…. The role of the shiftless, imbibing, but altogether lovable Lightnin' Bill Jones is played for every ounce of value by Will Rogers."

Mordaunt Hall, reviewer for the *New York Times,* commented:

> A happy hour or so awaits those who visit the Roxy this week, for at that theatre Will Rogers gives a delightful interpretation of the tipping, good-natured and understanding "Lightnin" Bill Jones. His acting is, if anything, superior to that of his previous characterizations in *They Had to See Paris* and *So This Is London,* pictures that have brought him a tremendous following, which was attested to by the crowds that filed into the big house for the first performance and by the fact that in spite of the wintry blasts a line of patrons was waiting outside…. This film is filled with genuinely good fun that kept an

> audience yesterday in gales of laughter. Mr. Rogers does not miss a single chance to make a line tell, and as Bill Jones he appears to enjoy his prevaricating as much as he does outwitting those for whom he has no liking.

However, some purists took offense. The *Film Spectator* worried that

> Will Rogers ... is being overdone by Fox. His pictures are coming out so rapidly that he is losing his status as America's most unique character, and is becoming merely a motion picture actor trying to compete in ordinary pictures with actors who have far more skill. Rogers is an institution, not a movie actor. He should not appear on the screen oftener than once a year, and then should be allowed to play himself.... *Lightnin'* is a worthy picture, but there are a score or more character actors in Hollywood who could have played the leading part with more skill than it was possible for Rogers to display.... A beautiful performance is contributed ... by that talented and lovable trouper, Louise Dresser; and Jason Robards also does notable work.

In October 1930, Will and Fox signed a new contract, yielding Will $1,125,000 for his next six films. Rogers received $100,000 in cash upon signing the agreement and the balance in eighty-two weekly installments of $12,500 each, beginning on the first day of November 1930. In addition to starring in these upcoming film productions, Will committed to assist Fox with writing original dialogues; to select and construct storylines; to choose the cast; and to compose, revise and adapt scenarios and titles. The contract

J. M. Kerrigan, Ruth Warren and Will Rogers in *Lightnin'* (courtesy Will Rogers Memorial).

Will Rogers on Fox lot preparing newspaper column (courtesy Will Rogers Memorial).

guaranteed Will exclusive star status in the six pictures and gave Fox exclusive right to his performance in any motion picture.

Along with his movie earnings, Will also earned considerable sums of money from product endorsements, radio shows, after-dinner speeches, book contracts and his newspaper columns. While other stars housed themselves in elaborate studio accommodations, Will hung out just about anywhere in and around the set. He could often be seen typing his next day's newspaper column while perched in his automobile.

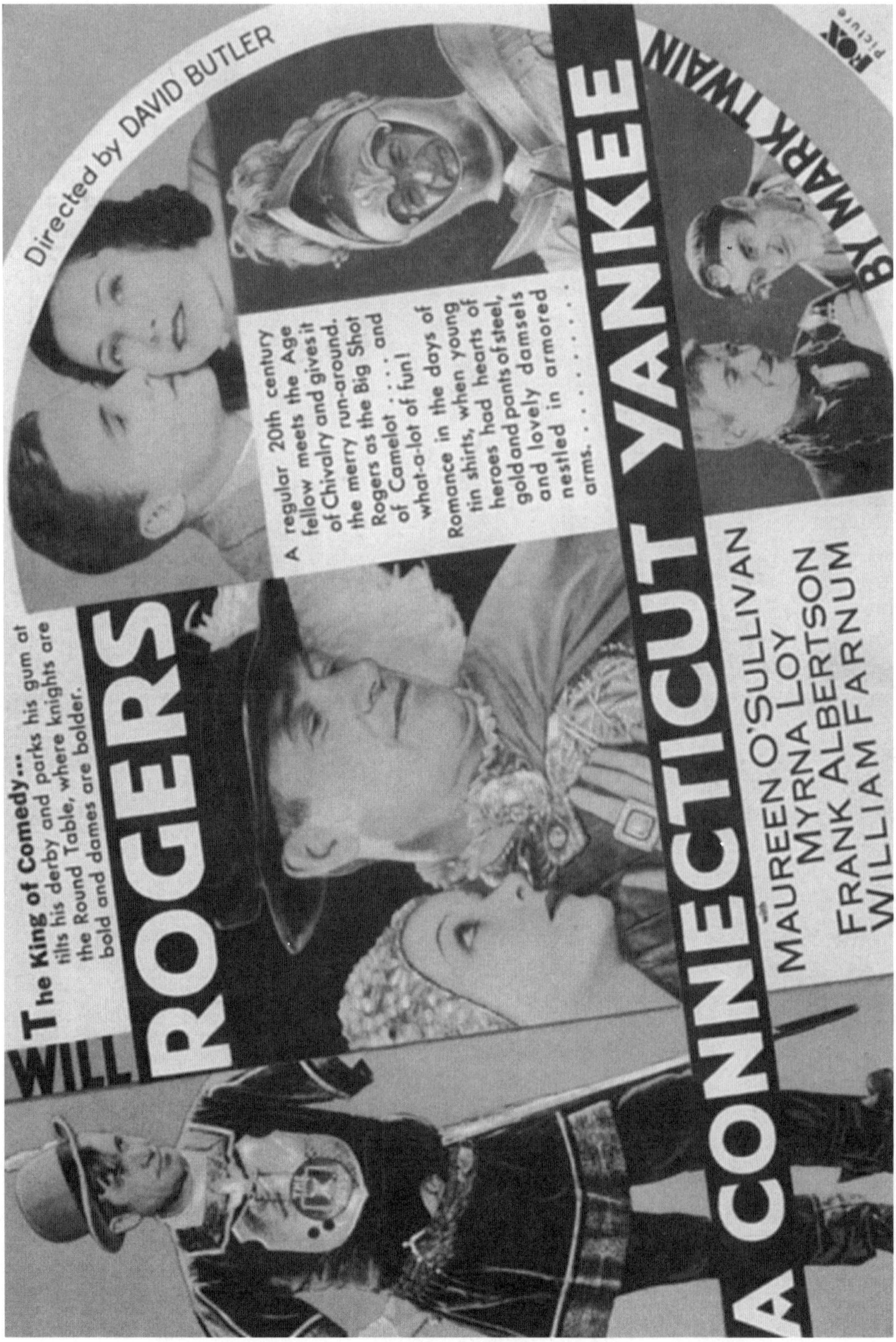
WILL
ROGERS
The King of Comedy... tilts his derby and parks his gum at the Round Table, where knights are bold and dames are bolder.
Directed by DAVID BUTLER
A regular 20th century fellow meets the Age of Chivalry and gives it the merry run-around. the Big Shot Rogers as the Big Shot of Camelot . . . and what-a-lot of fun!
Romance in the days of tin shirts, when young heroes had hearts of gold and pants of steel, and lovely damsels nestled in armored arms. . . . .
A CONNECTICUT YANKEE
MAUREEN O'SULLIVAN
MYRNA LOY
FRANK ALBERTSON
WILLIAM FARNUM
BY MARK TWAIN
FOX picture

The first picture under Will's new contract was the April 6, 1931, release of *A Connecticut Yankee,* adapted from the fantasy time travel Mark Twain story, *A Connecticut Yankee in King Arthur's Court.* This was the second of many film productions of the Twain classic. Fox had produced the first as a silent film in 1921 with Harry Myers. Paramount followed the Will Rogers treatment with its own interpretation, starring Bing Crosby, William Bendix and Rhonda Fleming, in 1949. An animated version followed in 1970 and a hip made-for-TV script came out in 1989.

Radio mechanic Hank Martin (Rogers) is called out on a stormy night to repair a radio. In the process he is knocked out and transported back to the time of the Knights of the Round Table. David Butler successfully directed Rogers, Myrna Loy, William Farnum, Frank Albertson and Maureen O'Sullivan through a number of amusing situations that have made this film a classic in its own right.

In her book *Myrna Loy: Being and Becoming,* Loy wrote of Will, "*A Connecticut Yankee* is memorable because of Will Rogers, another of those rascals who liked to tease me. I don't know why. Perhaps men need that as an excuse for contact, particularly shy men like Will.... He'd drive past me on the street and make a big fuss, waving and hollering, just to get a rise out of me. Around the studio, he'd always engage me in that innocent kind of corny way of his. But on the set ... he became extremely shy."

A Connecticut Yankee earned honors as one of the Best Pictures of the Month in the April 1931 *Photoplay,* while Will garnered recognition for giving one of the Best Performances of the Month. *Photoplay* also ranked the film number twelve on the Honor Roll of Films for 1931: "Mix Will Rogers with Mark Twain and you've got laughter medicine that'll cure anything from the megrims to depression-woe. This 1931 talkie of Twain's grand old story is better and funnier than was that silent ... that Harry Myers starred in some years ago.... As the Yankee, Will Rogers ... is a natural. His tongue fits Twain's words perfectly. William Farnum and sinuous Myrna Loy are excellent."

The *Film Daily* said, "With a modernized version of Mark Twain's famous story, Will Rogers scores heavily as a Yankee radio announcer (WRCO radio) who is transported back to the time of King Arthur.... It is filled with a lot of pleasant absurdities in a kidding manner that gets over for the laughs."

The *New York Times* rated *A Connecticut Yankee* in the tenth spot on its list of the year's best films: "Mr. Rogers fits his role marvelously. He makes the most of opportunities to drawl extemporaneous lines, and as Sir Boss he appears in a grotesque costume, with a white derby, and latterly in shining armor.... Myrna Loy also appears to advantage as Queen Morgan Le Fay."

Time commented, "Not until its present metamorphosis into a talking picture has a form been reached in which the many-faceted material is properly displayed.... Will Rogers' deliberate awkwardness, his shamble, mock shyness and ability on horseback, are all ideal for the role."

Silver Screen gave *A Connecticut Yankee* a "Great" rating and commented, "Will Rogers is ideally suited to the role of the Yankee who suddenly finds himself a prisoner in King Arthur's kingdom.... The thing is a riot from start to finish, and is recommended as a laugh tonic. The whole cast is great, and William Farnum makes a right royal King Arthur."

Opposite: **Ad for *A Connecticut Yankee* (1931) (authors' collection).**

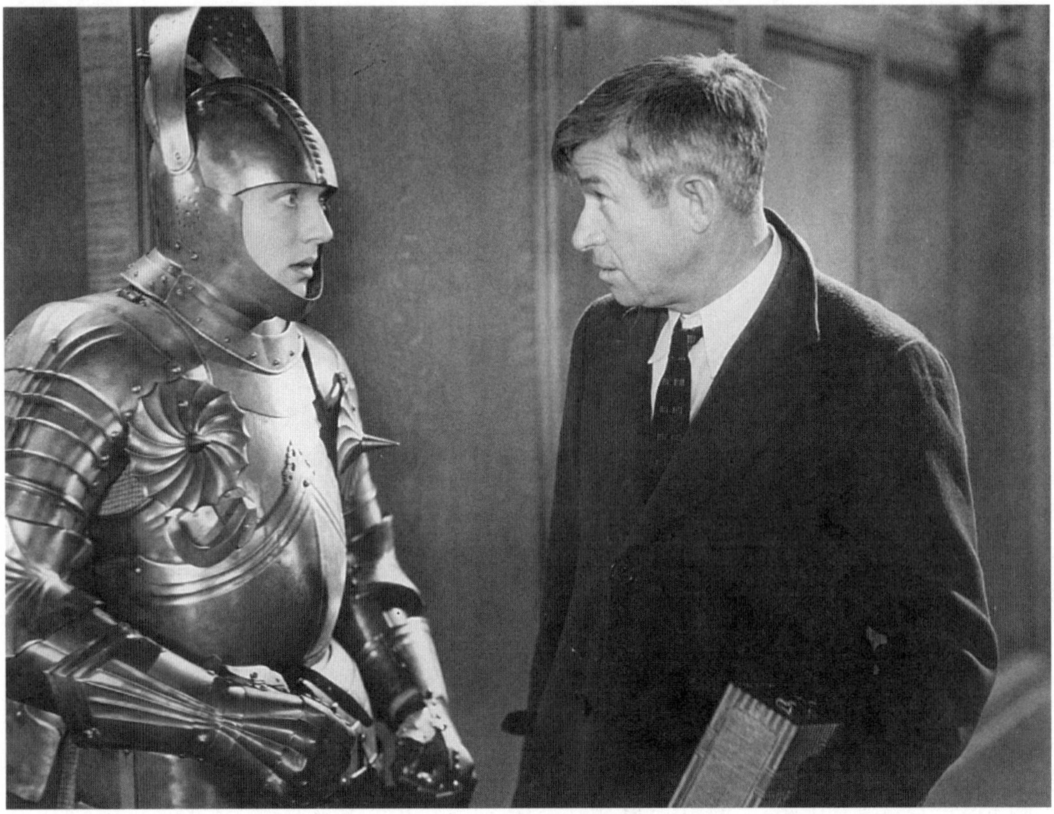

Frank Albertson and Will Rogers in *A Connecticut Yankee* (courtesy Will Rogers Memorial).

Variety proclaimed the movie, "Good deluxe comedy which has the Will Rogers name to make it class as strong b.o.... Rogers is at home all the way and there's a lot of action. That's a happy combination and ... ought to run up a lot of business."

Will ad-libbed his way into a number of great quotes:

"Can'st tellest me where in the hellest I am?"

"I don't care about King Arthur and his Court. I'm going home and get Amos 'n' Andy."

When Myrna Loy put her arms around his neck during one scene, Will turned bright red and edged away, saying, "Now looka here, Queen. You got me wrong. You must be lookin' for some other feller." Will later confided, "I feel like I've cheated on my wife."

"See here, I don't want to be bedecked, do your own bedecking."

Not missing the chance to plug Claremore, Oklahoma, Will asks, "Did you ever hear of Sir Rogers de Claremore? Its funny how they only find knights and lords as your ancestors. I guess they ship over all the horse thieves."

Will introduces King Arthur to a number of modern conveniences such as telephones, roller skates, factories, radio, hot dogs and advertising: "Makes you want to buy things you have been able to get along without."

In June 1931, Will, Wallace Beery, Douglas Fairbanks and Frank Lloyd sat together at a preparatory school graduation exercise. Will's daughter, Mary, was graduating as were relatives of the other three men. Will often made jokes about schooling, but his pride showed through among the jokes.

"All four of us just sat there and purred like four old tom cats basking in a little reflected sunshine."

"All the kids I know, either mine or anybody's, none of 'em can write so you can read it, none of 'em can spell so you can read it. They can't figure and don't know geography."

"Then they got some gag they call 'Credits.' If you do anything thirty minutes twice a week, why you get some certain 'Credit.' Maybe it's lamp shade tinting, maybe it's singing, maybe it's a thing they call 'music appreciation.' That used to drive my cowboy son Jim pretty near nuts. Some of 'em give you more 'Credits' for than others. If a thing is particularly useless, why it give you more 'Credits.' There is none at all for things that we thought constituted school."

"But us poor old dumb parents, we just string along and do the best we can, and send 'em as long as we are able, because we want them to have the same handicaps the others have."

About the same time as his daughter's graduation, Will refused an honorary doctorate of humanity and letters from Oklahoma State University: "What are they trying to do? Make a joke out of college degrees? They are in bad enough repute as it is, without handing 'em around to comedians. The whole honorary degree thing is hooey. I saw

William Farnum and Will Rogers in *A Connecticut Yankee* (courtesy Will Rogers Memorial).

Will Rogers and Fifi D'Orsay in *Young as You Feel* (1931) (courtesy Will Rogers Memorial).

some college is giving Mellon one, and he is a billion bucks short. I got too much respect for people that work and earn 'em to see 'em handed around to every notorious character." Will did concede, however, that he might accept an A.D. (Doctor of Applesauce).

In the August 1931 release, *Young as You Feel,* Will portrays meat packing business owner Lemuel Morehouse, who changes his obsession with routine to don a tuxedo and high hat to enjoy the high life with a saucy café society girl named Fleurette (Fifi D'Orsay). Will personally selected the George Ade story, which provides plenty of laughs and amusing situations for Rogers to play to the hilt.

"Will Rogers made the Roxy spectators forget the scorching sun outside yesterday afternoon by his performance in a humorous picture called *Young as You Feel* ... which has its quota of laughable incidents and merry patter," said the *New York Times* reviewer, Mordaunt Hall.

Photoplay named Will among its Best Performances of the Month in its July 1931 issue for his work in *Young as You Feel:* "Another grand Will Rogers film, funny enough to make you forget a toothache. In this Will is a drab, middle-aged business man who suddenly discovers that a little dash of champagne and Fifi D'Orsay are enough to make him younger than his sons. You'll hear plenty of risque lines, but no viciousness. Good cast, with Lucien Littlefield a scream, and Fifi doing her best work."

Life reviewer Harry Evans commented, "Some fun. And of course everybody should see Will in a high silk hat and tail coat. We sometimes think Fox is wasting its money

Sheet music for "The Cute Little Things You Do" from *As Young As You Feel* shows Fifi D'Orsay and Will Rogers (authors' collection).

hiring actors to appear in Will's pictures. During every one of his films ... we sat around in anticipation of the moments when he would come out with a Rogers paragraph. These short, bright remarks, delivered in the Rogers manner ... make his films worth while, regardless of what else goes on.... Fifi D'Orsay makes a fine foil for Mr. Rogers."

Variety took a dimmer view of the storyline: "If Will Rogers can stand up under this one Fox will. Outside of Rogers there's little to recommend, but that may be enough."

The *Hollywood Reporter* predicted that "Will Rogers will have them rolling out of their seats at this one ... maybe it has more of the risque tang to it than his former pictures, but the natural wholesomeness of Rogers and the vivacity of Fifi D'Orsay serve pretty well to offset any active feeling of distaste in the situations or dialog."

In a December 5, 1931, article in the *Film Weekly*, Fifi D'Orsay talked about working with Will on the set of *Young as You Feel*: "All the players know their lines, and we start rehearsing. It's only then that Monsieur Rogers looks at his dialogue for the first time. It's really funny. But he gets away with it, and, besides, he always changes the dialogue to make it to suit him. Leave it to Will Rogers.... When we started to make *Young as You Feel* I was supposed to be the 'sex element' in it. But oooo! la la! When it was finished and we saw it runoff in the rough in the studio, Monsieur Rogers was the 'sex appeal.' He was the one who had it.... The women surely will be crazy about him."

During one scene, Will and Fifi accidentally end up in the same bedroom. Fifi needs some help zipping up her dress, and Will first runs away but then reluctantly obliges amid stuttering comments of, "I'm all thumbs" and, "You certainly smell nice."

When Will asks the valet to lay out his suit (the one he only wears for funerals), the butler inquires, "Pardon me, sir, is anyone dead?"

Will and Fifi dance while she sings to him *The Things You Do, Do, Do*. Flustered, he blurts out, "I feel just like a kid seeing the only schoolhouse in town burn down."

In the movie, Will frequently pokes fun at the "art movement." He unveils one of his own art creations, a large boulder hauled in from a construction site. "This is Washington Crossing the Delaware. Turn it around and it's Washington Coming Back."

The final scene shows Will expounding on age: "There's no such thing as age. Age is just a word somebody invented that needed an alibi. Why, I was 108 at 35 and now at 51, I'm only 24. Say, from now on I'm growing backwards. And when I pass out of the picture, I'm going to have put on my tombstone, Lemuel Morehouse ... Died from infancy."

Will finished out 1931 with the November release of *Ambassador Bill*, based on Vincent Sheean's novel *Ambassador from the United States*. The storyline allows Will plenty of opportunity to make fun of politics and deliver more to-the-point homespun philosophy.

Harrison's Reports called the movie "A pleasant and entertaining comedy. There are not as many laughs in it as there are in Will Rogers' [other] pictures." The *New York Times* concurred, "The humor here is rather more subdued than in Mr. Rogers' other vehicles, but it is a good sketch with funny lines and ludicrous situations.... Greta Nissen is lovely as the siren, Lika. Marguerite Churchill serves the part of the Queen well.... Gustav von Seyffertitz is excellent as the sinister de Polikoff. And Mr. Rogers, as usual, never fails his audience."

Photoplay commented, "The cowboy star, Will Rogers, is again operating in a mythical kingdom, and while you are convulsed with laughter at some of his antics, the memory of 'King Arthur's Court' keeps bobbing up. Rabid Rogers fans won't mind this and there is fun enough to keep you hilarious for an hour. Marguerite Churchill is a very lovely queen while Greta Nissen makes an attractive vamp."

Will Rogers spiffed up in *Young as You Feel* (courtesy Will Rogers Memorial).

Ambassador Bill Harper (Rogers) arrives in Sylvania in time to experience this week's revolution. Upon arrival he believes the ongoing battle is his reception committee. When his hat is shot off in the melee before he gets to begin a speech, he remarks, "Why, I hadn't even said anything yet." As an armored vehicle picks him up to escort him safely to the embassy, he remarks, "Well, a Chicago taxi."

Ambassador Bill teaches Young King Paul (Tad Alexander) how to play baseball. After the king and the rival team's first baseman get into a scuffle, he orders the other youth shot. Ambassador Bill steps in and says, "Hey, wait a minute. I taught you the game of baseball and there's nothing in there about shooting a first baseman. An umpire maybe, that's different."

Senator Pillsbury (Ferdinand Munier) advises Ambassador Bill to keep his nose out of Sylvania's internal affairs: "It's absolutely contrary to the spirit of American government to mix or meddle in the affairs of any other country."

Ambassador Bill responds, "Yeah! Tell that to the Marines."

The senator continues as the target of Will's humor: "Put a US Senator with more than two people and t'aint any power on earth can keep him from making a speech," and "Look at the fine monument you'll get. Senator dies investigating."

When the cross-eyed butcher (Ben Turpin) is summoned to use an axe to free Ambassador Bill and Senator Pillsbury from a pair of handcuffs, Ambassador Bill asks, "You aint going to hit where you're looking are you!"

Business and Pleasure, with Jetta Goudal, Joel McCrea and Dorothy Peterson supporting Will, followed next, coming out in February 1932.

The storyline called for a peasant girl extra in one of the scenes. After much coaxing by his daughter, Mary, Will agreed to let her play the extra. However, he never let on

Ad for ***Ambassador Bill*** (1931) (authors' collection).

Arnold Korff and Will Rogers in *Ambassador Bill* (authors' collection).

to anyone on the set that she was his daughter. Mary worked under the name Mary Howard, which she later used in her own brief movie career.

Irene Rich was originally scheduled to team up again with Will in *Business and Pleasure*, but the shooting schedule conflicted with her daughter's graduation from Smith College and she was replaced.

Business and Pleasure, adapted from Booth Tarkington's novel *The Plutocrat,* centered around the exploits of razor-blade manufacturer Earl Tinker (Rogers) and his travels to the Middle East and adventures with a femme fatale (Goudal).

Photoplay voted *Business and Pleasure* one of the Best Pictures of the Month and gave the nod to Will for giving one of the Best Performances of the Month despite finding fault with the story: "If it weren't for Will Rogers, this would be just another movie, and not so much of a one at that. But thanks to the man's inimitable drolleries, it's lifted into the worthwhile entertainment class.... When Rogers is talking, the film is a riot."

Variety found "some of the passages between husband and wife are honestly amusing, and a few of Rogers' gag lines pack a laugh. But for the most part the main appeal is rural."

The *New York Times* ranked *Business and Pleasure* number thirteen in its list of Notable Films of 1932. Mordaunt Hall, movie reviewer for the *Times*, wrote, "Will Rogers, who never fails to give motion picture audiences their full money's worth of laughter, is

Ad for ***Business and Pleasure*** **(1932) (authors' collection).**

as successful as ever in his latest venture.... The Roxy was well filled for the first showing ... and many a chuckle, giggle and guffaw was evoked by the comedian's special brand of dry wit.... Mr. Rogers' performance is capital, and it is obvious that he improvises many of his lines, which adds to the humor of the piece."

Harrison's Reports regarded *Business and Pleasure* as "a good comedy. There are not many really hearty laughs in the picture but it keeps one amused all through out."

The film opens aboard ship where Madame Momora (Goudal) warns Earl Tinker (Rogers) of much danger ahead for him. Enthralled by Momora, Tinker tells his wife (Peterson) he was out playing poker with the boys. When Madame Momora's dog comes into the staterooom with him, Mrs. Tinker inquires, "Oh, did the dog play poker too?"

After Tinker discovers that Madame Momora has been in cahoots with his competitor, he says, "What do you know about that. What a fine old fool I've been. I might have known a beautiful woman like that wouldn't be wasting her time on an old bird like me."

Tinker masquerades as a swami to trick Madame Momora into revealing his competitor's secrets. While he is still dressed in the swami costume, his wife visits to have her fortune told. Realizing he has not been recognized, he starts out with, "You was not always a blonde and you have come to see about your husband." When his wife offers

Will Rogers and Jetta Goudal in *Business and Pleasure* (courtesy Will Rogers Memorial).

to pay the fee, he refuses, "No, I can't take it, lady. This one was too easy. It's on the house."

Two other laugh-getting lines deserve mention: "The US Government is making every effort to get Congressmen and Senators off the dole," and, "I want you to meet the wife, she's a great little woman when she's in a good humor."

Will took time off from filming to attend the funeral of Florenz Ziegfeld, who died in July 1932. Will personally handled all of the funeral arrangements. "Ziggy gave me my start. If there is anything I can do to repay him, nothing could be too much."

In August 1932, William Sheehan, vice president and general manager of Fox Film Corporation, announced the signing of Will Rogers to a new contract, calling for Will to star in four more Fox productions over a two-year period at a salary of $125,000 a picture. The new contract went into effect after Will completed *Down to Earth*, a September 1932 release produced under the direction of David Butler. Will and Butler had previously worked together on *A Connecticut Yankee* and *Business and Pleasure.*

Down to Earth derived its storyline from a novel by Homer Croy, author of *They Had to See Paris*, an earlier Rogers film. It continued the theme of the exploits and adventures of a nouveau riche American family, this time plagued by a financial crisis.

Harrison's Reports described *Down to Earth* as "good entertainment. It has human interest and some good homely philosophy that will be understood and enjoyed by the

Will Rogers reading Oklahoma paper in *Down to Earth* (1932) (courtesy Will Rogers Memorial).

masses. Men will particularly emphasize with Rogers who, hit hard financially, cannot make his wife and son realize the significance of the depression. Several situations are funny as well as pathetic."

Photoplay wrote, "Will Rogers and his rich, four-flushing family lose their butlers and Rolls Royces and learn to like it! Not a new theme, by any means, and a picture that might have been one of Will's best if it were not quite so sketchy and obvious. Will gets off some real depression philosophy that is comforting to us all, and maybe it's not such a bad depression as depressing things go!"

The *New York Times* commented, "This little tale, which evidently pleased the audience, turns out happily, with Pike wearing an apron while he cooks a meal. He is at last freed from the gaze of the omnipresent butler. He is down to earth. Mr. Rogers fortifies his part by his drawl and his amusing demeanor."

Pike Peters (Rogers) continually rails against his wife's extravagance, elaborate entertaining and desire to keep up with the neighbors. "Bet we've got more guests and less friends than any family in America."

When times turn bad and his business is in financial trouble, he philosophizes, "You can see the handwriting on the wall. The only trouble nowadays is that none of us stay home long enough to look at the wall."

Will Rogers and Jetta Goudal in *Business and Pleasure* (authors' collection).

After the stock market crash, Peters is found cutting up shares of stock into paper dolls, and his sanity is challenged. "Buying them was a state of insanity, cutting 'em up is a sign I'm getting my sense of reason back."

In an attempt to salvage his business, Peters invites the bank's board of directors over for dinner to show how he and his wife have cut back drastically on their lavish lifestyle. Not knowing the reason for the dinner, Mrs. Peters (Irene Rich) goes all out to impress the bankers. Multiple servants serve the meal on a table decorated with gardenias. To the bankers, Peters says, "You notice, I hope, they ain't orchids."

After a separation, Peters and his wife reconcile: "No woman will ever believe a man that he's not worthy of her … until after they are married."

The December 1932 release *Too Busy to Work* brought back the endearing Jubilo character Will Rogers made famous. Jubilo's appearance in a small town changes the destinies of members of a prominent family. Rogers' portrayal of Jubilo in this film ranks among the best of his human interest roles.

The *Film Daily* regarded *Too Busy to Work* as a "good family picture with Rogers giving enjoyable characterization in dandy all-around comedy-drama. Playing one of his most likable roles, Will Rogers is a real treat in this story. Which has a neat romance and some effective human interest in addition to plenty of Will Rogers' humor."

The *Tulsa Daily World* wrote, "The popular and beloved comedian was never so keen of wit and so razor-edged in repartee as he is in his latest Fox picture. Nor has he ever before demonstrated such exceptional emotional qualities."

Top: Will Rogers in ***Too Busy to Work*** (1932) (authors' collection). ***Bottom:*** Dick Powell and Will Rogers in ***Too Busy to Work*** (courtesy Will Rogers Memorial).

The *New York Times* reviewer, Mordaunt Hall, commented, "In his latest picture, *Too Busy to Work,* Will Rogers, who without a doubt is one of Hollywood's most industrious inhabitants, portrays a tramp with a decided distaste for even the simplest form of toil.... During this chronicle Mr. Rogers goes through his part admirably."

All movie critics were not pleased with the picture, however. The *New York Sun* found *Too Busy to Work* "the weakest of the Will Rogers talkies. Certainly it is the most obvious and slowest."

Jubilo (Rogers) hops off a freight train and approaches Dan Hardy (Dick Powell). Hardy asks, "Are you broke?" Jubilo replies, "Well, my assets are temporarily frozen."

Rose (Marian Nixon) admonishes Jubilo for continually avoiding work. "How can you be so lazy?" she inquires. "It's not very hard. You jes don't do anything about it and first thing you know, it takes care of itself," answers Jubilo.

Jubilo watches Axel (Constantine Romanoff) pluck the feathers off a chicken and remarks, "Wall Street couldn't do a better job on a client than that."

Jubilo comments on human nature: "People are funny. They'll believe any kind of lie if it sounds like the truth but they won't believe the truth if it sounds like a lie."

Will's first 1933 release, *State Fair,* premiered on January 26 at Radio City Music Hall in New York City. Will starred with Louise Dresser, Janet Gaynor and a prize hog named Blue Boy. Fox ran a full-page ad for the movie in the March 1933 issue of *Photoplay* with

Will Rogers and Janet Gaynor promotion shot for *State Fair* (1933) (courtesy Will Rogers Memorial).

pictures of the major stars and ad copy calling the film "Another sensational screen treat from Fox."

Will said, "Me and the hog nap along together. I'll do anything they want, even to wrestling with the boar, but I never read the script or the book. I never do, because I don't want to be disappointed in the picture."

Both Will and Janet Gaynor won honors for Best Performances of the Month in the April 1933 issue of *Photoplay*, while the movie achieved ranking among the Best Pictures of the Month: "When you add to this fine cast a whimsical tale that fairly breathes the charm side of life on the farm; introduces chuckles and laughs ... you'll probably feel that there's no fun to improve upon that at state fairs. All in all, beyond question here's superb entertainment for the whole family."

Other honors followed. The National Board of Review voted *State Fair* one of the Ten Best Films of the Year and the *New York Times* and *Film Daily* rated the film number four and number five, respectively, in their listings of top films of the year. *Film Daily* headlined, "Great Cast and Ace Entertainment.... Fine human interest story packed with laughs and heart punch" while the *New York Times* reviewer called *State Fair* "an easy-going offering which will appeal both to those who know all about state fairs and those who do not.... Will Rogers gives a most pleasing characterization."

Vanity Fair commented, "Among the many pleasant surprises in this movie, is that ubiquitous, homespun humorist Will Rogers. For the first time since his silent picture days, Mr. Rogers is made to act and not comment. He plays stooge to a champion hog called Blue Boy, and he does it with a great deal of skill.... I congratulate ... Mr. Rogers.... *State Fair* is a good job."

"I feel what Henry King, the director, has done with this film is almost remarkable.... He has toned down Will Rogers ... handled the relentless wistfulness of Janet Gaynor with a nice tact," wrote the *New Yorker* reviewer.

Will used his association with Blue Boy to his best advantage: "You and me, just a couple more hams for Hollywood. You're certainly some hog. When it comes to pork, there's nothing like you, even back in Washington."

When the hog offered no grunt in response, Will continued, "Hmmm. Just as talkative as a stock speculator before a Senate investigating committee."

During one scene, the hog steadfastly refused to be positioned as the director wanted in the pen. Will salvaged the situation: "You're probably lining up on the wrong side of his profile. Tell you what, I'll switch over to the right side. It doesn't make any difference with my face. After all, it is his pen." In another scene, Abel Frake (Rogers) uses Melissa Frake's (Dresser) hair brush to groom Blue Boy. Mrs. Frake says, "The next thing you know, he'll be wearing my silk stockings."

As Abel frets over Blue Boy's listlessness, Mrs. Frake admonishes, "Abe, will you get your mind off that hog." Just then they walk by the girlie show and Abel responds, "Mind's off the hog now, Ma."

When Margy Frake (Gaynor) bemoans the fact that the state fair is a year away, Abel comments, "If you don't think next year will roll around quick, just wait till you are old enough to pay taxes."

After completion of the movie, the producers suggested that Will buy Blue Boy. He declined, saying, "I can't do it. I jus' wouldent feel right eating a fellow actor."

Louise Dresser and Will Rogers in *State Fair:* "Mind's off the hog now, Ma" (courtesy Will Rogers Memorial).

Will teamed up with director John Ford in his portrayal of a small-town doctor in the film production of a James Gould Cozzens novel, *The Last Adam,* released in August 1933 under the title *Doctor Bull.* Ford later recalled, "*Doctor Bull* was a downbeat story but Bill managed to get a lot of humor into it … and it became a hell of a good picture. It was one of Bill's favorites." *Photoplay* ranked *Doctor Bull* as number twenty-five of the Year's Best Films: "Will Rogers brings personality to the tale of a country doctor struggling with a community that misunderstands; mild, except for Will."

Will had convinced Fox to change the name of the film from *Life's Worth Living* to *Doctor Bull.* The *New York Times* reported:

> The humor of Will Rogers brought the comedian a victory this week when Fox acceded to his request that the name of his newest picture be called *Doctor Bull.* Behind the change is an amusing inside story which indicates how Mr. Rogers has won points in the innumerable controversies he has had with the studio…. The executives were determined about the title. Every one but Mr. Rogers thought he was beaten. A meeting of sales and studio executives was held recently in Atlantic City and to this Mr. Rogers dispatched a telegram…. "I hear you are having a convention back there. I thought con-

ventions passed out with the Republicans. There is nothing as useless, outside of a Rogers close-up, as a convention. But as you are gathered to do some good anyhow, put the name *Doctor Bull* on our next picture. Some half-wit suggested *Life's Worth Living*. Now we find that they have tried to hang that title on every Fox picture since *Over the Hill* so they finally said give it to Rogers. Somebody must be winning a bet if he gets that title on some picture whether it fits or not so you hyenas have a chance to help pass it along to some other poor devil to use. *Life's Worth Living* sounds like a graduation essay. As a matter of fact, if we don't make some better pictures life won't be worth living and it will come to the point where the exhibitor is as bad off as he says he is."

Mordaunt Hall, reviewer for the *New York Times*, wrote, "As Dr. Bull, Mr. Rogers shows a fighting spirit and no little artfulness in outwitting his enemies.... It is a characterization which suits Mr. Rogers particularly well and he gives a really human characterization."

Harrison's Reports recommended *Doctor Bull* as "good entertainment.... The action is rather slow and the story is not particularly exciting but there is enough of the Will Rogers brand of humor and quips to hold the interest of most audiences. Comedy is brought about by the picture of small-town life, with its smugness, gossip and interference in the private lives of neighbors."

The *Literary Digest* commented, "Will Rogers makes a homespun field day out of

Louise Dresser, Will Rogers and Janet Gaynor in *State Fair* (courtesy Will Rogers Memorial).

Director John Ford and Will Rogers on the set of *Doctor Bull* (1933) (courtesy Will Rogers Memorial).

that successful novel, *The Last Adam.* You are more likely to enjoy it if you haven't read the book."

Two of Will's lines in the picture stand out. During one scene he asks to use a phone and is told by the family, "Ain't got a phone, doctor." Dr. Bull responds, "Well, guess you're lucky."

After spending all night delivering a baby, Dr. Bull muses, "Get some sleep. We have to die to get any sleep."

Will's final 1933 release, *Mr. Skitch,* premiered at the Roxy Theatre in New York City during December. The cast included the versatile Florence Desmond giving the audience a taste of her unique impressions of Hollywood actresses, the deadpan antics of ZaSu Pitts and the lovely Rochelle Hudson as the ingenue. Will's daughter, Mary, interviewed for the ingenue part under the stage name of Mary Howard.

Worth noting, perhaps, are two films Will did *not* make in 1933. One was allegedly planned to be his life story. The December 30, 1932, issue of the *Tulsa Daily World* had reported that Will was beginning work on *Arizona to Broadway*, an original story by William Conselman patterned after Will's life story from cowboy to star in the Ziegfeld *Follies.* The January 21, 1933, issue of the *New York Sun* mentioned that Will postponed

Doctor Bull **lobby card (courtesy Will Rogers Memorial).**

an airplane vacation in order to make a screen dramatization of his own life, *Arizona to Broadway.*

"They've been talkin' of doing the story of my life, but that's an old gag. They do that between pictures all the time. Always somethin' about startin' in the West and goin' to the *Follies*. Shucks, we had too much o' that in the beginning of the talkies, and I have no hankerin' to star in one of those backstage stories. Besides, my life wouldn't be of any interest to nobody, not even to my own folks. You never get credit for playing yourself, just blame; better play a character."

In April 1933, the *Tulsa Daily World* reported Will pulling out of the *Arizona to Broadway* project: "In the raw [it] didn't look so hot to Will Rogers when he read it the first time. 'Thumbs down,' he said. Will Rogers read it a second time and it looked better to him, especially when he found it was going to be a big picture with music, girl ensembles and other trimmings. His reaction came too late, for Jimmy Dunn had already been given the part."

James Dunn and Joan Bennett starred in the 1933 Fox release of *Arizona to Broadway*. The storyline bore no resemblance to Will's life story. Instead it involved a confidence man, a girl and a Broadway setting.

Also in 1933, Will declined to appear in a film based on a story written especially for him, *If I Were President,* because it criticized President Herbert Hoover and his administration. He commented that making the picture might not be a good thing for the country at the present time. The *Tulsa Daily World* also reported that Will's next picture would be based on a magazine story, *The Handshaker*, and would be adapted by Jane Storm. No other mention of this project could be found.

Will received honors for one of the Best Performances of the Month in the February 1934 issue of *Photoplay*, which also gave a rave review to Desmond: "Florence Desmond's impersonations of well-known movie stars are nigh perfect, and are the high spots of the picture. The whole family will enjoy the Rogers humor."

Silver Screen reported that *Mr. Skitch* played to a full house for three days and nights in Neosho, Missouri. A New York reviewer wrote that *Mr. Skitch* was kept over for a second week: "No one seems to object to the review last Sunday which called *Mr. Skitch* the best picture Will Rogers ever made. The only complaints the Uptown has had since the picture has been there have come from a pet store five blocks away whose manager declares the Uptown audiences are laughing so loudly the parrots can't hear themselves think."

The *Hollywood Reporter* concluded, "It has plenty of comedy, enough pathos to keep it from getting monotonous, and is filled with Rogerisms that are funnier than usual." The *New York Times* said, "Although Will Rogers' latest vehicle, *Mr. Skitch*, ... is never

Gloria Jean Robb, Cleora Joan Robb, ZaSu Pitts, Will Rogers and Rochelle Hudson in *Mr. Skitch* (1933) (authors' collection).

ZaSu Pitts, The Robb twins, Florence Desmond, Will Rogers and Harry Green in *Mr. Skitch* (authors' collection).

particularly dramatic, it possesses that human quality that may make the spectator glad or sad, according to what happens to the likable but sometimes foolish Mr. Skitch.... Mr. Rogers is just as natural and pleasing as he was in *Doctor Bull.* Miss Pitts adds to the general interest."

Variety found fault with literary flaws, illogical goings-on and loose ends: "Critics can make mincemeat of *Mr. Skitch* for by standards of excellence it is a grave sinner. Yet this is probably wiped away for the general public by the laughs. Performances are generally good.... It should be a moderate grosser on Will Rogers' name plus that of ZaSu Pitts."

In December 1933, Will and Fox Film Corporation came to agreement and signed another multi-film contract, this time calling for Will to star in five Fox films for a salary of $125,000 per film. The new agreement kept Will Rogers the highest-paid film star in Hollywood. The contract was well earned. Will ranked as the number one male box office draw in 1933 over such other lead actors as Eddie Cantor, Wallace Beery and Clark Gable. Only Marie Dressler outpaced Will in the listings.

Will chose Edward Noyes Westcott's novel *David Harum* for his next starring role. The movie premiered at Radio City Music Hall in March 1934 and co-starred Louise Dresser, Evelyn Venable, Kent Taylor and Stepin Fetchit.

Will Rogers and Kent Taylor in *David Harum* (1934) (courtesy Will Rogers Memorial).

Talking about his role as a small-town banker and horse trader (David Harum is honest except when it comes to horse-trading), Will said, "I never saw a man in the trotting horse business under 80. The only thing I had to recommend me was that I looked as old as a driver."

Photoplay heaped praise on *David Harum* and Will Rogers, giving them nods for inclusion in the listings of Best Pictures of the Month and Best Performances of the Month, respectively: "Comedy-Drama close to the Will Rogers pattern, with all the genuine charm of his previous endeavors. The character of David Harum, a small-town banker who indulges in horse-trading on the side, fits Will like a glove. He discovers that his balky horse will break records to 'ta-ra-ra-boom-de-ay' which saves the day in the big race. Evelyn Venable and Kent Taylor supply romance. Some of the trades will have you in stitches."

The *New York Times* wrote, "*David Harum* is another of those welcome, refreshing pictures, which, judging by the constant outbursts of laughter, was enjoyed greatly by an audience at its first exhibition.... Mr. Rogers is at the height of his form here. He makes one forgive any extravagant ideas. Miss Dresser does nicely as Polly and Miss Venable is charming as Ann."

Harrison's Reports found *David Harum* "a pleasant homely type of comedy. The story is very thin and the action slow, but Rogers excels in his quips, making up for the other defects."

Among the quips that rate mention are:

"I go a long way on a man's character and then a longer way on his collateral."

"It's a heap easier to get a hook into a fish's mouth than it is to get it out."

When Ann Madison (Venable) asks if John Lennox (Taylor) is married, Harum (Rogers) answers, "No he seems perfectly sane to me."

While on the Fox set for *David Harum*, Will became friends with rising child star Shirley Temple.

Will Rogers and Shirley Temple on the set of *David Harum* (courtesy Will Rogers Memorial).

Will Rogers served as master of ceremonies for the 1932-1933 Academy of Motion Pictures Arts and Sciences Awards on March 18, 1934. He personally handed out a number of the major award categories: Best Actor (Charles Laughton in *The Private Life of Henry VIII*), Best Actress (Katharine Hepburn in *Morning Glory),* Best Motion Picture (*Cavalcade),* Art Direction (William S. Darling, *Cavalcade*), Cinematography (Charles Bryant Lang, Jr., *A Farewell to Arms),* Directing (Frank Lloyd, *Cavalcade)* and Sound Recording (Paramount Studio Sound Department, Franklin Hansen, sound director, *A Farewell to Arms*). Will's movie *State Fair* also received a nomination for Best Motion Picture.

Will proved to be a master at being master of ceremonies with lines such as:

"It's a racket. If it wasn't, we all wouldn't be here in dress clothes."

"If the movies are an art, I kinda think it'll leak out somehow without bein' told; and if they're a science ... then it's a miracle."

"It takes great restraint to stand there and hand out tokens of merit to inferior actors. There is great acting in this room tonight, greater than you will see on the screen."

"We all cheer when somebody gets a prize that everyone of us in the house knows should be ours. Yet we smile and take it. Boy, that's acting."

"An adapter is one who wants to bet you won't recognize your own story. Original writers are men who have had good enough lawyers to protect them from plagiarism."

"I have never seen any of these pictures. They don't look at mine and why should I go see theirs?"

The successful musical *Stand Up and Cheer,* featuring Shirley Temple, originated from a story idea put forth by Will Rogers and Philip Klein. The film premiered at Radio City Music Hall in New York City on April 19, 1934. Fox placed a two-page ad for *Stand Up and Cheer* in the May 1934 issue of *Photoplay,* crediting Rogers and Klein for the story idea.

Several other proposed movie productions were linked to Will in 1934. An early 1934 Fox press release promised a new Will Rogers picture with Janet Gaynor, *One More Spring,* based on the novel by Robert Nathan and being adapted by Edwin Burke. The April 11, 1934, issue of the *Tulsa Daily Herald* reported that *One More Spring* would feature many of Fox's "biggest and best stars" and would be directed by Henry King. Will never did appear in this movie, but Fox released it in 1935 with Janet Gaynor and Warner Baxter assuming the star roles.

Will was also mentioned in connection with another upcoming film, *What Am I Bid?* That production scheduled him in the role of an auctioneer with a supporting cast of James Dunn, Rosemary Ames, Claire Trevor and John Bradford. A movie with a similar storyline was eventually produced by Liberty International in 1967. The July 1, 1934, issue of the *New York Times* mentioned both of the above projects and another one, *What's a Lawyer For?* No further reference can be found regarding the latter proposed production.

Will spoke out in July 1934 on the subject of censorship and cleaning up the movies. "They had it comin' to 'em. Oh Lord! I'm not mixed up in that. My pictures are so clean they're not interestin'."

Will's performing career took on a new direction in 1934. After George M. Cohan's critical acclaim in Eugene O'Neill's stageplay, *Ah, Wilderness!*, producer Henry Duffy persuaded Will to star in the West Coast presentation. Will traveled to New York in January 1934 to see the production in person.

Will explained, "Yeah. Well, they want me to do Cohan's part when it comes to the coast ... they take these plays around, y'know, and they stay awhile sometimes ... and I thought I'd take a look at Georgie in it first.... I've been away from the stage for a long time and I'd like to get back, just for awhile.... Getting back on the stage now and then is good for a person; it keeps them on their toes.... I don't know whether I can get away with it at all or whether I'll be a flop but I'm certainly going to try it for all it's worth."

The West Coast production of *Ah, Wilderness!* with Will Rogers in the role of Nat Miller began rehearsal in April 1934 under the direction of Russell Fillmore. The show opened at the Curran Theatre in San Francisco on April 30, 1934, with a supporting cast that included Charlotte Henry, William Janney and Anne Shoemaker.

For once in his life, Will stuck to his lines as written and passed up the opportunity to ad-lib. "Why should I change anything? O'Neill has got along all right so far and I don't see why I should begin to help him now."

Will explained why he never faced the audience in his role of Nat Miller: "On the stage every big star always fixes it so's there's some place during the evening he can play facing the audience and count the house. But it aint necessary for me to do that, 'cause I'm on a straight salary."

Will received an ovation as the curtain dropped on his first dramatic West Coast performance at the opening night of *Ah, Wilderness!* Will remained modest about his portrayal of Nat Miller and any comparison to George M. Cohan. During one performance, Will came out between acts and remarked, "Anybody who's seen George M. Cohan in this show in New York can get half their money back at the box office."

The *New York Times* wrote,

> Will Rogers made his debut as an actor of straight roles in a regular play tonight at the Curran Theatre ... before an audience that represented society, the arts and civic and political life.... If Mr. Rogers had hunted the world over he could not have found a character more suited to his purposes.... He made Nat Miller a delightful personage.... There was a husky quality in his voice in the few emotional speeches of the part that caused misty eyes in the audience.... The house was packed. It had been sold out for more than a week. Mr. Rogers had a welcome on his first appearance that lasted several minutes. There was an ovation after the play and a speech in the best Rogers manner.

The *New York Telegraph* commented, "Will Rogers ... was acclaimed an instant success here last night."

The *Los Angeles Examiner* also praised Rogers: "Will Rogers ... made theatrical history last night.... In the O'Neill play Mr. Rogers not only finds a characterization which fits him brilliantly, but the audience also finds a theme of terrific interest, and a plot of importance, too. Mr. Rogers presents a role with a sincerity which makes the word 'actor' sound ridiculous. His earnestness and humor are all keyed to the spirit of honesty and simplicity of that period, and in his every speech and gesture the characterization is perfect."

"The shrewd, simple philosophy of Nat Miller might have been written for Mr. Rogers, so easily does he slip into the part and make it his own," commented *Newsweek.*

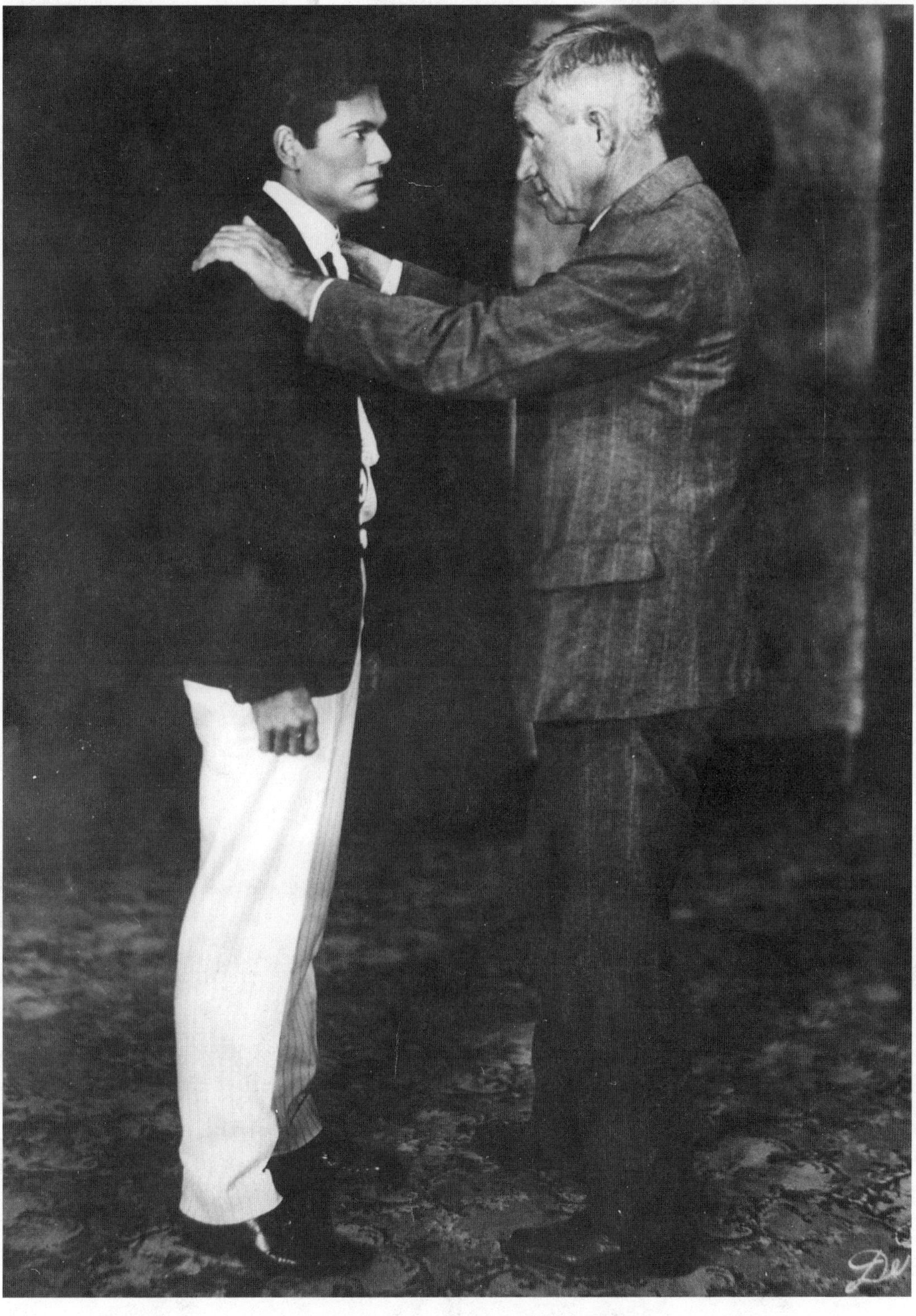

William Janney and Will Rogers in *Ah, Wilderness!* (1934) (authors' collection).

He's Busted Loose Again . . .
There's no stopping him . . . nor the laughs either when he starts stepping as you never dreamed he would. Absolutely the funniest comedy of his career
WILL ROGERS
in
HANDY ANDY
A FOX Picture with
PEGGY WOOD
CONCHITA MONTENEGRO
MARY CARLISLE • ROGER IMHOF
ROBERT TAYLOR
Produced by
SOL M. WURTZEL
Directed by
DAVID BUTLER
Based on the play "Merry Andrew" by Lewis Beach

The *Hollywood Reporter* gave Will a big thumbs up: "Will Rogers is nothing short of sensational in his role."

Characteristically, Will brushed aside the favorable comments and accolades: "'Taint me, it's the play and the other members of the cast. We're fooling 'em in large numbers up in San Francisco and we'll be here to do the same thing."

After running in San Francisco for three weeks and another six weeks at the El Captain Theatre in Los Angeles, the show closed and Will embarked on a world tour. There was some talk about Will assuming the Nat Miller role in the movie version of O'Neill's play, but the role in the Metro-Goldwyn-Mayer movie eventually went to Lionel Barrymore.

Handy Andy premiered at the Roxy Theatre in New York City in August 1934. The picture featured a variety of animals ranging from twenty-four homing pigeons to a Great Dane and a cat and her litter of kittens. Will called the film "an animal picture, with actors."

During a Mardi Gras costume ball scene, Will dons a loincloth and pink tights and performs an adagio dance with fireball Conchita Montenegro. Will shucked off the performance: "First time I ever tried that, but, of course, when a feller's been in the *Follies* like I have, well..."

Above: **Peggy Wood and Will Rogers in *Handy Andy* (1934) (courtesy Will Rogers Memorial). *Opposite: Handy Andy* promotional material (authors' collection).**

Will Rogers and Stepin Fetchit in *Judge Priest* (1934) (courtesy Will Rogers Memorial).

"In this *Handy Andy* there are many hilarious incidents, and, whether they are comedy or farce, Mr. Rogers copes with what he is called upon to do or say in his usual dependable fashion.... Proof of the film as an eminently satisfactory entertainment were the frequent outbursts of laughter that greeted Mr. Rogers' performance as Andrew Yates.... Mr. Rogers attacks this new homespun role in his accustomed easy fashion and it is evident that he had a hand in the writing of quite a number of his lines. Some of them are very funny, but others are somewhat stale ... the picture has proved so popular that it has been continued for a second week," wrote the *New York Times.*

The *American* concurred: "That classic national figure, the 'downtrod' American husband, strides the screen through trial to triumph at the Roxy this week in one of Will Rogers' more amusing vehicles.... Of course, it's a Will Rogers picture, and the star who knows a lot more than he reads in the papers, makes it ninety per cent his show. But Miss Wood, charming and clever, arrogates many moments to herself, while Mary Carlisle and Robert Taylor provide pleasant if subordinated young love interest."

Photoplay said, "As an apothecary, Will Rogers does another of his priceless characterizations. Besides an A-1 cast — Peggy Wood, Mary Carlisle and Frank Melton — there is good dialogue and believable burlesque."

The show opens with druggist Andrew Yates (Rogers) mixing up a concoction of medicine: "It may not cure 'em but it will certainly take their mind off their illness."

When a hunter comes into the drugstore attired in a vest covered with shotgun shells, Yates remarks, "Where are you going, to a disarmament conference?"

When asked to attend the Mardi Gras costume ball in New Orleans, Yates replies, "I used to shake a leg, in fact, they shake yet but not in the same way."

Will's next picture, *Judge Priest*, premiered at Radio City Music Hall in October and ranked as one of the top grossing 1934 films, helping to boost Will Rogers to the status of number one box office star that year over such noted actors and actresses as Clark Gable (number two), Janet Gaynor (number three), Wallace Beery (number four) and Mae West (number five).

Judge Priest claims the distinction of being one of Will's best movies, both from a box office and dramatic perspective, as well as one of director John Ford's classic films. Over 400 national film critics voted *Judge Priest* number twelve on the Honor Roll of the Year's Best Films. While Will did manage to get in a few one-liners for laughs, he delivered a stirring dramatic performance as Judge William Pitman Priest. Will worked on *Ah, Wilderness* and *Judge Priest* around the same time and undoubtedly the dramatic roles in each production helped Will hone his skill for the other performance.

The *Tulsa Daily World* described Will's performance in *Judge Priest*: "The star's portrayal of Judge Priest has the mark of authenticity upon it … the unique blending of a splendid talent with a rich and splendid role."

Will Rogers gives romantic advice to Tom Brown in *Judge Priest* (authors' collection).

Henry B. Walthall, Will Rogers and Berton Churchill in *Judge Priest* (authors' collection).

Photoplay rated *Judge Priest* one of the Best Pictures of the Month in its December 1934 issue and rewarded Will with a Best Performance of the Month accolade: "As Irvin S. Cobb's favorite character, eccentric Judge Priest, Will Rogers is type-perfect.... Henry B. Walthall and David Landau play their parts to perfection. Rochelle Hudson, Frank Melton, Charley Grapewin, Berton Churchill, Francis Ford contribute valuable moments. Indispensable local color is provided by Hattie McDaniels and Stepin Fetchit in some grand scenes and music."

"The photoplay ... presents the cowboy Nietzsche in one of the happiest roles of his screen career.... Put *Judge Priest* down as a thoroughly delightful sentimental comedy, and let it remind you Will Rogers, although he bears the burdens of the nation on his shoulders, continues to be a remarkedly heart-warming personality," wrote the *New York Times*.

Variety commented, "But when the tailpiece fades Rogers has made the old judge completely his own, so much so as to suggest other Judge Priest stories to follow.... It is not a fine piece of writing, but it's a wonderful chance for the star, and he gives out more than the authors put into their work.... Rogers gives one of the best performances of his career. He does as well in his serious moments as in his comedy moods, and holds absolute attention. He invests the character so strongly with his personality that readers of the Priest stories will not visualize other than Rogers ... the handling of the action is a credit to John Ford. He did much for the picture."

The *Hollywood Reporter* put it simply: "It is beautiful, it is human. It has drama and a great, quiet, universal humor," while the *Literary Digest* regarded *Judge Priest* as "a decidedly engaging film."

After Judge Priest (Rogers) hears that barber Flem Tally (Melton) had been cut during a ruckus, he remarks, "Whoever cut him up couldn't have cut him much if he used a barber's razor."

Will's first release in 1935, *The County Chairman,* came out just after the New Year and represented a classic spoof of the actions of politicians based on George Ade's stageplay about politics in Tomahawk County, Wyoming. A number of humorous situations show Will at his satirical best beginning with wiley Jim Hackler (Rogers) trading away his dog, Oscar, in order to get his law partner nominated for county prosecutor. Will is supported by a fine cast that includes Berton Churchill, Louise Dresser, Stepin Fetchit, Kent Taylor, Evelyn Venable and a rising young star named Mickey Rooney. *The County Chairman* captured enough votes to be ranked number thirty-three on the Honor Roll of Best Movies of 1935.

The *Literary Digest* commented, "Will Rogers is up to his usual homespun tricks—but in a definitely engaging way—as a cynical, but instinctively noble and philosophical, politician of thirty years ago.... It is a pleasant film in its slow-paced fashion."

Mickey Rooney, Kent Taylor, Will Rogers and Eleanor Wesselhaeft in *The County Chairman* (1935) (authors' collection).

Will Rogers and Mickey Rooney in *The County Chairman* (authors' collection).

Will earned Best Performance of the Month honors from *Photoplay* and the following review: "Will Rogers leads all Hollywood's stars at the box office — far and away. Very possibly the reason he does so is that he gets closer to the American scene than any other star. People love him because they know him.... As Rogers repeats throughout the entire film, it will be 'good politics' to take the whole family."

"Will Rogers is having a grand time — and his audiences with him — in the film of George Ade's play. *The County Chairman,* now at the Roxy.... Its screen treatment provides an amusing excursion into the fertile fields of bucolic politics and rustic romance.... Mr. Rogers shines in a role that perfectly suits his personality, talent and his voice.... Members of the supporting cast are uniformly excellent in their roles."

The *Hollywood Reporter* headlined, "Rogers, Direction and Cast All Score.... Will's aptitude for the discussion of politics is given free rein.... The laughs are built on the campaigning methods of Rogers, who kids every political speech ever made and throws hooks into all politicians and their works at every opportunity."

Political pro Jim Hackler (Rogers) explains, "He's no geat shucks maybe as a lawyer, but he's never been in jail and he's an orphan and he won an oratory contest up at the school and Presidents been nominated on less than that."

After trading his dog for his partner's nomination, "You get the best of it, the dog's worth more than the office."

Discussing the convention proceedings, "We opened up with the Harmony Program and then we all started in to fight."

"He's been talking like that for twenty years, he ain't said nothing yet."

"There's only two things in politics, personality and promises.... It don't make sense but it's good politics."

"Say, that was a good speech, you talked just enough and said as little as the cards called for."

"The next morning after an election, people don't come around and say, Did you conduct a clean and honorable campaign? No sir, they just come around and say, Boy, did you win? That's politics in a nutshell."

"I'll print the truth, the whole truth and nothing but the truth. It's such an unusual thing to do in a campaign that the novelty of it is liable to appeal to the voters."

After an automobile starts on fire, Hackler remarks, "Reading the other day about some fella up in Detroit. Named Henry something. Don't know his last name, probably never hear it again. Well, he says someday there'll be more of them things than there is horses. Imagine a man predicting a thing like that."

Will Rogers and Evelyn Venable in *The County Chairman* (authors' collection).

Top: Life Begins at Forty **(1935) with Will Rogers and hog caller Bill Bletcher (authors' collection).**
Bottom: Life Begins at Forty **lobby card with Will Rogers and Richard Cromwell (authors' collection).**

In March 1935, the *New York Times* reported that Will Rogers and Fox Film Corporation had signed a new three-year contract, extending the relationship to ten years and a record of tenure, upon completion of the contract, of any actor at one studio up to that time.

In a *Movie Mirror* article, Will discussed the contract negotiation process:

> I'm going to tell you the secret of the picture business. It's made up of two lines of figures. One's in black ink, the other in red. At the end of the year when it's time to talk about a new contract for Rogers or discuss whether the old fellow should be dropped, they pull out those rows of figures.
>
> If the Rogers pictures show a good profit, they want to sign Rogers again. They don't stop to say, "Well, it's because Walthall was so good and Stepin Fetchit certainly made him look bad." So the more good work the others do and the better parts they have, the better it is for old Rogers.
>
> Why, when I ride over the range down in Santa Monica I see many a piece that Step's acting has paid for — I even got a canyon there that I call Fetchit Canyon.

Radio City Music Hall audiences in New York City were the first to be treated to Will's next 1935 release, *Life Begins at Forty*, beginning on April 4. The *New York Times* found the movie less than up to par for a Rogers vehicle but praised Will: "The star himself is a thorough delight regardless of what he is doing, and his country editor takes its place in his gallery of warm and sagacious homespun portraits."

Photoplay honored Will with a listing in its Best Performances of the Month category and ranked the movie one of the Best Pictures of the Month: "Every recent Will Rogers picture seems to get better and better. And here's another smash hit for 'Mark Twain of the Screen.' Rogers can move into more excellent roles than any other star. He's perfect as the ink-stained tank-town crusader. More than usual, this picture is spiced with typical Rogers pithy observations and dry witcracks. You won't have a minute's recess in laughing at Will.... Don't dare miss it."

The *Literary Digest* found "the plot is just a framework for the excellent humor of Rogers ... and it is the most delightful of his vehicles."

Variety predicted, "It's a cinch box office hit and no worry attaching to it in New York or elsewhere.... Plenty of hoke but cleverly handled and right over the home plate. Besides Rogers there's a fine supporting cast. George Barbier being a perfect foil to Rogers."

Motion Picture commented, "Will spouts epigrams by the yard and delves into politics en route. The result is one long laugh that leaves your sides pleasantly aching.... *Life Begins at Forty* comes pretty close to top rating AAA 1/2."

During the filming, Rogers noticed that the sign for the newspaper office only read the *Plainview Citizen*: "Every paper has to have a slogan, you know." The next day, when the director arrived on the set, the sign sported an added line, "All the news $1.00 a year entitles you to."

After unloading a box of canned goods, Will remarks, "The American eagle ought not to be our national emblem ... ought to be a can opener. The man who invented this thing was public enemy #1. I can think of no quicker way of starving this country to death than to invent a can opener that nobody knows how to work."

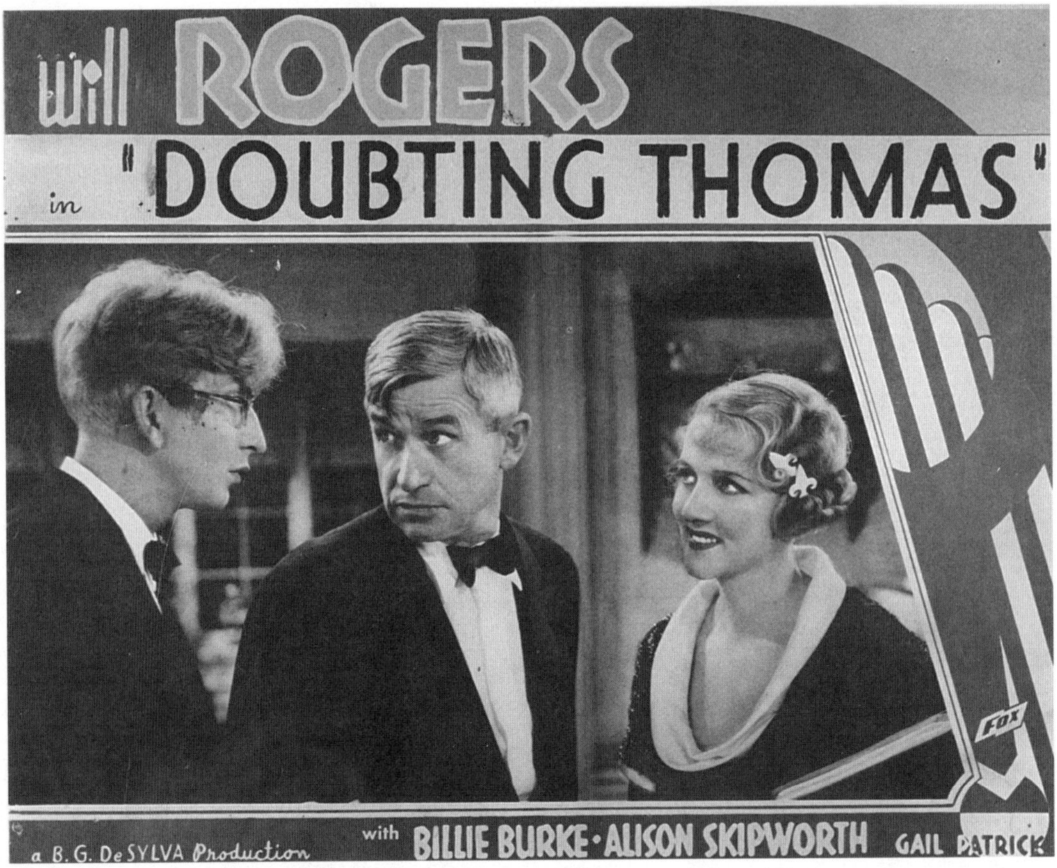

Lobby card for *Doubting Thomas* (1935) with Sterling Holloway, Will Rogers and Helen Flint (courtesy Will Rogers Memorial).

"America will feed everybody who don't live close to them."

"With everything working by machinery, the American born 100 years from now won't have any head, arms or legs. He'll just have a thumb to push a button with."

Will's next feature film, *Doubting Thomas,* reached theaters across the nation in July 1935 and featured fellow Ziegfeld *Follies* star and wife of the late Florenz Ziegfeld, Jr., Billie Burke, as Will's wife. The *Tulsa Daily World* promised, "You'll laugh your fill when Billie Burke, under the influence of Allison Skipworth, who plays an amateur impresario, wants to make a career of the stage until Rogers finally effects a cure by hiring a bogus Hollywood director."

Photoplay called *Doubting Thomas* "one of the best Will Rogers pictures and a howl from start to finish." The *New Republic* commented,

> I meant to say of *Doubting Thomas* … that though its rewrite of *The Torch Bearers* seemed a terribly old pack of cards, there had been more aces shuffled into the comedy as a whole, in the way of people and high management, than might seem possible.... There was always a tendency to confuse Rogers with the national boobies to whom his frequent social pronouncements linked him. But he was in the first place a show figure; even in his worst things one

Frances Grant, Will Rogers and Billie Burke in *Doubting Thomas* (courtesy Will Rogers Memorial).

> could not help recognize him as a very good one.... In this created character he was a valuable property. Just as he would be in real life, heckling the cows and squinting at the tarnal weather. He was one of the naturals of show business.

The *New York Mirror* wrote, "A brutal lampoon of amateur actors, *Doubting Thomas* is particularly timely.... It has not aged at all since it delighted Broadway theatre audiences. It has life, sparkle, wit and lusty slapstick clowning. Especially, it now has Will Rogers, who contributes to it one of his finest comedy performances."

The *New York American* concluded that the movie saved "the original zest and humor of the popular play ... and in addition there are a number of interpolations which add to the high hilarity of the modernized piece. The picture's a pleasure through and through....The honors go to Mr. Rogers.... Billie Burke is superb in the dizzy part of the wife."

The *New York Times* panned the movie but credited the actors: "Giving the cast its due, the players without exception draw the fullest measure of comedy out of every stock situation.... Mr. Rogers is too good a humorist and too valuable as a homespun philosopher to be hidden under this type of story.... *Doubting Thomas* is pretty old hat for 1935."

Among Rogers' observations and quips that received laughs in *Doubting Thomas*:

"Acting is just like the measles. If you catch it when you're young, why, you can get over it, but if you catch it when you get older ... it's sometimes fatal."

After her performance, Billie Burke asks, "Didn't you like me?" Will responds, "I did until I saw you act."

Will moved from starring in an Irvin S. Cobb story, *Judge Priest*, to playing rival riverboat captains with Cobb in the September 1935 release, *Steamboat Round the Bend.* It was actually Will's last picture filmed but was released before the previously completed film, *In Old Kentucky. Steamboat Round the Bend* became the first Will Rogers movie to reach the public after his death with Wiley Post in Alaska. Will posthumously received a Best Acting of the Month Award, sharing honors with Henry Fonda, from the Screen Actors' Guild for his work in *Steamboat Round the Bend.*

As usual, Will took license to promote his home state of Oklahoma, his home town of Claremore and his heritage. Two of the riverboats in the movie bear the names *Claremore Queen* and *Cherokee.* The riverboat movie proved to be one of the top grossing

Will Rogers and Berton Churchill in *Steamboat Round the Bend* (1935) (authors' collection).

Anne Shirley and Will Rogers in *Steamboat Round the Bend* (authors' collection).

films of 1935 and one of two Rogers films that headed Fox's top producers that year. Both Will Rogers and Anne Shirley were heralded for Best Performances of the Month by *Photoplay*, while the film garnered honor as one of the Best Pictures of the Month: "Romance, dramatic, laugh-laden, this Will Rogers picture is perfect entertainment. It is, surprisingly enough for a Rogers vehicle, actually a young love story, and even without Will's persuasive wit, it could stand alone as a tender romance ... it's beautifully played by the star, Anne Shirley, John McGuire ... and a large, fine cast."

The *Hollywood Reporter* described the movie as a "real knockout.... There has never been a Will Rogers picture like this. It marks a complete change of pace for the comedian, gives him for the first time a dramatic characterization and a chance to act. And how he takes off his coat and tears into it!"

Andre Sennwald, reviewer for the *New York Times*, wrote, "Immersed, like all the good Rogers films, in mood and atmosphere rather than the complexities of plot structure, *Steamboat Round the Bend* is in the rich comic tradition of Mark Twain and those great days on the Mississippi. If the photoplay is not the finest of Mr. Rogers' works, it is close to the top, and it finds America's favorite philosopher at his homespun best."

"Doc" Pearly (Rogers) lassoes New Moses (Berton Churchill) off of a wharf along the riverbank as the *Claremore Queen* skims by, dragging him through the water and on deck in order to get New Moses to testify on Duke's (John McGuire) behalf and prevent him from being hung for murder. New Moses protests, "I've got souls to save." Doc responds, "You've got a life to save and the Good Lord don't care which you do first."

Will was well known for his sentimentality. During the shooting of the scene in which Duke and Fleety Belle (Anne Shirley) are being married in jail, Will's role called for him to hand over the ring and say, "It belonged to your mother." However, when the time came, Will was so full of emotion that he couldn't utter a word. All he could do was pass the ring to Duke in silence. Eugene Pallette, who was playing the role of Sheriff Rufe Jetters and officiating in the wedding ceremony, picked up the cue and ad-libbed, "It's mighty old fashioned, looks as if it might have belonged to your mother." Will mustered all his emotion and nodded while he let out a choked-up, "It was."

Those two words and slight nodding of the head captured Will's heartfelt compassion and sentimentality. When Director John Ford wrapped up the shooting of the scene, everybody in the cast and crew could be seen wiping tears from their eyes. The scene was left exactly as shot. It was one of the few times Will Rogers was ever at a loss for words.

Will's final release, *In Old Kentucky,* played to packed houses beginning with its opening at the Roxy Theatre in New York City in late November 1935. *Photoplay* ranked the movie among its Best Pictures of the Month and praised Will and Charles Sellon for giving the Best Performances of the Month in its September 1935 issue: "Many an 'old southern custom,' including a feud, is brought out in this latest Will Rogers picture, which is a laugh from beginning to end.... It's a film for every type of movie-goer, well-balanced in humor and action, with fast moving and modern dialogue.... Will Rogers is his lovable homely self, trying to fix up everything for everybody, all of whom put in well sustaining performances."

The *New York Times* honored Will with a final tribute:

> The last page in the golden book of Will Rogers' screen comedies is turned with *In Old Kentucky,* which opened at the Roxy yesterday. ... There is poignance and grief in the realization that there will be no new characterizations, no new plot structures for Mr. Rogers to animate.... With the usual sly Rogers humor, with extremely fine comedy performances by Charles Sellon and Etienne Girardot, with the romantic interest carried gently by Dorothy Wilson and Russell Hardie and with Bill Robinson to tap away the duller moments, *In Old Kentucky* can be listed as a first-rate comedy and a handsome epitaph to twentieth century America's first humorist.

Variety also handed out its last applause for Will: "It's no less fitting that Will Rogers' last picture should be one of his best. *In Old Kentucky* is a delightful comedy.... As a foil for Rogers and excellent on his own, Bill Robinson hoofs his way to importance.... *In Old Kentucky* will merit future attention whenever Rogers revivals are played. Its immediate box office record should be nifty."

Time, perhaps, said it best: "Good humored, unpretentious, *In Old Kentucky* is somehow more suitable than something grander would have been as the swan song of a man beloved because he created laughter and dispensed with stuck-up ways.... If a box office record broken by *Steamboat Round the Bend* means anything, *In Old Kentucky* may be further proof that Rogers was the first star in cinema history who could draw even better dead than he could alive."

Naturally the plot of *In Old Kentucky* involves horse racing. Rogers plays the part of

Dorothy Wilson, Bill "Bojangles" Robinson and Will Rogers in *In Old Kentucky* (1935) (authors' collection).

Steve Tapley, a horse trainer caught between rival horse-racing families. As always, he gets in his share of one-liners. For example, Tapley explains the picture of Lille Langtry on his wall: "I bought it thinking it was Mae West."

During one scene he admonishes Wash Jackson (Robinson) to take good care of Greyboy's legs: "His feet are more valuable than yours."

Consulting an almanac to forecast rain for race day, he says, "I don't exactly believe in them but I'd just as soon have them on my side."

Tapley convinces Jackson to teach him how to dance after Miss B says, "If you could dance like that, I'd marry you."

For the pre-race dance, Tapley rents a suit once owned by a former senator: "It's a good suit all right. That's one thing you know about those Republicans ... they had good clothes."

To escape from jail, Tapley masquerades as Jackson, who smuggles in some burnt cork to blacken Tapley's face. After applying the burnt cork, he asks Jackson, "How you think I look?" Jackson takes one look and responds, "Well, that makes you look better. If I was you, I'd keep that on all the time."

Will was scheduled to appear in the 1936 Fox production of *A Country Doctor*, the story of the Dionne quintuplets, but Jean Hersholt was selected to play the role of Dr. John Luke after Will's passing. Fox tried unsuccessfully to groom Irvin S. Cobb to fill

Will's shoes with Cobb appearing as the lead actor in the role of William Franklin in the 1936 Fox film *Everybody's Old Man.*

Even after his death in August 1935, Will Rogers ranked as the number one 1935 male box office draw and trailed only Shirley Temple in the overall ratings. Through his Ziegfeld *Follies,* radio, stage, film and after-dinner speaker performances and his writings, Will Rogers left a lasting legacy that endures today.

Chapter 4

Lasting Legacy

On the Air

They sent what they call the Budget to Congress. It took the head men of every Department in Washington six months to think up that many figures.... Well I went down and I found that what little I was supposed to have, been put in a sinking fund. There is things in there that you had no idea existed. Federal Radio Commission grabbed us in advance for ...$364,027.25. That's just for static alone.

Will's radio career went on concurrently with his stage and movie careers. As mentioned earlier, his first radio appearance took place in 1922 on Pittsburgh's KDKA. Over the years, Will's involvement with radio grew from sporadic appearances to contract engagements with major corporate sponsors. During the 1924 election coverage, Will added a few quips to the coverage of returns on WEAF in New York, the first regional broadcast of national elections. In November 1926, he appeared on the debut for NBC's *Eveready Hour* with a monologue called "Fifteen Minutes with a Diplomat," which included an imitation of President Calvin Coolidge.

Although Will felt uncomfortable in front of a microphone, he explained his attraction to the new medium: "Radio is too big a thing to be out of.... I like this new racket. It's a lot of fun. They ought to give a few Congressmen a chance at it, too. They could talk themselves to death into a microphone."

In January 1928, Will served as master of ceremonies for an unprecedented transcontinental, 45-station hookup for the *Dodge Victory Hour*. Millions of people throughout the country listened as Will talked from his Beverly Hills home, Al Jolson performed from the Roosevelt Hotel in New Orleans, Fred and Dorothy Stone sang duets from Chicago and the Paul Whiteman Orchestra played *Rhapsody in Blue* from New York City.

The broadcast cost Dodge in excess of $1,000 per minute and helped launch its new automobile.

Will's parody of Coolidge met with uproarious laughter across the nation. "Ladies and Gentlemen. It's the duty of the President to deliver a message to the people on the condition of the country. I am proud to report that the condition of the country as a whole is prosperous. I don't mean by that the whole country is prosperous. But as a Hole, it's prosperous. That is it is prosperous for a Hole. There is not a 'hole' lot of doubt about that."

Pharmaceutical manufacturer E. R. Squibb & Sons contracted with Will in 1930 to produce a series of twelve broadcasts lasting between twelve and fifteen minutes during April, May and June for a payment of $77,000, amounting to almost $430 per minute. The company also produced a pamphlet giving the text of each of the broadcasts. Will's topics (in order of broadcast date) included the Arms Conference, Charles Lindbergh, President Hoover, Vice President Curtis, Alfred E. Smith, Mother's Day, the Prince of Wales, Dwight Morrow, Henry Ford, Prohibition, Boston, and Chicago. A number of these talks survive on tape recordings.

"You know I don't mind telling you brothers that geography has been mighty good to us. It's wonderful to pay honor to Washington and Lincoln, but I want to tell you we ought to lay out one day a year for the old boy that laid out the location of this country. I don't know who he was, but boy he was a sage, that bird was."

"Coolidge has the best idea on this farm relief. He went out and spoke to the farmers one time in Minneapolis. He said, 'Farmers, you are in a hole. I can't help you, but I will get in with you.' He did."

"I always did want to see him [Hoover] elected. I wanted to see how far a competent man could go in politics. It has never been tried before."

"They never figured there might be something worse as a profession than acting, and there is, and [Al] Smith found it. It's politics."

"You know, there ought to be some kind of a star given to any woman that can live with a comedian. Now, that little compliment ought to repay for the flowers that I forgot to get today."

"The War come pretty near ruining royalty. It was pretty near as hard to get a King after the War as a three-minute speaker. Kings went out about as quick as silk shirts."

"I asked Mr. Ford, I know it is rather inquisitive, but in case these opposition things get to cutting the prices and all, just how cheap could you sell your car? He said, 'Well, Will, that is kind of personal but if the worst comes to the worst, I could give it away, as long as we retain the selling of the parts. You know, Will, one of these things will shake off enough in a year to pay for itself.'"

"A Ford car and a marriage certificate is the two cheapest things there is. We no more than get either one than we want to trade them in for something better."

"City people seem to be more excited about Prohibition. Country folks seem to be more excited over making a living."

"From all the people in the studio it looks like Ben Lyon and Bebe Daniels' wedding, only nobody brought nice presents, that is the only thing. Bebe Daniels got married yesterday—her and Ben and this is their freshman wedding. That is unusual in Hollywood, for anybody to get married the first time."

Will Rogers at radio microphone (courtesy Will Rogers Memorial).

"Why this [Chicago] is just a great, big, overgrown home-loving town, that is all. Of course, they do have these gangs here, and they do kill each other. Well, that is their privilege."

Will also teamed up with Standard Oil Company in 1930 to do a fifteen-minute spot for which he received $15,000. In February 1931, Will appeared on the New York WEAF radio network with Mary Pickford and Governor Franklin D. Roosevelt. During a 1931 NBC broadcast to raise $10 million for the American Red Cross drought relief, Will followed former President Coolidge and President Hoover to the microphone.

"I don't know why they put me on here after hearing all these serious talks.... Pinch hitting, as usual, I guess.... We ought to be worrying more, though, about where our poor folks are going to get something to eat instead of our rich folks getting a drink."

To the drought sufferers he said, "Congress may help you but you won't live to receive it."

Will appeared with Billie Burke on the inaugural *Ziegfeld Follies of the Air Show* on April 3, 1932, and followed that up with several guest appearances over the next few months. In 1933, Will signed a contract to appear on a series of 53 radio broadcasts for Gulf Oil Corporation called *The Gulf Show.* The broadcasts began on April 30, 1933, and Will finished the last broadcast under the contract on June 9, 1935. The show included the music of the Al Goodman Orchestra and the Revelers Quartet and other guests such as fellow actor and author Irvin S. Cobb.

Will divided the $50,000 he received for the first seven broadcasts between the Salvation Army and the Red Cross. Per his telegrams to the two organizations, "I am going to preach for seven Sundays for the Gulf Oil Company and I am going to turn all the oil over to you. I ain't got nothing to lose but my voice, and I haven't lost it yet. The only one who can lose is Gulf—that is, if they don't sell enough gas to pay me for my gas. Don't thank me, thank the Gulf people, or better yet, the radio listeners—they will be the sufferers."

This generous act of kindness represented many more that Will bestowed on numerous organizations and people throughout his career. He truly felt a kinship with all peoples and felt it his duty to share his good fortune by helping those in need. He gave unselfishly of his time and his money.

"The hardest thing over this radio is to get me stopped. I never know when to stop. So, tonight, I got me a clock here.... When that alarm clock goes off, I am going to stop, that is all there is to it. I don't care whether I am in the middle of reciting Gunga Din or the Declaration of Independence, I am going to stop when that rings."

"Well, that is about all the news I know tonight. Good night!"

When Will crashed in Alaska, CBS and NBC went off the air for 30 minutes in tribute.

Literary Efforts

> *I got a little idea for a debate—maybe to help the unemployed. I'll probably debate with some old college professor at one of the State colleges up in the Northwest. We'll argue about "Ignorance versus Knowledge," and I'm going to be Ignorance. Knowledge has got us where we are today, and we'd be better turning the country back to ignorance.*

As mentioned earlier, Will's literary career blossomed along with his other endeavors. In addition to his newspaper columns, Will penned several books: *Rogerisms* (1919), *The Cowboy Philosopher on the Peace Conference* (1919), *The Cowboy Philosopher on Pro-*

hibition (1919), *Rogerisms: What We Laugh At* (1920) (possibly unpublished), *Illiterate Digest* (1924), *Letters of a Self-Made Diplomat to His President* (1926), *There's Not a Bathing Suit in Russia and Other Bare Facts* (1926) and *Ether and Me, or Just Relax* (1927).

On Prohibition:

"You won't find this country any drier than this book."

"If you saw a drunk in the old days it was a sign of no will power, but if you see one drunk now it's a sure sign of wealth."

"Ohio was voted wet by the people and dry by their misrepresentatives."

"Instead of weddings being jolly parties, from now on they are going to be as they should, very solemn affairs."

On Russia:

"Russian men wear their shirts hanging outside their pants. Well, any nation that don't know enough to stick their shirt tail in will never get anywhere."

Will lent his writing and humor to the books of others as well. In 1927, Will wrote an introduction to Charles M. Russell's' posthumous book, *Trails Plowed Under*. The following excerpts originate from that introduction:

> Hello Charley old hand, How are you? I just thought I would drop you a line and tell you how things are a working on the old range since you left. Old Timer you don't know how we miss you. Gee but its been lonesome since you left.... There aint much news here to tell you. You know the big Boss gent sent a hand over and got you so quick Charley, But I guess He needed a good man pretty bad.... But we all know you are getting along fine, You will get along fine anywhere.... I bet you Mark Twain and Old Bill Nye, and Whitcomb Riley and a whole bunch of those old Joshers was just waiting for you to pop in with all the latest ones.... Course we are all just a hanging on here as long as we can. I dont know why we hate to go, we know it is better there, Maby its because we havent done anything that will live after we are gone.

Will wrote the introduction to another 1927 book, *Annie Oakley: Woman at Arms* by Courtney Ryley Cooper.

> "Little Miss Sure-Shot"—that was what they called her, was not only the greatest rifle-shot for a woman that ever lived, but I doubt if her character could be matched outside of some saint. She and her fine husband, Frank Butler, were great friends of Fred Stone and family, and I first became acquainted with her there, years ago. I had heard cowboys who had traveled with the Buffalo Bill Show speak of her in almost reverence. They loved her. She was a marvelous woman; kindest hearted, most thoughtful, a wonderful Christian woman.
>
> I went out to see her last spring in Dayton.... She'd been bedridden for months, but she was just as cheerful. I told her I would see her in the Fall ... and tried to cheer her up in the usual dumb way we have of doing those things. She said I would not come back. She says, "But I will meet you...." Well, she will certainly keep her end of the bargain.

The next year, 1928, Will provided a foreword to Chet Byers' book on a topic dear to Will's heart, *Roping: Trick and Fancy Rope Spinning*.

> Chet sent me word he was going to write a book. Well he wasn't where I could get at him to choke him off, and then again he is of what they call

> "lawful age, free born, and sound of mind and body," that is he is as sound of mind as a man can be who spends the best part of his life making rings with a piece of rope and going through life trying to jump through 'em, then when he does get through on the other side he immediately wants to get back on the side he just come from.
>
> Now I can't give a man much "marking" on his intellect, when he will continually keep doing a thing like that. But it's just men and women do fool things like that, that write all these books. So just let Chet take his old trick rope and start whipping it down on some good white paper, I don't know how tangled up he is liable to get in it, I do know this, that statistics have never shown where any trick roper, for the good of posterity has ever been fortunate enough to choke himself with his own rope.
>
> I doubt if the book will be any good, for it's on a subject. And all the books I ever read on subjects were written by men that dident know anything about the subject. And people read them and think they are pretty good. So I hate to see Chet pick out the subject of Ropes. I would have had more confidence in it if he had picked out something that he dident know anything about.
>
> Now Chet knows ropes, and Chet knows Roping, so it is liable to be awful uninteresting, and be contradicted by the 109 million that dont know ropin. So Chet shows he dont know nothing about Authoring right there....

In 1931, Will provided the introduction to Wiley Post and Harold Gatty's book, *Around the World in Eight Days*, heralding their landmark flight. "We are gathered...to do honor to two gentlemen who knew that the World was cockeyed. But wasent right sure it was round.... Mr. Post the Pilot is another Oklahoman. He did live in Texas as a child, But even Texas children grow up. Post used to be on a Cotton farm, it wasent ambition that drove him to the air, it was the bo-weevil. If it hadent been for the bo-weevil and a Republican Administration he might have remained an underfed, overmortgaged, Farmer."

In 1934, Will's radio tribute to Marie Dressler was used as the foreword for her autobiography, *Marie Dressler, My Own Story.* "Marie Dressler has more friends among our real people of this country—I mean from the President on down. Why, she visited the White House—regardless of political faith, or anything of that kind, she has entree into places where none of us connected with the movies—where we couldn't get our nose in—And that's all been done simply on a marvelous personality and a great heart."

That description holds true for Will Rogers as well.

Will Rogers Testimonials and Memorials

If you live right, death is a joke to you as far as fear is concerned.

News of Will Rogers' and Wiley Post's airplane crash on August 15, 1935, shocked the world as it flashed around the globe. Everyone from presidents to kings and from bit actors to movie moguls to the average man and woman deeply felt a personal loss. Americans especially had suffered the loss of a dear friend, someone they frequently turned to for laughter, common sense, news and entertainment.

An immediate outpouring of grief ushered forth and continued through the decades, exhibiting itself in a variety of memorials and testimonials. A sampling helps bring home how Will Rogers, a simple man from Claremore, Oklahoma, touched and continues to touch the soul of America.

"His death will be a great loss to the country, as well as to his family and his myriad friends and admirers. He was a staunch American, and his powerful and patriotic influence was always exercised for the good of his country and his countrymen"—William Randolph Hearst.

"The memory of the sweetness and light which Will Rogers brought to the world is something that will be cherished as a hallowed recollection by the American people for many years to come. His was a unique talent. And it was not kept hidden under a bowl. The wit and wisdom which were uniquely his and his alone were given freely to all who had ears to hear and eyes to see. A truly great man passed when Will Rogers died"—Larry Reid.

"I have lost a great friend. The stage and screen have lost a great artist. America has lost her greatest humorist since Mark Twain. I am too deeply affected to say more"—Samuel Goldwyn.

"He was one of the kindest men and best friends in the world.... Mr. Rogers was like a brother to me"—Billie Burke.

"Will Rogers was probably the most beloved man of our time. He was the one man in the entertainment world who more than balanced by his exemplar life any of the scandals involving people of the theater.... He was the most charitable, most tolerant man I have ever known"—Eddie Cantor.

"It is not the length of time we remain in this present human sphere that is important. It is what we do with this time. Will Rogers and Wiley Post gave gloriously of every moment, enriching our lives with the treasures of their accomplishments. I am consoled by knowing that the qualities they possessed and shared so generously with the world will endure beyond time, space and human finiteness"—Mary Pickford.

"I was shocked to hear of the tragedy which has taken Will Rogers and Wiley Post from us. Will was an old friend of mine, a humorist and philosopher beloved by all.... Both were outstanding Americans and will be greatly missed"—Franklin Delano Roosevelt.

"They were great souls and I feel a sense of deep personal loss in their passing"—Herbert Hoover.

"Rogers' death is a national calamity. The world has lost a great man and I have lost my best friend"—Fred Stone.

"He was a friend to all the world. Men like him, I'm sure, don't come along oftener than once in a century"—Irvin S. Cobb.

Writer Bruce McKinstry of the *Wenatchee Daily World* in Wenatchee, Washington, wrote (in Will's voice) a letter to his readers of which Will surely would have approved.

> Well, Wiley and I got tangled up in the scenery today, folks. Looks like we was through. But don't go blaming aviation for that. Of course we knew it was dangerous, flying around here next door to the North Pole, and bad weather to boot. But we wanted to see the country and we took our chance. That don't mean that regular flying is dangerous. It's as safe as regular walking.

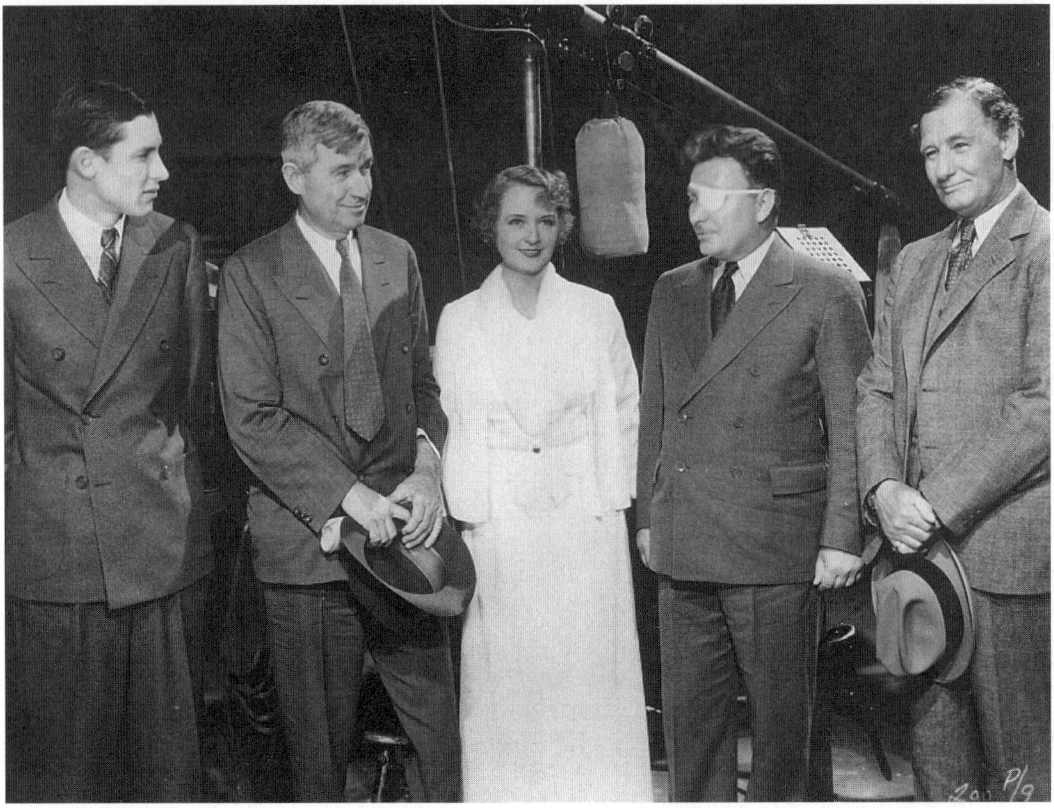

***Left to right*: Will Rogers, Jr., Will Rogers, Billie Burke, Wiley Post and Fred Stone (courtesy Will Rogers Memorial).**

> This country needed Wiley Post, but don't you folks go spending a lot of time feeling bad over an old buckaroo like me. I had my fling and did the best I knew how and had a fine time doing it. You just think of the ones that are left, help the ones that need it, and enjoy yourselves as you go along.
>
> Yours, Will

More than 150,000 people paid their respects to Will Rogers in person, filing past his casket at Forest Lawn Memorial Park. His funeral ceremony, like his life, was simple. World figures, actors and his fellow men paid tribute to this man of the people. The motion picture industry darkened the screens of 12,000 theaters, production ceased in Hollywood and each of the studios held its own memorial services. At Twentieth Century–Fox, George Jessel gave a stirring eulogy, concluding it with a traditional Jewish Kaddish.

Within weeks, friends of Will's, spurred by a plea by Marian Davies, initiated an international broadcast campaign to raise money for a fitting memorial to the humorist. George M. Cohan acted as the master of ceremonies and speakers included Billie Burke, Irvin S. Cobb and Eddie Cantor. Messages were read from President Roosevelt and the prince of Wales.

In November 1935, the theatrical world donated $1.5 million to the Will Rogers

Will Rogers and Eddie Cantor (courtesy Will Rogers Memorial).

A posthumous musical tribute to Will Rogers (authors' collection).

Memorial Fund in the form of a million dollars in property value, including a sanitarium at Lake Saranac, New York, and $500,000 in cash, to be used to treat handicapped children of stage and screen players.

Among other honors and memorials to Will Rogers:

—Betty Rogers received the Spirit of St. Louis Medal for Will's contribution to aviation. (October 1935)

—Shirley Temple formally opened the new $500,000 Will Rogers soundstage at Twentieth Century–Fox. (November 1935)

—The Wiley Post/Will Rogers Airway Beacon, with 1.8 million candlepower, visible for 64 miles and at an altitude of 15,000 feet, was installed on the George Washington Bridge in New York City. (November 30, 1935)

Rogers seems to be giving a final farewell in this cheery shot from the 1930s (authors' collection).

—Andrew A. Trimble portrayed Will Rogers in the MGM production *The Great Ziegfeld*. William Powell played Florenz Ziegfeld and Myrna Loy played Billie Burke. (1936)

—The Will Rogers Library opened in Claremore, Oklahoma. Will had donated $4,000 to the town a year before he died and suggested that the money "be given to a poor lady to buy herself a cow." This library has since been replaced by a modern Will Rogers Library. (August 1936)

—Andrew A. Trimble again portrayed Will Rogers, this time in *You're a Sweetheart,* a Universal production with Alice Faye in the role of a star of a show bound for Broadway. The film was remade in 1943 as *Cowboy in Manhattan.* (1937)

—A Will Rogers ice sculpture (22 feet high, 100 tons) was built in Hibbing, Minnesota, during the Junior Chamber of Commerce Baby Olympics. Will appeared in Hibbing several times during his speaking tours. (January 1937)

—The Will Rogers Shrine of the Sun was dedicated on Cheyenne Mountain near Colorado Springs, Colorado. The ceremony was officiated by Oklahoma Chief Fred Lookout, a friend of the cowboy philosopher. Outside of the 103-foot tower stands a granite pedestal with a bronze bust of Will Rogers by noted sculptor Jo Davidson. (September 6, 1937)

—20,000 people gathered on a hilltop above Claremore, Oklahoma to dedicate the $200,000 Will Rogers Memorial. Presently, the memorial has been expanded and includes an excellent collection of Will Rogers memorabilia, tracing his life from the earliest days

Postcard of the Will Rogers Library in Claremore, Oklahoma (authors' collection).

in Oklahoma to stardom. Exhibits include a replica of the family's Santa Monica Ranch family room, lobby cards from Will's movies and a theater showing Will's films. The museum also includes excellent research materials on Will Rogers and his papers. After Betty Rogers' death in 1944, her body and Will's were moved to their final resting place on the grounds of the Will Rogers Memorial. When George M. Cohan visited the memorial in 1939 and looked at the Will Rogers statue, he remarked, "It's marvelous. It is he." The Memorial spurred Roy Rogers to preserve his own legacy. (November 1938)

—The Will Rogers/Wiley Post Memorial, built from Oklahoma stone, was dedicated near Point Barrow, Alaska. A new monument was erected in 1992. (August 15, 1938)

—A Will Rogers statue was unveiled in Statuary Hall of the Capitol Rotunda. The Congress gave Will the opportunity to "always keep an eye on Congress to see what they're up to." (July 13, 1939)

—Betty wrote a series of eight articles about Will for the *Saturday Evening Post* under the title "Uncle Clem's Boy." (October 5–November 30, 1940)

—Betty published a book on her life with Will titled *Will Rogers: His Wife's Story.* (September 12, 1941)

—Oklahoma City airport was renamed Will Rogers Field, now called the Will Rogers World Airport. (June 2, 1942)

—Betty Rogers and Irene Rich launched the SS *Will Rogers* Liberty Ship. (November 8, 1942) The ship was torpedoed by a German submarine in December 1943, beached, repaired and returned to service. A five-foot model of the ship, the ship's flag and service bars are on exhibit at the Will Rogers Memorial.

—The family's Santa Monica Ranch became the Will Rogers State Park after the death of Betty. It includes 186 acres and a polo field used on a regular basis. Visitors can

Will Rogers ice sculpture in Hibbing, Minnesota (courtesy Aubin Studio, Hibbing, Minnesota).

tour the main ranch house and grounds as well as view some of Will's movies in the theater adjacent to the ranch house. (1944)

—General Dwight D. Eisenhower unveiled a statue of Will Rogers on a horse in front of the Will Rogers Memorial Center in Fort Worth, Texas, on Will's birthday. The president's daughter, Margaret Truman, assisted in the dedication ceremony. The Will Rogers Memorial Center includes the Will Rogers Auditorium, Will Rogers Coliseum and Will Rogers Equestrian Center. (November 4, 1947)

—The American Film Company released *Gaslight Follies*, a compilation of film clips from the era of silent comedy featuring Will Rogers as well as Douglas Fairbanks, Mary Pickford, Marie Dressler, Rudolph Valentino and Charlie Chaplin. (1948)

—Will Rogers was honored with a 3-cent postage stamp First Day Issue on his birthday at Claremore, Oklahoma. (November 4, 1948)

—RKO Radio Pictures released *The Golden Twenties,* a chronicle of America's Jazz Age, featuring clips of Will Rogers. (1950)

—Fox Feature Syndicate released a Will Rogers comic book. (1950)

—*Life* magazine published an 11-page article, "The Legend of Will Rogers," and *Coronet* published an 8-page article, "Will Rogers: American Legend." (January 1950)

—The American Chicle Company sponsored a 26-week radio program using five-minute excerpts from Will Rogers' 1930s radio broadcasts. (1951)

—Transcontinental Highway 66 was dedicated as the Will Rogers Highway for the full length of its 2,200-mile route. Warner Bros. erected markers along the highway. (July 1952)

—Will Rogers, Jr., starred as his father in the Warner Bros. movie *The Story of Will Rogers.* (July 1952)

—The New York to Los Angeles skyway was named for Will Rogers. (August 1952)

Postcard of Will Rogers Shrine of the Sun near Colorado Springs, Colorado (authors' collection).

Top: **Postcard of Will Rogers Memorial in Claremore, Oklahoma (authors' collection).** ***Bottom:*** **A recent photograph of the memorial (courtesy Will Rogers Memorial).**

—Jesse Stubbs, a 72-year-old boyhood friend of Will Rogers, hiked 300 miles from Anchorage to Fairbanks before accepting a plane ride to Point Barrow. He then hauled his construction materials over mushy snow and tundra to erect a monument at the spot where Will Rogers and Wiley Post crashed in 1935. (1953)

—The Will Rogers Memorial in Roxbury Park, Beverly Hills, was dedicated. (November 1956)

—Robert Youngson produced a documentary, *The Golden Age of Comedy,* featuring clips of Will Rogers. (1957)

—Bob Hope narrated *The Story of Will Rogers* on NBC. (March 28, 1961)

—Mike Wallace narrated *Will Rogers: A Biography,* a television documentary by Wolper Productions. (1962)

—The Will Rogers portrait at the National Hall of Fame for Famous American Indians in Anadarko, Oklahoma, was dedicated. (October 15, 1965)

—The United States commissioned the SS *Will Rogers* Polaris nuclear submarine, which served until 1992. (1969)

—James Whitmore launched *Will Rogers' U.S.A.* for a long-running tour, bringing the message and the humor of Will Rogers to millions of Americans. (1970)

—The New York Museum of Modern Art hosted a tribute to Will Rogers, celebrating the receipt of a collection of Will Rogers films by the museum's Department of Film from the Will Rogers Memorial. (May 18–June 7, 1972)

—Will Rogers was elected to the Aviation Hall of Fame and honored at Dayton, Ohio. (July 23, 1977)

The statue of Will at the Will Rogers Memorial (courtesy Will Rogers Memorial).

—A documentary, *Will Rogers' 1920s: A Cowboy's Guide to the Times* by Peter C. Rollins, was shown on television. (1978)

—The Will Rogers Centennial was celebrated on the cover of the official state of Oklahoma map, with many photos of Will inside. (1979)

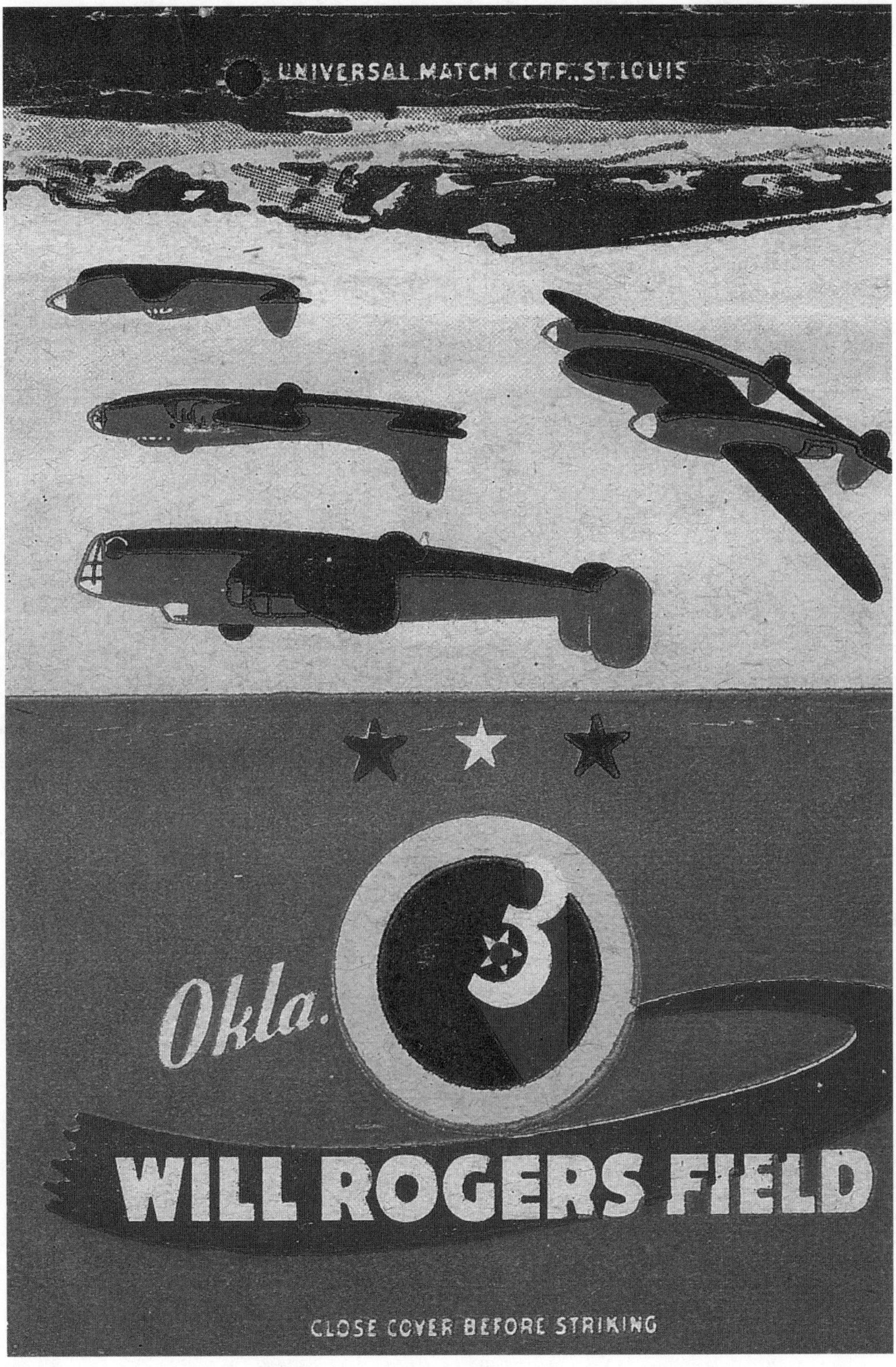

World War II Will Rogers Field matchbook cover (authors' collection).

—The Academy of Motion Pictures Arts and Sciences paid tribute to Will Rogers in honor of his centennial with showings of Will Rogers films in the academy's Samuel Goldwyn Theatre. Academy historian Anthony Slide headed the tribute, with comments by actors from Will's films, including Fifi D'Orsay, Sterling Holloway and Evelyn Venable. (October 1979)

—The US Congress declared November 4, 1979, as Will Rogers Day. (1979)

—A film essay, *Will Rogers: One Hundred Years*, was shown on television. (November 1979)

—A First Day Issue of the Will Rogers/Performing Arts stamp was issued at Claremore, Oklahoma, on Will's birthday. (November 4, 1979)

—An HBO special, *Will Rogers: Look Back in Laughter,* appeared on television. (May 1987)

—Fox released a number of Will Rogers' movies on video. (1990)

—Keith Carradine, Mac Davis and Larry Gatlin portrayed Will Rogers in the popular Broadway production *The Will Rogers Follies: A Life in Revue.* Tommy Tune choreographed and directed the show, which garnered more awards for Best Musical than any other show of the decade. *The Will Rogers Fol-*

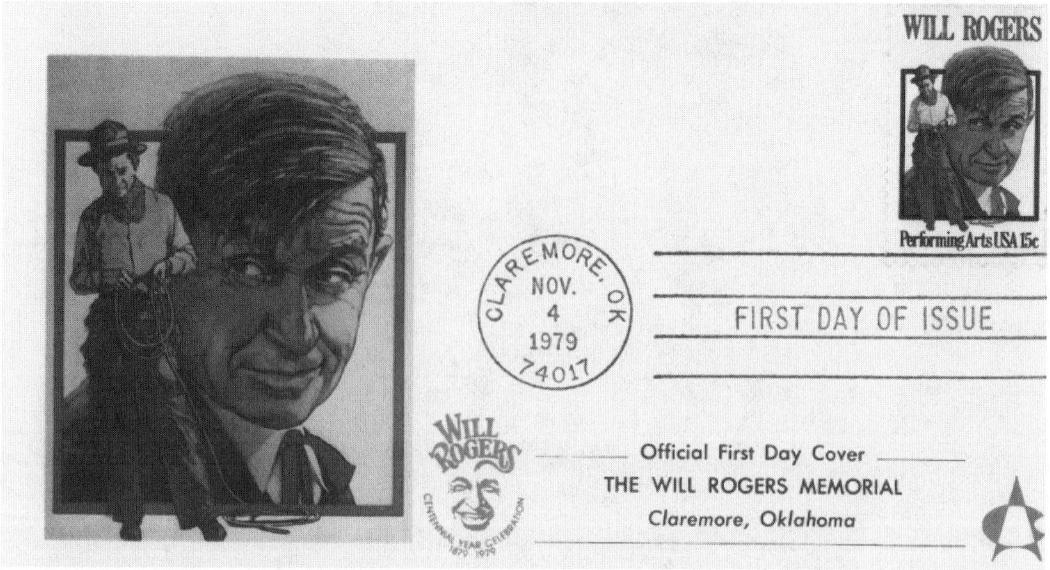

Top: **1948 Will Rogers stamp. Actual size: ⅞" × 1", excluding perforated edges (authors' collection).**
Bottom: **Will Rogers/Performing Arts First Day Cover (authors' collection).**

Will Rogers was featured in the eightieth Celebration of Oklahoma Statehood (1987). Will Rogers in Celebration of Oklahoma Statehood poster (authors' collection).

lies premiered at the Palace Theatre, where Will played in vaudeville decades before. It played 981 performances at the Palace, went on national tour and then played in 1994 at the Will Rogers Theatre in Branson, Missouri, with Pat Boone as Will Rogers. (May 1, 1991, premiere)

—In the tradition of Will Rogers, Mac Davis, who portrayed Will in *The Will Rogers Follies* on Broadway, spoke as Will Rogers at the Democratic National Convention in New York City. Will made his own mark at the 1924 Democratic Convention, the last time it was held in New York City. After 17 days and 103 ballots, Will quipped, "The thing has got to end. New York invited you people here as guests, not to live." (1992)

—Thirteen/WNET and Oklahoma Educational Television Authority co-produced a documentary, *Rediscovering Will Rogers,* for broadcast on PBS. (November 1994)

—A modern sculpture, featuring hat, chaps and lasso, called "Virtual Will" by artist David Venezky, was installed at the Will Rogers Elementary School in Santa Maria, California. (1996)

Other memorials of Will Rogers include the Will Rogers State Beach near Malibu, California; a crimson Will Rogers Rose; the Will Rogers Elementary School in Edmond, Oklahoma; the Will Rogers Scout District in Oklahoma; the Will Rogers Salvation Army Camp in Calabasas, California; the Beverly Hills Will Rogers Optimist Club; Will Rogers Junior High School in Long Beach, California; the Will Rogers Bank and Trust Company in Oklahoma City, Oklahoma; the Will Rogers United Methodist Church in Tulsa, Oklahoma, and two stars (movies and radio) on the Hollywood Walk of Fame.

Second Generation Stars

Dad never encouraged or discouraged our entering the movies. He let us make our own decisions but when he found out you were interested in something, then he piled in.

—Jimmy Rogers

Mary Rogers

Mary sneaked into performing before the camera by convincing her father to let her play a bit part in a café scene in his 1932 film *Business and Pleasure.* She was determined to make it on her own and tested for parts under the screen name of Mary Howard. At age eighteen, she earned a bit part as Diana Griffith in the Fox Film Corporation production *My Weakness,* directed by David Butler and starring Lillian Harvey and Lew Ayres. The film was released in September 1933.

The *Los Angeles Times* reported that Mary was being screen-tested for one of Will's movies, *There's Always Tomorrow.* The part went to another actress (the film was released as *Mr. Skitch*). Shortly thereafter, the *New York Times* reported that Mary Rogers' brief film career was over and quoted Will as saying, "She's back in the kitchen."

However, that did not keep Mary from performing. In early 1934, she entered stock theater with the Lakewood Players in Skowhegan, Maine, taking on the role of the ingenue

Mary Rogers in Fox publicity still (courtesy Will Rogers Memorial).

in the June 1934 production of *Her Master's Voice.* The May 1934 issue of *New Movie* carried a full-page story on Mary.

Will flew to Maine to see the production and gloated, "I saw Mary in a play and she did right good.... Next week she is to play the leading role in a drama. I was surprised at her improvement and she might make an actress yet."

Next Mary went on the road with a Canadian company's stage production of *Reunion in Vienna.* She was scheduled to debut on Broadway in the play *The Saint's Husband* in mid–October 1934, but the production was canceled at the last minute. In early January 1935, Will saw Mary perform in the ingenue role in *On to Fortune* at the National Theater in Washington, D.C. The January 9, 1935, issue of the *New York Times* announced that Mary Rogers would reach the Broadway stage after all, in *On to Fortune* playing at the Fulton Theatre.

Brooks Atkinson, theater reviewer for the *New York Times,* described Mary Rogers as "the daughter of His Excellency, Will of the Cracker Barrel, who sprinkles salt on his gum."

Another reviewer noted,

> A distinguished first night audience agreed that the 19-year-old Mary, blonde and chic and lovely, is considerably easier to look upon than her old man.... Will Rogers probably would have grinned and blushed tonight, and he probably would have been unusually proud. His daughter, determined to be an actress, tripped upon the Broadway scene for the first time in a role that was merely the usual minor ingenue part, and in a play that will hardly send the Pulitzer prize committee dashing for their ballot blanks. But Mary ... captivated a blasé first night audience with her adeptness at playing a minor role in a way that made her measure up to the more mature, experienced performers in the cast.

Next Mary appeared in *Ten Minute Alibi, Remember the Day* and *Stag at Bay* in June and July 1935 at Skowhegan, Maine. She was rehearsing for her role in an aviation melodrama, *Ceiling Zero,* when news of her father's death reached her in August. She left immediately to join her mother in California.

Mary returned to Maine and then appeared in her first Broadway leading role as Phyllis in *Crime Marches On*, which opened at the Morosco Theatre on October 23, 1935. The *New York World Herald* wrote, "Mad, merry, melodramatic and malicious, *Crime Marches On* turned up at the Morosco and had the audience in a dither. Nobody knew where the piece was going. Nobody cared. For it was always on the move with cockeyed irrespon-

Mary Rogers in Fox publicity still for *My Weakness* (courtesy Will Rogers Memorial).

sibility.... That it is melodramatic, that it is a farce is not to be denied. At the same time it is something more. Of satire there is a goodly portion aimed at the theater's pet abomination, old devil radio. There is also romance."

The *Daily Mirror* added, "The premierites liked *Crime Marches On*. And there's a lot about the piece to like.... Mary Rogers, daughter of the late Will Rogers, is excellent as a sympathetic secretary who tries to keep the poet from falling a victim to the vices of high pressure exploitation."

The *New York Times* also praised Mary's performance: "Mary Rogers, daughter of the lamented Will and a beautiful young actress in her own very winning right. She remains cool and lovely in the vortex of a shrill version of *Donnybrook Fair.*"

In January 1936, Mary was scheduled to appear in *Three Wise Fools* with noted 80-year-old actor William Gillette, who was returning to the stage after a four year absence. On January 19, Mary had to withdraw from the cast and was replaced by Elisabeth Love. Newspapers reported that Mary Rogers could not stand the strain of a constant stream of well-wishers who wanted to reminisce about her father.

Mary never again appeared in a New York production and finished out her stage career in a minor role in the July 1936 Skowhegan, Maine, production of *Feather in the Breeze.* The June 1, 1936, issue of *Vogue* carried a photo of Mary modeling a white crepe short jacket and skirt, and the *Encyclopedia of Film* mentions Mary's appearance in a Fox film called *The Last Slaver.* No other mention of this film could be found.

For the rest of her life, Mary traveled and lived in various locations around the world. She painted and wrote poetry for her own enjoyment and died in December 1989 at age 76. She is interred in the family sarcophagus at the Will Rogers Memorial in Claremore, Oklahoma.

Will Rogers, Jr.

Will Rogers, Jr., played a bit role in the September 1921 release of *The Jack Rider* along with Will, Sr.'s sidekick, Guinn "Big Boy" Williams. Charles R. Seeling directed the western for Aywon. Will, Jr., also joined "Big Boy" in the October 1921 release of another western, *The Vengeance Trail,* Williams' first leading role in a full-length western.

In 1924, Will, Jr., won a Little Theater Tournament with his play *Judge Lynch.* Six years later, he acted as co-master of ceremonies with Frank Albertson at the premiere of his father's movie *So This Is London.* In 1931, he decided on a newspaper career and went to work as a cub reporter for the *Star-Telegram* in Fort Worth, Texas, at the age of nineteen. When Will heard about his son's decision to enter the newspaper business, he said, "They'll probably put him on the street corner selling papers."

Will, Jr., continued his interest in publishing through schooling at Stanford University, where he ran the student weekly. In November 1935, at age twenty-four, he purchased a 75 percent interest in the *Beverly Hills Citizen* for $75,000. He said he was starting at the bottom of the newspaper ladder in spite of his title of managing editor and that his salary was "too small to talk about."

In 1942, he enlisted in the army as a private and received a commission as a second lieutenant after completing OCS training. He ran for and was elected to Congress in 1942 and left active service. In Congress, he served on the Foreign Affairs Committee, visited England under the blitz and helped write the soldier voting bill.

During his term in Congress, he turned down an offer by Warner Bros. to play the part of his father in a movie about the famous humorist: "I do not intend to make any picture at all until after the war is won and the peace is settled."

After one term in Congress, he resumed his military service. He was sent overseas

Will Rogers, Jr., in *The Story of Will Rogers* (1952) (authors' collection).

with the 814th Tank Destroyer Battalion, participated in the Normandy invasion and the Battle of the Bulge, got wounded in action and received a Purple Heart before being discharged in January 1946. A month later, he announced his intentions to run for the US Senate. He was defeated in a general election but kept his hand in politics as campaign manager in southern California for President Harry Truman's reelection campaign.

In addition to running his newspaper, Will, Jr., reentered the movie business. He appeared in *The Search* (1948) and *Look for the Silver Lining* (1949) before Warner Bros. resurrected the story of his father's life, *The Story of Will Rogers,* in 1952. Will, Jr., played the lead role of his father opposite Jane Wyman as Betty Rogers and Noah Beery, Jr., as Wiley Post.

Time wrote, "It is in Will Rogers Jr.'s performance that his father comes most alive on the screen; the familiar slouch with hands jammed in pockets, the unruly forelock, the sheepish grin, the shambling wisecracks delivered in his famous gumchewing drawl."

The *New York Times* reviewer, Barry Crowther, commented, "Considering that Will Rogers Jr. is vastly natural in the role of his dad, it is not surprising that this gush of admiration should have a certain genuineness on the screen ... it gives a tender reflection of a character that many people loved." The June 7, 1952, issue of *Collier's* featured Will Rogers, Jr., on the cover, with some *Follies* dancers included on an inside two-page spread.

Famous rodeo cowboy and trick roper Montie Montana taught Will, Jr., rope tricks for the movie, served as a double for Will, Jr., during the filming and performed all of the horse-roping scenes in the movie. Montie had first met Will many years earlier at one of the rodeos on the circuit, had been out to Will's Santa Monica Ranch a number of times and had appeared with Will in several shows and parades over the years. In an early meeting of the two, Will watched Montie perform at a Rose Bowl charity. After observing awhile, Will strode up to Montie and asked if Montie minded if he used his horse and big loop.

"He took my rope and tested it. He said he didn't think the honda was heavy enough, and he asked me if he could tie another knot in it. I still have the rope just as Will left it that day. I treasure it," said Montie 63 years after Will's passing. "It was a real honor to work on *The Story of Will Rogers*. He was a great man I admired very much."

Will, Jr., also played his father in the 1953 release *The Eddie Cantor Story* and in 1954 earned the lead role in *The Boy from Oklahoma*. In 1953, the year he sold the *Citizen*, he played himself in *Rogers of the Gazette*, a 30-minute show on CBS radio. He returned to films in the 1958 western *Wild Heritage*.

Over the years Will, Jr., turned to various projects, including touring in a solo stage show called *My Father's Humor*, taking the lead role in a revival of *Ah, Wilderness* at the Pasadena Playhouse, hosting the CBS *Good Morning Show* in New York, serving as chairman of the California State Park Commission and as special assistant to the commissioner of Indian Affairs, narrating a film on Alaska, producing a video tour of ghost towns and

Will Rogers, Jr., Jane Wyman and James Gleason in *The Story of Will Rogers* (authors' collection).

acting in a series of stories on American Indian culture. He was named the American Indian Exposition's Outstanding Indian of 1960. Will, Jr., died in 1993 at age 81 and is buried next to his wife in Arizona.

Jim Rogers

Jim Rogers appeared as a child actor in a number of his father's silent movies, including *Jes' Call Me Jim* (1920), *The Strange Boarder* (1920) and *Doubling for Romeo* (1921), but making movies for a living never crossed his mind.

He was always partial to horses and riding the range. Will Rogers set him up on a horse when he was three and had him playing polo as soon as he could hold the stick to whack the ball. After working at the Los Angeles stockyards, he and a friend partnered the leasing of 160,000 acres of land to raise cattle. The government ended up taking over the land for Camp Cook (now Vandenberg Missile Base), and Jim headed down to Los Angeles to look after the newspaper while Will, Jr., was in the service.

Jim's movie career started to take shape at age twenty-six, when Hal Roach offered him $500 a week to act in some "oaters" with Noah Beery, Jr. "I thought I hit the jackpot," said Jim.

Jim made three pictures co-starring Beery for Roach: *Dudes Are Pretty People* (1942),

Noah Berry, Jr., and Jim Rogers in *Calaboose* (1943) (courtesy Will Rogers Memorial).

Calaboose (1943) and *Prairie Chickens* (1943). Beery used to say that their pictures were like Laurel and Hardy with horses. Jim's contract with Roach required that under no circumstances would his father's name be used in any studio publicity or theater marquee billing.

After the first three Roach pictures were in the can, the government took over the Roach studio for use by the Army Photography Corps, leaving Jim Rogers without movie work. Six months later, he went to work for Harry Sherman in army training films and then followed that up with six "Hoppies," Hopalong Cassidy films starring William Boyd for United Artists/Paramount: *False Colors* and *Riders of the Deadline* (both 1943) plus *Forty Thieves, Lumberjack, Masquerade* and *Mystery Man* (all 1944).

Jim spent a stint in the US Marines Corps in the latter part of World War II as a writer/correspondent and thereafter returned to ranching. As of the late 1990s, he owned a riding stable and preferred to hang around "horse people."

Asked why he never returned to the movies after the Marines, Jim responded, "Movies were just like the Marines ... hurry up and then sit and wait. Besides, I was too busy ranching. I don't have any regrets. I guess you could say I'm an old brush country mountain cowboy at heart."

Will would have liked it that way.

Epilogue

Heroing is one of the shortest lived professions there is.... This thing of being a hero, about the main thing is to know when to die. Prolonged life has ruined more men than it ever made.

Will Rogers starred in dozens of silent movies and then successfully made the transition to headline in 21 "squawkies," as he liked to call them. Will Rogers entertained people around the world but, more important, he befriended and deeply touched all he came in contact with along his life's journey: a hero for his time and all time.

Filmography

Laughing Bill Hyde

Release Date: September 30, 1918. Goldwyn Pictures Corporation. Rex Beach Pictures. Distributed by Goldwyn Distributing Corporation. 6 reels, 5,970 feet. Based on the story by Rex Beach.

Credits Director: Hobart Henley. Assistant Director: Walter Sheridan. Scenario: Willard Mack. Camera: Arthur A. Cadwell. Art Director: Hugo Ballin.

Cast Mabel Ballin (Alice), Robert Conville (Denny Slevin), Joseph Herbert (Joseph Wesley Slayforth), Anna Lehr (Ponotah), Dan Mason (Danny Dorgan), Clarence Oliver (Dr. Evan Thomas), Will Rogers (Laughing Bill Hyde) and John Sainpolis (Black Jack Burg).

Synopsis Will Rogers portrays an escaped convict in his debut role in *Laughing Bill Hyde.* He manages to get Danny Dorgan (Mason), his wounded fellow escapee, to Dr. Evan Thomas (Oliver) but not in time to save his life. Hyde (Rogers) then leaves for the Alaskan goldfields aboard ship. He encounters the doctor en route while attempting to ransack and rob what turns out to be the doctor's stateroom. Instead of turning Hyde in, the doctor calls him friend and asks Hyde to go straight. The two become fast friends. Upon arriving in Alaska, Hyde befriends a half-breed Indian maiden, Ponotah (Lehr), the former owner of a gold mine that Joseph Wesley Slayforth (Herbert) swindled her out of. In turn, Slayforth's superintendent, Black Jack Burg (Sainpolis), and foreman, Denny Slevin (Conville), are chiseling Slayforth out of most of the mine's gold production. Hyde recovers Ponotah's money and wins her as a bride by plying his previous profession of thief for the last time. Hyde follows Black Jack and his partner and discovers where they had buried their purloined gold. He digs it up and uses part of it to salt a worthless mine the doctor had received as payment for medical services rendered. As anticipated by Hyde, greedy Slayforth falls for the plot and purchases the doctor's worthless mine. The doctor now has enough money to marry his girlfriend, and Hyde wins over Ponotah with the balance of the gold, which was rightly hers. Justice triumphs again when Black Jack and Slevin have a falling-out over the gold disappearance and shoot it out, to their mutual demise.

Despite being hindered by title cards, Will got in some great lines:

"I'm looking for work, and I'm afraid I'll find it."

"You wouldn't give a duck a drink if you owned Lake Erie."

"I ain't no Romeo, so don't try to feint me into a clinch. I would not wish myself onto nobody."

Reviews *Motion Picture News* summed up the critics' and public's acceptance of Will Rogers as a movie actor: "Whether he would make good in this art was a question that many wiseacres of Broadway were dubious about. So much of his success depended on his delivery and his lines. Well, Will Rogers has made good, there is no doubt about that. His face was meant for the camera and in *Laughing Bill Hyde* he gives ample proof of this....Will Rogers turns out to be such a fine screen actor that you would never know he was acting....The most famous wit of the speaking stage turns to pictures and is an instantaneous success."

Almost a Husband

Release Date: August 12, 1919. Goldwyn Pictures Corporation. Distributed by Goldwyn Distributing Corporation. 5 reels, 4,818 feet. Based on the novel *Old Ebenezer* by Opie Percival Read.

Credits Director: Clarence G. Badger. Camera: Norbert Brodin and Marcel A. Le Picard.

Cast Ed Brady (Zeb Sawyer), Sidney DeGray (John Caruthers), Clara Horton (Jane Sheldon), Cullen Landis (Jerry Wilson), Will Rogers (Sam Lyman), Gus Saville (Jasper Stagg), Herbert Standing (Banker McElwyn) and Peggy Wood (Eva McElwyn).

Synopsis Sam Lyman (Rogers), a country teacher, moves to a small town and participates as the groom in a mock wedding with the banker's daughter, Eva McElwyn (Wood). As it turns out, the person performing the mock wedding is a bona fide minister, and the marriage is deemed valid. A rich mule dealer, Zeb Sawyer (Brady), makes a move on Eva, but she convinces Sam to stay married to her to protect her from marrying Zeb. Zeb tries to drive Sam out of town by slandering him and having him horsewhipped by a gang of night riders. Zeb also stages a run on Eve's father's (Standing) bank. Just in time, Sam saves the day, using his advance money from a book sale to prevent the bank's collapse. Sam proposes for real this time, and he and Eva become husband and wife in fact.

Reviews *Harrison's Reports* stated, "*Almost a Husband* will surely be enjoyed by picture patrons. There is much human appeal in it, as well as comedy and thrills." The Sunday, October 12, 1919, issue of *The New York Times* carried coverage of the film's New York premiere at the Strand Theatre: "Personality Plus! The one essential asset to make a picture star is a screen personality. Will Rogers has it in every bit of business he does before the camera — he has favored the sophisticated theatregoers of New York for years with his personality — his droll wit — his clever comedy — and in this newest picture of his he puts over a fine story in a big way with this same genuine personality of his."

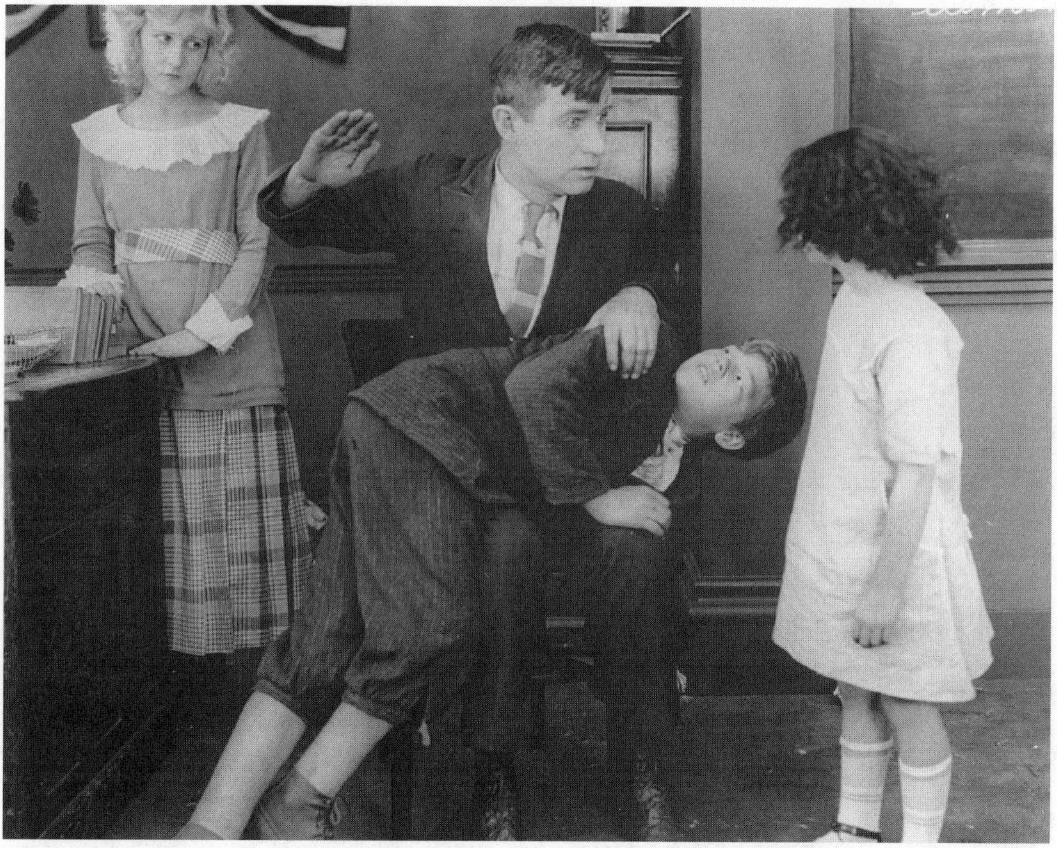

Will Rogers as schoolteacher Sam Lyman in *Almost a Husband* (1919) (courtesy Will Rogers Memorial).

In addition to praising Rogers' performance, *Wid's Daily* found favor with Will's co-star, "Peggy Wood as the banker's daughter was consistently good throughout." *Almost a Husband* received such popularity that the January 1930 issue of *Photoplay* mentioned Will Rogers and the picture in its "Ten Years Ago" section.

Jubilo

Release Date: December 7, 1919. Goldwyn Pictures Corporation. Distributed by Goldwyn Distributing Corporation. 6 reels. Based on a story by Ben Ames Williams in the *Saturday Evening Post.*

Credits Director: Clarence G. Badger. Scenario: Robert F. Hill. Camera: Marcel A. Le Picard.

Cast Charles French (James Hardy), Willard Louis (Sheriff Nate Punt), James Mason (Bert Rooker), Will Rogers (Jubilo) and Josie Sedgwick (Rose Hardy).

Synopsis A ne'er-do-well tramp, Jubilo (Rogers), begrudgingly hires out on James Hardy's (French) ranch to earn a home-cooked meal. Contrary to his hobo nature, the

Will Rogers as Jubilo and Josie Sedgwick as Rose Hardy in *Jubilo* (1919) (courtesy Will Rogers Memorial).

regular work and living pattern, not to mention the rancher's attractive daughter, Rose Hardy (Sedgwick), stirs an interest in living a productive life. Jubilo works at the ranch and helps the rancher get out of difficulty when he is implicated in a train robbery. Jubilo falls in love with Rose and decides to settle down.

Reviews *Motion Picture News* called *Jubilo* a picture that "just naturally reaches out and takes hold of your heart strings. And it keeps you enchanted to the very end. A well-balanced cast of perfect types artistically portray the various roles.... The story is a simple one of humor and pathos.... It sounds simple, and it is simple,—but it's great."

The "Exhibitors' Box Office Reports" section of the January 31, 1920, issue of *Motion Picture News* reported, "Will Rogers scores in charming picture. This is simply great, one of the best the Goldwyn organization has turned out in the new series. Delightful, splendidly received, well cast, good direction and good photography. Predict good future for Rogers. Big business seven days."

The character of *Jubilo* stayed with Rogers for many years. The December 17, 1921, issue of *Movie Weekly* included the following poem:

Jubilo

Man, but he's an awkward feller,
Green as grass and pumpkin yeller;
Bashful as a country girlie—
Homely! Boys, he knocks 'em curly!
But he's sure one bunch of cherro,
Never lets his smile touch zero.
When the road with ruts is bristlin'
He comes shufflin' long, a-whistlin'.
He's the prince of carefree codgers—
Who? Why honest big Bill Rogers!

Will Rogers returned to Ben Ames Williams' *Jubilo* storyline with the release of *Too Busy to Work* in 1932.

Water, Water Everywhere

Release Date: February 8, 1920. Goldwyn Pictures Corporation. Distributed by Goldwyn Distributing Corporation. 5 reels, 4,207 feet. Based on the novel *Billy Fortune and the Hard Proposition* by William Rheem Lighton and Louis D. Lighton. *The Saturday Evening Post* serialized the novel.

Credits Director: Clarence G. Badger. Scenario: Robert F. Hill. Camera: Marcel A. Le Picard.

Cast Milton Brown (Sam Beecher), Wade Boteler (Ben Morgan), William Courtwright (Daddy Sammett), Sydney DeGrey (Red McGee), Lillian Langdon (Fay Bittinger), Rowland Lee (Dr. Lyman Jennings Jordan), Marguerite Livingston (Martha Beecher), Victor Potel (Steve Brainard), Irene Rich (Hope Beecher), Will Rogers (Billy Fortune) and Lydia Yeamans Titus (Mrs. Red McGee). Some early sources cite Rowland Lee playing the role of Arthur Gunther. The January 18, 1920, issue of *The New York Times* mentioned that Will Rogers' son Jimmy would play a tiny role in *Water, Water Everywhere.*

Synopsis Cowboy Billy Fortune (Rogers) tries to reform a habitual drunkard, Dr. Ben Morgan (Boteler) despite the fact that the girl Fortune pines for, Hope Beecher (Rich), is in love with the doctor. Widow Fay Bittinger (Langdon) leads a temperance movement to close the local saloons. Billy Fortune and the boys draw lots to see who will be charged with wooing the temperance leader to get her to stop the drive against alcohol. Fortune's luck runs out, and he is chosen to move in on Bittinger but flees when she becomes too amorous for his taste. Taking another tack, the boys turn the saloons into soda water parlors with pretty waitresses doing the honors. The new social entertainment attracts the town's married men, causing the womenfolk to abandon their temperance crusade. Closing out the picture, a mine explosion allows the doctor to redeem himself by coming to the rescue of injured miners and shedding his dependence on booze.

Reviews The March 1920 issue of *Photoplay* commented, "Will Rogers, as every screen follower knows by this time, is one of the rare personalities of the screen. I suspect him of writing half his own titles (the better half) and of developing many of his own best scenes." The *Dramatic Mirror* proclaimed, "Goldwyn has in this actor one of their strongest stars, for no man can look at a Rogers picture without a few squirms of delight before the final fadeout.... A pleasant feature of this picture is Irene Rich as Hope Beecher. She is good to look at and lends the atmosphere of a wholesome woman to all her scenes." Taking a somewhat negative view of *Water, Water Everywhere, Variety* called the story "rambling and lacking in coherency.... Rogers does some corking riding stunts.... If he [Rogers] is to continue to grow as a picture star, he will have to be fitted with better yarns than this."

The Strange Boarder

Release Date: May 11, 1920. Goldwyn Pictures Corporation. Distributed by Goldwyn Distributing Corporation. 5 reels, 4,575 feet. Based on a story by Will Payne.

Credits Director: Clarence G. Badger. Scenario: Edfrid A. Bingham. Camera: Marcel A. Le Picard.

Cast Lionel Belmore (Jake Bloom), Sydney Deane (Dawson), Louis J. Durham (Sergeant Worrill), James Mason (Kittie Hinch), Doris Pawn (Florry, Hinch's Wife), Irene Rich (Jane Ingraham), Jake Richardson (Westmark), Jimmy Rogers (Billy Gardner) and Will Rogers (Sam Gardner).

Synopsis Arizona rancher Sam Gardner (Will Rogers) promises his dying wife to take their son, Billy (Jimmy Rogers), east to be educated. When they arrive in the big city, Sam is swindled out of his life savings. A crook, Kittie Hinch (Mason), saves Billy from being run over by a truck and becomes friends with Sam. Sam takes up residence in a boardinghouse where Jane Ingraham (Rich) takes a motherly interest in the boy. Sam and Hinch visit a gambling den where a man makes advances toward Hinch's wife, Florry (Pawn). Hinch later murders the man in revenge, but the police arrest Sam for the shooting. Hinch escapes to Mexico where he sends a telegram back to the police inspector admitting his guilt. Sam is freed and marries his son's new friend, Jane.

Will most likely had a hand in writing the titles for *The Strange Boarder.* During one scene, Jane remarks that you could tell that the man was a murderer by his face. Will responded, "If you could hang a man on account of his face, look where I'd have been."

Reviews Will's son, Jimmy, garnered some good press on his own. The *Exhibitor's Trade Review* of April 17, 1920, said, "Little Jimmy Rogers, a chip off the old block, makes his appearance as a star with his father and exhibits all the talents that contributed to the success of the elder. Even to the nonchalance and grimaces. The entire cast is worthy of individual mention, the characters being perfectly selected for characteristic roles."

Jes' Call Me Jim

Release Date: May 30, 1920. Goldwyn Pictures Corporation. Distributed by Goldwyn Distributing Corporation. 6 reels, 5,700 feet. Based on the novel *Seven Oaks* by James G. Holland.

Credits Director: Clarence G. Badger. Scenario: Edward T. Lowe, Jr. Adaptation: Thompson Buchanan. Camera: Marcel A. Le Picard.

Cast Lionel Belmore (Belcher), Nick Cogley (Mike Conlin), Samuel De Grey (Sam

Yates), Raymond Hatton (Paul Benedict), Irene Rich (Miss Butterworth), Jimmy Rogers (Harry Benedict), Will Rogers (Jim Fenton), Sheldon the Hound Dog (himself) and Bert Sprotte (Buffum).

Synopsis Miss Butterworth (Rich) convinces Jim Fenton (Will Rogers) that prominent businessman Belcher (Belmore) stole Paul Benedict's (Hatton) invention and improperly committed Benedict to an insane asylum. Jim breaks Benedict out of the asylum and hides him in his backwoods cabin.

When Belcher hears of the breakout, he goes to find Benedict only to come face to face with his ghost. Miss Butterworth brings a suit in the name of Harry Benedict (Jimmy Rogers) to recover money from Belcher. Paul appears in court to prove he has been defrauded, Belcher is arrested and Jim marries Miss Butterworth.

Reviews The *New York Times* applauded Will Rogers but panned the film: "Rogers gives character to this Jim and the touches of genuine humor in his acting, though uniquely his own, become definitely Jim's for the time being.... If it were not for Rogers' personality and his definite, if apparently artless, impersonation of Jim Fenton, this work would be a melodrama of the most farfetched and unconvincing type."

Irene Rich, Jimmy Rogers and Will Rogers in *Jes' Call Me Jim* (1920) (courtesy Will Rogers Memorial).

Cupid, the Cowpuncher

Release Date: July 25, 1920. Goldwyn Pictures Corporation. Distributed by Goldwyn Distributing Corporation. 5 reels, 5,000 feet. Based on the novel *Alec Lloyd, Cowpuncher* by Eleanor Gates.

Credits Director: Clarence G. Badger. Scenario: Edfrid A. Bingham. Camera: Marcel A. Le Picard.

Cast Cordelia Callahan (Mrs. Bergin), Helene Chadwick (Macie Sewell), Roy Laidlaw (Dr. Billy Trowbridge), Nelson McDowell (Sheriff Bergin), Tex Parker (Monkey Mike), Andrew Robson (Zack Sewell), Will Rogers (Alec Lloyd), Katherine Wallace (Rose), Lloyd Whitlock (Dr. Leroy Simpson) and Guinn "Big Boy" Williams (Hairoil Johnson).

Synopsis Bar X cowpuncher Alec Lloyd (Rogers) earns his nickname, Cupid, by marrying off his fellow cowpokes but achieves small success in getting himself hitched. When ranch owner Zack Sewell's (Robson) daughter, Macie (Chadwick), returns from boarding school, Cupid gets speared by his own arrow, and Alec falls head over heels for her. Their first meeting sets the tone for what follows. As Macie rides by, a bucking bronco throws Alec into a large mud puddle.

Shyster Dr. Leroy Simpson (Whitlock) eyes the Sewell fortune and sets out to woo Macie. Macie plans to leave for New York to pursue an opera career. The doctor finds out her plans and plots to take the same train and romance her. Alec lassoes the doctor's car and gets him to admit his fortune-hunting ambitions to Macie's father. Macie returns to marry Alec.

Reviews The *New York Times* review gave Rogers a thumbs up: "Rogers is becoming, for many he has become, one of the established screen characters. His personality is a substantial thing, apparently, that can be photographed — at any rate.... His smile, his homeliness, his awkward manner, his odd gestures, are, of course, part of his make-up, but if they were an end in themselves they would soon become tiresome. Their charm is in the fact that they serve to convey thoughts and feelings; they are expressive. In other words, Rogers acts."

Motion Picture News reported, "This picture belongs to Will Rogers, lock, stock and barrel. He appears in 99 44/100 per cent of the scenes, does his famous rope stunts, rides a bucking bronco and has quite evidently contributed most of the titles along with his share of the entertainment.... Great Entertainment with Star in Ideal Role."

In addition to writing the titles for the picture, Will obviously had his hand in naming some of the characters such as Hairoil Johnson and Monkey Mike.

Honest Hutch

Release Date: September 19, 1920. Goldwyn Pictures Corporation. Goldwyn Distributing Corporation. 6 reels, 5,349 feet. Based on a *Saturday Evening Post* story, *Old Hutch Lives Up to It* by Garret Smith.

Credits Director: Clarence G. Badger. Scenario: Arthur F. Statter. Camera: Marcel A. Le Picard.

Cast Mary Alden (Mrs. Hutchins), Priscilla Bonner (Ellen), Nick Cogley (Hiram Joy), Tully Marshall (Thomas Gunnison), Byron Munson (Thomas Gunnison, Jr.), Will Rogers (Ort Hutchins, or "Honest Hutch") Eddie, Jeanette and Yves Trebaol (Hutchins Children) and nine dogs from the pound (Themselves). The working title of this film, *Old Hutch,* was picked up in 1936 for the MGM remake starring Wallace Beery.

Synopsis Another lazy ne'er-do-well's life changes when he stumbles upon a buried strong box filled with $50,000 in bank robbery loot. In order not to arouse suspicions over his newfound wealth, Hutch (Rogers) reburies the money and goes to work to establish a new reputation. His new industriousness turns him into a prosperous farmer. When he returns to recover his money, he finds it gone. At first disheartened, he then realizes he has become a successful self-made man.

In a full-page ad for *Honest Hutch*, Goldwyn Pictures immodestly proclaimed, "We consider Will Rogers' performance in *Honest Hutch* one of the finest screen characterizations since the birth of the celluloid drama. We think that *Honest Hutch* comes close to being the greatest comedy ever made. We believe that this picture will put Will Rogers across for good and all as the most lovable male star in pictures.... We add our little note of praise to the nation-wide tribute which Will Rogers' greatest picture is going to evoke, knowing instinctively that for once the exhibitor will accept it at its honest face value,

Mary Alden and Will Rogers in *Honest Hutch* (1920) (courtesy Will Rogers Memorial).

and act accordingly.... We'd have the same opinions about *Honest Hutch* if it were produced by another firm."

Guile of Women

Release Date: December 26, 1920. Goldwyn Pictures Corporation. Distributed by Goldwyn Distributing Corporation. 5 reels, 4,496 feet. Based on a *Saturday Evening Post* story by Peter Clark MacFarlane.

Credits Director: Clarence G. Badger. Assistant Director: James Flood. Scenario: Edfrid A. Bingham. Camera: Marcel A. Le Picard.

Cast Lionel Belmore (Armstrong), Nick Cogley (Captain Stahl), Doris Pawn (Annie), Will Rogers (Yal), Charles A. Smiley (Captain Larsen), Bert Sprotte (Skole), Jane Starr (Maid) and Mary Warren (Hulda).

Synopsis Yal (Rogers), a Swedish sailor unlucky at love, works hard to save money to have his sweetheart, Hulda (Warren), join him in America. He sends her the money for the journey but never hears from her again. Then he gets involved with Annie (Pawn) and puts her in charge of a delicatessen he purchases. When he wants to get his money

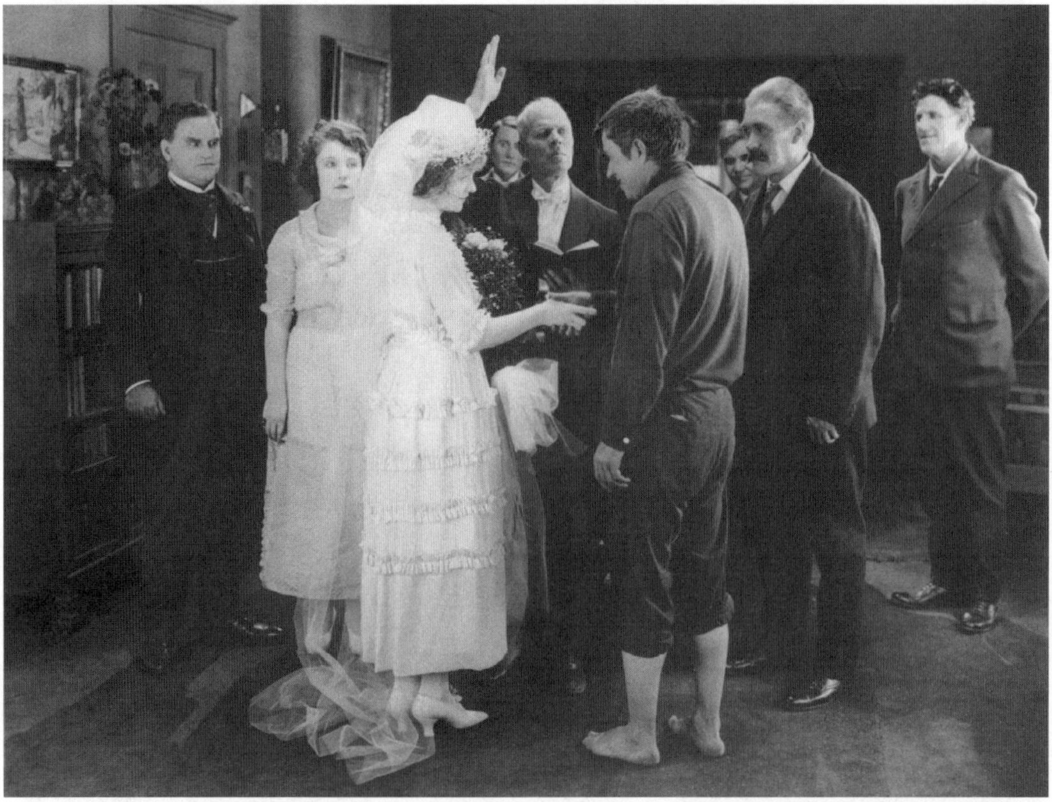

Mary Warren and Will Rogers wed at last in *Guile of Women* (1920) (courtesy Will Rogers Memorial).

out to buy a ship, Annie laughs at him. As he put it, "Yal was t'rough with vimean." He sees Hulda on the waterfront and finds out his money never arrived. She pretends to be Captain Larsen's (Smiley) maid. In reality, Larsen has adopted Hulda. Larsen dies and leaves his fishing fleet to Hulda. She reveals her status to Yal and they marry.

Reviews *Motion Picture News* called *Guile of Women*, "Exceptional story material both in plot and development and homely old Bill Rogers in a role eminently suited to his particular talents makes this very fine entertainment for audiences appreciating something that gets away from the orthodox.... He plays with a finesse and skill worthy of emulation by the greatest stars and depends less on his particular tricks and mannerisms than in any picture in which he has previously appeared.... Rogers, Good Story and Clever Titles Make This Fine Entertainment."

Boys Will Be Boys

Release Date: February 27, 1921. Goldwyn Pictures Corporation. Distributed by Goldwyn Distributing Corporation. 5 reels, 4,300 feet. Based on the *Saturday Evening Post* story by Irvin S. Cobb and play by Charles O'Brien Kennedy.

Credits Director: Clarence G. Badger. Scenario: Edfrid A. Bingham. Camera: Marcel A. Le Picard.

Cast Sidney Ainsworth (Cassius Sublette), Cordelia Callahan (Mrs. Hunter), Nick Cogley (Aunt Mandy), Burton Halbert (Farmer Bell), May Hopkins (Kitty), Edward Kimball (Judge Priest), C. E. Mason (Tom Minor), Irene Rich (Lucy), Will Rogers (Peep O'Day), H. Milton Ross (Bagby) and C. E. Thurston (Sheriff Breck).

Synopsis Orphan Peep O'Day (Rogers) finds himself heir to a small fortune and embarks on recovering his lost childhood. "You see, folks, I never had no boyhood. I reckon every man that grows up is entitled to a been a boy once in his life time." Crooked attorney Cassius Sublette (Ainsworth) arranges for an impostor to pose as Peep's niece to steal his fortune. Sublette hauls Peep in front of Judge Priest (Kimball) to get Peep declared insane. Peep's friend Lucy (Rich) testifies and convinces the judge that Peep is sane. The "niece" exposes Sublette and his dual plots to defraud Peep of his inheritance and Lucy of her house. All ends well with Peep playing Santa to the boys at the orphanage.

Reviews The June 11, 1921, *Movie Weekly* expressed its approval: "The Will Rogers brand of humor, the sly smile, the funny facial expressions, the droll mannerisms, are enough to keep a person in good humor for a week."

An Unwilling Hero

Release Date: May 8, 1921. Goldwyn Pictures Corporation. Distributed by Goldwyn Distributing Corporation. 5 reels, 4,759 feet. Based on the story *Whistling Dick's Christmas Stocking* by O. Henry.

Credits Director: Clarence G. Badger. Scenario: Arthur F. Statter. Camera: Marcel A. Le Picard. Art Director: Cedric Gibbons.

Cast John Bowers (Hunter), Nick Cogley (Servant), Jack Curtis (Boston Harry),

Larry Fisher (Hobo), Darrel Foss (Richmond), Dick Johnson (Hobo), Edward Kimball (Lovelyo), George Kunkel (Hobo), Molly Malone (Nadine), Will Rogers (Whistling Dick) and Leo Willis (Hobo).

Synopsis Whistling Dick (Rogers) rides the freight rails south to escape the winter cold and work: "The curse of the world." He learns of his fellow hobos' plan to rob a southern plantation on Christmas Eve with the aid of Richmond (Foss), a guest at the plantation and a suitor of Nadine (Malone), the plantation owner's daughter. Nadine, in turn, loves Hunter (Bowers), the plantation overseer. Dick refuses to participate in the robbery (too much like work) and sneaks off. He meets Nadine and Hunter on the road and they give him a Christmas present. He tells them of the plot to rob the plantation and as gratitude they offer him employment. Not wishing to change his preferred lifestyle, Dick refuses and resumes his wandering ways.

Reviews *Motion Picture News* predicted, "Mr. Rogers will have the distinction, when the history of the American screen is written, of being not only one of its leading actors, but one of the most appreciated humorists as well. Ever since the days when he won fame for his monologues delivered at the *Follies,* on Broadway, this star has been considered one of the quaintest humorists that America has produced. His titles in *An Unwilling Hero* are an example of the most appealing and exquisite comedy."

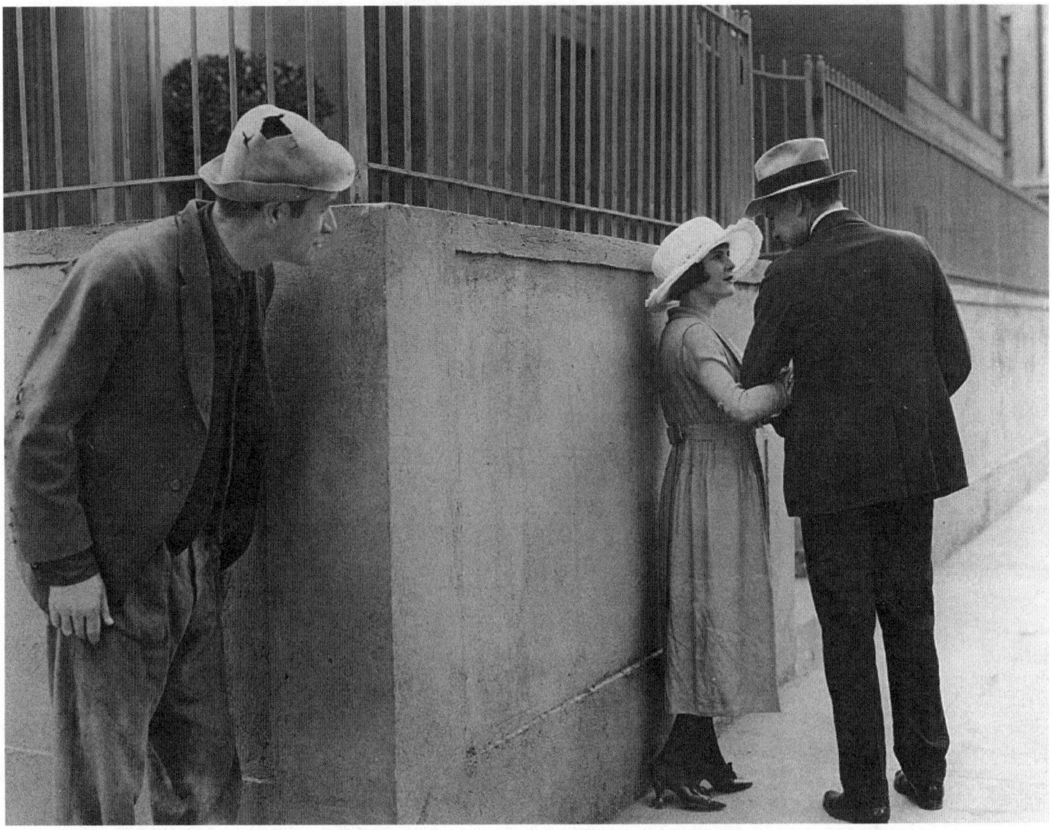

Will Rogers tails Molly Malone and John Bowers in *An Unwilling Hero* (1921) (courtesy Will Rogers Memorial).

Doubling for Romeo

Release Date: October 21, 1921. Goldwyn Pictures Corporation. Distributed by Goldwyn Distributing Corporation. 6 reels, 5,304 feet. Based on *Romeo and Juliet* by William Shakespeare. Adaptation by Elmer L. Rice and Will Rogers.

Credits Director: Clarence G. Badger. Scenario: Bernard McConville. Camera: Marcel A. Le Picard. Art Director: Cedric Gibbons. The working title for this film was *The Bashful Romeo.*

Cast Sidney Ainsworth (Pendleton/Mercutio), Sylvia Breamer (Lulu Foster/Juliet), Cordelia Callahan (Maid Maggie), John Cossar (Foster/Capulet), Al Hart (Big Alec/Tybalt), Raymond Hatton (Steve Woods/Paris), William Orlamond (Movie Director), Jimmy Rogers (Jimmie Jones), Will Rogers (Sam Cody/Romeo), Roland Rushton (Minister/Friar), C. E. Thurston (Duffy Sauders/Benevolio) and Guinn "Big Boy" Williams (Cowboy).

Synopsis Sam Cody (Rogers), a shy Arizona cowpoke, laments his sweetheart, Lulu Foster (Breamer), pining over a photograph of Douglas Fairbanks and chiding Sam, "How wonderfully he makes love. Oh, if only I could be made love to like that." Determined to win his girlfriend's undivided attention, Sam goes to a movie studio to learn how to make love firsthand. He obtains a job as a double and plenty of hilarious scenes ensue.

He finally gets a chance to play the role of a lover but fails miserably and is fired. Upon returning to Arizona, he falls asleep while reading *Romeo and Juliet.* In his dreams, he and his friends take on romantic roles, out-romancing and out-swashbuckling Fairbanks and his ilk.

> Ah! Fair One. Speak not of Romeo to me,
> With his fancy pants cut off at the knee,
> Silk socks, I do despise, also frilly lace,
> But if you crave beauty, just gaze upon my face,
> And lady! Lady! When I commence to woo,
> You'll see that I'm not a fool
> Because I took the whole darn course of love
> From the Acme Correspondence School!

Finally, Sam awakens and, inspired by his dream episodes, sweeps Lulu off her feet.

Reviews *Doubling for Romeo* was the first of several Rogers films to spoof the movie industry and movie stars. As reported in the *Los Angeles Times,* "Rogers' sub-titles 'kidding' other celebrities in filmland will alone be worth the price of admission. He says he has done his bit in this picture to help publicize Doug Fairbanks, Mary Pickford, Bill Hart, Charlie Chaplin, Charles Ray, Wallie Reid and many others in the screen world."

The National Board of Review's *Exceptional Photoplays* found favor with Will's farcical western Shakespeare: "*Doubling for Romeo* has what is perhaps the rarest quality in a motion picture story—genuine wit. Many motion pictures have real humor, and not only of the slap-stick variety, but those that are distinguished for their wit can still be counted on a one-armed man's fingers.... The whole picture is a delicious burlesque of the conventional film.... It is easily the best picture Mr. Rogers has ever done."

Will Rogers in *Doubling for Romeo* (1921). Guinn "Big Boy" Williams stands directly behind Rogers (authors' collection).

Motion Picture News continued the praise: "The picture is a farce comedy vehicle for Mr. Rogers but it is one of the most original offerings of the season. Titles written by the star add not a little to the comedy provided.... The personality of Will Rogers, titles contributed by the star, which are the acme of wit and appropriateness, a wealth of truly humorous incidents and one of the most ingenious picture ideas ever to be used, all contribute in making *Doubling for Romeo* fine entertainment."

A Poor Relation

Release Date: November 29, 1921. Goldwyn Pictures Corporation. Distributed by Goldwyn Distributing Corporation. 5 reels, 4,609 feet. Based on a comedy-drama in three acts of the same name by Edward E. Kidder.

Credits Director: Clarence G. Badger. Scenario: Bernard McConville. Camera: Marcel A. Le Picard.

Cast Sidney Ainsworth (Sterrett), Sylvia Breamer (Miss Fay), Robert De Vilbiss (Rip), Wallace MacDonald (Johnny Smith), Molly Mallone (Scallops), Walter Perry

(O'Halley), Will Rogers (Noah Vale), Jeanette Trebaol (Patch) and George B. Williams (Mr. Fay).

Synopsis Poor Noah Vale (Rogers) cares for two adopted orphans, Rip (De Vilbiss) and Patch (Trebaol), while working hard to perfect an invention. He appeals to a rich relative, Mr. Fay (Williams), for help in marketing the invention, but Fay refuses, thinking Noah is simply asking for a handout. Fay's daughter (Breamer) takes an interest in Noah. Fay's partner, Sterrett (Ainsworth), steals the invention, thinking there is a great fortune to be made. However, the invention proves worthless. Fay's secretary, Johnny Smith (MacDonald), asks for Fay's daughter's hand. In response, Fay fires him. Smith visits Noah, discovers some of Noah's writings and takes them to a publisher. The writings prove commercially successful. Noah quits inventing and pursues a writing career. Smith earns enough money to marry Miss Fay.

Reviews *Moving Picture World* said, "*A Poor Relation* enforces what many people have long contended, that Rogers is one of the most versatile character actors the screen boasts today, and that he is not by any means limited to the shy cowboy or self-sacrificing bashful tramp role."

One Glorious Day

Release Date: January 22, 1922. Famous Players–Lasky Corporation. Distributed by Paramount Pictures. 5 reels, 5,100 feet.

Credits Director: James Cruze. Adaptation: Walter Woods. Scenario: Walter Woods and A. B. Barringer. Camera: Karl Brown. The working title for this movie was *Ek*.

Cast Clarence Burton (Bert Snead), John Fox ("Ek," a spirit), Alan Hale (Ben Wadley), Lila Lee (Molly McIntyre), George Nichols (Pat Curran), Emily Rait (Mrs. McIntyre) and Will Rogers (Ezra Botts).

Synopsis Ezra Botts (Rogers), a bashful psychology professor, secretly loves his housekeeper's daughter, Molly McIntyre (Lee), but is too timid to tell her. Ezra puts himself into a trance, sending his spirit out of his body. In its place comes "Ek," a rambunctious unborn spirit seeking a body.

The revitalized Ezra shocks the entire town, routing scheming politicians and winning over Molly by soundly thrashing his romantic rival, Ben Wadley (Hale). However, all good things come to an end and "Ek" leaves Ezra's body after "one glorious day." Ezra does not remember anything of the previous day's adventures but finds out that Molly loves him. Impressed with his strength and honesty, the town nominates him for mayor.

Reviews "Can anything imaginative come out of Hollywood?" asked the *New York Times*. "It can. It has. It is *One Glorious Day* and it is at the Rivoli this week. Many people outside the studiously unoriginal studios have dreamed of both the dramatic and comic possibilities of spiritism on the screen, but most of them have about given up hope of ever seeing any of these possibilities realized. They may now take heart.... It is a spiritistic spree.... Will Rogers, as Professor Botts, is a revelation. See him first when the Professor's spirit is at home, and then when Ek occupies his body, and you'll say again that Will Rogers can be a good deal more on the screen than just himself."

The Ropin' Fool

Release Date: October 29, 1922. A Will Rogers production. Released by Pathé Exchange, Inc. 2 reels, 2,000 feet.

Credits Director: Clarence G. Badger. Scenario: Will Rogers. Camera: Marcel A. Le Picard.

Cast John Ince (The Stranger), Russ Powell (The Medicine Doctor), Irene Rich (The Girl), Will Rogers ("Ropes" Reilly, the Ropin' Fool), Bert Sprotte (The Sheriff) and Guinn "Big Boy" Williams (Curley Bowman, the Foreman).

Synopsis "Ropes" Reilly (Rogers), a cowboy obsessed with roping, even lassoes his girl (Rich) with a wedding ring hitch. After being fired by the foreman (Williams), "Ropes" returns to town, where he performs a series of rope tricks. Accused of injuring a man with his lariat, "Ropes" barely escapes a hanging—his own.

The Ropin' Fool, Will's first attempt at movie production, runs on a simple storyline but makes up for that with exceptional shots of many of Will's roping tricks. Also noteworthy is the innovative use of slow-motion photography illustrating the intricacy of Will's roping feats.

Reviews Will's hometown paper, the *Claremore Daily Progress,* declared, "Bill's latest comedy full of laughs and chuckles, showing just as he is. Don't miss this excellent comedy, it is his very latest."

The Headless Horseman

Release Date: November 5, 1922. Sleepy Hollow Corporation. Distributed by Hodkinson Pictures. 7 reels, 6,145 feet. Based on the story *The Legend of Sleepy Hollow* by Washington Irving.

Credits Producer: Carl Stearns Clancy. Director: Edward Venturnin. Assistant Director: Warren V. Fromme. Adaptation: Carl Stearns Clancy. Camera: Ned Van Buren. Sets: Tec-Art Studios. The working title for this movie was *Legend of Sleepy Hollow.*

Cast Mary Foy (Dame Martling), Charles Graham (Hans Van Ripper), Ben Hendricks, Jr. ("Brom" Bones), Lois Meredith (Katrina Van Tassel) and Will Rogers (Ichabod Crane).

Synopsis Washington Irving's infamous schoolmaster Ichabod Crane's (Rogers) adventures range from romancing Katrina Van Tassel (Meredith), the daughter of a wealthy farmer, to meeting the ghost of the Headless Horseman. Ichabod's rival for Katrina's hand, "Brom" Bones (Hendricks) spreads rumors that Ichabod is practicing witchcraft on the community's schoolchildren and concocts the legend about the Headless Horseman to spook Ichabod. On the way home from a party one evening, Ichabod encounters the Headless Horseman on the road. As Ichabod makes a mad dash to escape across a lonely bridge, the Headless Horseman hurls his head and hits Ichabod squarely. The next day the schoolroom is deserted and the schoolmaster is never seen again.

Reviews *Harrison's Reports* found *The Headless Horseman* "well directed, for the most part well acted and realistically produced. Mr. Rogers' comedy in places is rather forced." On the other hand, *Film Daily* remarked, "Lois Meredith is a pretty Katrina Van

Tassel although she is not the buxom coquette you might expect. Will Rogers, while not as lanky as Irving's Ichabod, is the right one for the part. His humorous touches never fail and he makes Ichabod a likeable fellow regardless of his appetite and bad proportions. Rogers gets the most out of the role and never misses a chance for a comedy bit."

Fruits of Faith

Release Date: December 24, 1922. A Will Rogers Production. Distributed by Pathé Exchange, Inc. 2 reels. Based on the original story and screenplay by Mildred and William Pigott.

Credits Director: Clarence G. Badger. Camera: Marcel A. Le Picard.

Cast Irene Rich (The Girl/Wife), Jimmy Rogers (Child) and Will Rogers (Larry, the Tramp).

Synopsis Larry (Will Rogers), a likable tramp, comes upon a lost boy (Jimmy Rogers) and a mule in the desert and takes them under his wing after an itinerant preacher advises him of the wonders of faith. When the boy cries for a mother, Larry marries a

Will Rogers, baby and Irene Rich in *Fruits of Faith* (1922) (courtesy Will Rogers Memorial).

girl (Rich) and takes on a respectable life. The boy's real father arrives on the scene to claim him but leaves after sensing the child's happiness and family love.

Reviews *Exhibitors Trade Review* advised, "There's a kick of real size in the third and final part of Pathe's *Fruits of Faith* in which Will Rogers is starred.... Mr. Rogers is in his best and most whimsical vein—and the remark applies to his manner and to the characteristic titles that adorn the action."

One Day in 365

Produced in 1922 but never released. A Will Rogers Production. To have been distributed by Pathé Exchange, Inc. 2 reels. An August 1922 newspaper article stated, "Will Rogers, directed by Clarence Badger, has completed two two-reel subjects, entitled *Fruits of Faith* and *The Ropin' Fool.* Irene Rich plays opposite the star in both productions. Mr. Rogers is now making another picture, entitled *No Story at All.* His wife and children comprise the cast." Working titles for *One Day in 365* included *No Story at All* and *Home Folks.*

One Day in 365 focuses on one day in the life of the Rogers family and the trials and tribulations of living in Beverly Hills during the early 1920s among famous neighbors. In one scene, Will shows a carload of tourists from Iowa the way to Doug Fairbanks' and Mary Pickford's house. In another humorous scene, Will sits on the steps, with a dejected look on his face, next to a real estate agent. "Lots are sold so quickly and often out here that they are put through escrow made out to the twelfth owner. What's worrying me is who is going to be the last owner?"

Hollywood

Release Date: August 19, 1923. Famous Players–Lasky Corporation. Distributed by Paramount Pictures. 8 reels, 8,197 feet. Based on the story appearing in *Photoplay* by Frank Condon.

Credits Producer: Jesse L. Lasky. Director: James Cruze. Adaptation: Tom Geraghty. Camera: Karl Brown.

Main Cast Roscoe "Fatty" Arbuckle (Fat Man in Casting Director's Office), George K. Arthur (Lem Lefferts), Luke Cosgrave (Joel Whitaker), Hope Drown (Angela Whitaker), Bess Flowers (Hortense Towers), Harris Gordon (Dr. Luke Morrison), Ruby Lafayette (Grandmother Whitaker), Eleanor Lawson (Margaret Whitaker) and King Zany (Horace Pringle).

Star and Celebrity Cast Gertrude Astor, Mary Astor, Agnes Ayres, Baby Peggy, T. Roy Barnes, Noah Beery, William Boyd, Clarence Burton, Robert Cain, Charles Chaplin, Edythe Chapman, Betty Compson, Ricardo Contez, Viola Dana, Cecil B. De Mille, William De Mille, Charles De Roche, Dinky Dean, Helen Dunbar, Snitz Edwards, Douglas Fairbanks, George Fawcett, Julia Faye, James Finlayson, Alec Francis, Jack Gardner, Sid Grauman, Alfred E. Green, Alan Hale, Lloyd Hamilton, Hope Hampton, William S. Hart, Gale Henry, Walter Hiers, Mrs. Walter Hiers, Stuart Holmes, Sigrid Holmquist, Jack

Holt, Leatrice Joy, Mayme Kelso, J. Warren Kerrigan, Theodore Kosloff, the Kosloff Dancers, Lila Lee, Lillian Leighton, Jacqueline Logan, May McAvoy, Robert McKim, Jeanie Macpherson, Hank Mann, Joe Martin, Thomas Meighan, Bull Montana, Owen Moore, Nita Naldi, Pola Negri, Anna Q. Nilsson, Charles Ogle, Guy Oliver, Kalla Pasha, Eileen Percy, Carmen Phillips, Jack Pickford, Mary Pickford, Chuck Reisner, Fritzi Ridgeway, Will Rogers, the Sennett Girls, Ford Sterling, Anita Stewart, George Stewart, Gloria Swanson, Estelle Taylor, Ben Turpin, Bryant Washburn, Maude Wayne, Claire West, Laurence Wheat and Lois Wilson.

Synopsis Angela Whitaker (Drown) goes to Hollywood in the company of her grandfather, Joel Whitaker (Cosgrave), to break into the movies. Instead, directors latch onto grandpa while his granddaughter cannot find work. The rest of the family comes to Hollywood to see gramps in the movies. All end up with jobs except Angela, who finally ends up marrying her boyfriend, Lem Lefferts (Arthur), from back home. Will Rogers appears in a brief scene, lassoing a group of players to hurry them along to catch a train.

Reviews The *New York Times* wrote, "As a smart satire with sparkling wit *Hollywood,* James Cruze's latest production, overwhelms all other screen efforts in its line." *Photoplay,* which first published the story, commented, "By laughing at himself and his crowd Mr. Cruze has turned out a rattling good film … the result is one of the most successful of Paramount pictures."

Jus' Passin' Through

Release Date: October 14, 1923. Hal Roach Studios, Inc. Distributed by Pathé Exchange, Inc. 2 reels.

Credits Producer: Hal E. Roach. Director: Charles Parrott (C. Chase) with Percy Pembroke. Scenario: Hal E. Roach.

Cast Marguerite Bourne, Earl Mohan, Marie Mosquini and Will Rogers.

Synopsis Will leaves his lariat behind as he portrays a hobo "jus' passin' through" a town where hobos are not allowed. Hungry, he gets himself arrested in order to partake in the Thanksgiving feast due the town's jail prisoners.

Hustlin' Hank

Release Date: November 11, 1923. Hal Roach Studios, Inc. Distributed by Pathé Exchange, Inc. 2 reels.

Credits Producer: Hal E. Roach. Director: Percy Pembroke. Scenario: Hal E. Roach. Camera: Robert Doran and Otto Himm. Editor: T. J. Crizer.

Cast Ed Baker, Billy Engle, Gus Leonard, Earl Mohan, Marie Mosquini, Will Rogers (Hustlin' Hank), Vera White and Noah Young.

Synopsis Hustlin' Hank (Rogers) works hard at creating a life without work and beating everybody to the chow line. His life changes and the fun begins when the boss's sister arrives to photograph the Wild West, and Hustlin' Hank becomes her cameraman.

Reviews *Moving Picture World* found *Hustlin' Hank* "all very good entertainment, well marked with the star's distinctive personality and talent."

UNCENSORED MOVIES

Release Date: December 9, 1923. Hal Roach Studios, Inc. Distributed by Pathé Exchange, Inc. 2 reels.

Credits Producer: Hal E. Roach. Director: Roy Clements with Percy Pembroke. Scenario: Hal E. Roach. Camera: Robert Doran and Otto Himm. Editor: T. J. Crizer.

Cast Ena Gregory, Henry Langdon, Earl Mohan, Marie Mosquini, Will Rogers (Lem), Mary Tansay, Ben Turpin, Guinn "Big Boy" Williams, Leo Willis and Noah Young.

Synopsis Doing a take-off within a take-off, Lem (Rogers), a representative of the "Cleaner Screen League" (lampoons the production of *Hollywood* in which Will had a cameo role), visits Hollywood to investigate and report on its "evils." Rogers adds to the humor with well-skilled impersonations and burlesques of a number of movie notables.

Reviews *Moving Picture World* called *Uncensored Movies* "one of the best of the new series of Will Rogers' two-reelers.... The titles and action are in Rogers' best style and there are a number of laughs and several subtle touches."

Rogers as William S. Hart in *Uncensored Movies* (1923) (courtesy Will Rogers Memorial).

TWO WAGONS, BOTH COVERED

Release Date: January 6, 1924. Hal Roach Studios, Inc. Distributed by Pathé Exchange, Inc. 2 reels.

Credits Producer: Hal E. Roach. Director: Rob Wagner with Roy Clements, D. Ross Lederman and Percy Pembroke. Scenario: Will Rogers. Titles: Will Rogers.

Cast Ed Baker, Billy Engle, Earl Mohan (Sam Woodhull), Charles Lloyd (Jesse Wingate), Marie Mosquini (Molly Wingate), James O'Neil, Will Rogers (William Banion/Bill Jackson), Leo Willis and Noah Young.

Synopsis Will Rogers plays the dual roles of William Banion and Bill Jackson in this spoof of James Cruze's successful movie *The Covered Wagon.* Both sagas follow a wagon train on its journey west. Will is also credited with the story idea and writing much of the screenplay. His touches are especially notable in the dislike between the two lead characters (both portrayed by Rogers) and the feared attack by the "Escrow Indians" (California real estate agents with long, onerous contracts).

Reviews The December 12, 1923, "Preview" section of the *Los Angeles Times* treated *Two Wagons, Both Covered* with two pages of excellent coverage: "Mr. Rogers' best medium in the motion picture field obviously is his own particular brand of satire. It sears, but it doesn't hurt—and it literally dumps at his feet a vast amount of material."

The Cowboy Sheik

Release Date: February 3, 1924. Hal Roach Studios, Inc. Distributed by Pathé Exchange, Inc. 2 reels.

Credits Producer: Hal E. Roach. Director: Jay A. Howe with Roy Clements, D. Ross Lederman, Percy Pembroke and Rob Wagner. Scenario: Hal E. Roach. Titles: Will Rogers.

Cast Ed Baker, Helen Gilmore (The Cook), Earl Mohan (Slicky), Marie Mosquini (The Schoolteacher), Will Rogers ("Two-Straw" Bill), Leo Willis and Noah Young.

Synopsis "Two-Straw" Bill (Rogers) falls in love with the schoolteacher (Mosquini) but is afraid to let her know. In turn, the cook (Gilmore) aggressively pursues "Two-Straw" with romance in mind. "Two-Straw's" propensity for using straws to make decisions gets him into a number of amusing situations.

The Cake Eater

Release Date: March 2, 1924. Hal Roach Studios, Inc. Distributed by Pathé Exchange, Inc. 2 reels.

Credits Producer: Hal E. Roach. Director: Jay A. Howe with D. Ross Lederman and Percy Pembroke. Scenario: Hal E. Roach. Titles: Will Rogers.

Cast Ed Baker, Billy Engle, Al Forbes, Earl Mohan, Marie Mosquini, Patsy O'Byrne, Will Rogers, Grace Woods and Noah Young.

Synopsis Will Rogers appears as a cowboy trying to escape the pursuit of two spinster ranch owners who have taken a romantic interest in him. Following the old adage that the way to a man's heart is through his stomach, they make him eat their homemade cake. When he feigns illness, they care for him. All of this creates interesting situations captured by Will's subtitles.

Reviews *Moving Picture World* said, "There are quite a few laughs and some of Rogers' characteristically witty sub-titles.... It is up to his usual standard in entertainment value."

Big Moments from Little Pictures

Release Date: March 30, 1924. Hal Roach Studios, Inc. Distributed by Pathé Exchange, Inc. 2 reels.

Credits Producer: Hal E. Roach. Director: Jay A. Howe with D. Ross Lederman, Percy Pembroke and Rob Wagner. Scenario: Hal E. Roach.

Cast Ed Baker, Billy Engle, Marie Mosquini, Will Rogers and Noah Young.

Synopsis Will impersonates a number of top box office draws, including Rudolph Valentino in a bullfight scene from *Blood and Sand*, the Keystone Cops and Douglas Fairbanks as Robin Hood. All of the above lead to hilarious situations and great fun.

Reviews *Exhibitors Trade Review* commented, "Rogers is funny in his imitations and he gets laughs in his 'big scenes.' His imitation of Fairbanks in a scene from *Robin Hood* is especially funny."

High Brow Stuff

Release Date: April 27, 1924. Hal Roach Studios, Inc. Distributed by Pathé Exchange, Inc. 2 reels.

Credits Producer: Hal E. Roach. Director: Rob Wagner with D. Ross Lederman and Percy Pembroke. Scenario: Hal E. Roach. The working title for this film was *The Little Theater Movement.*

Cast Ed Baker, Marie Mosquini, Will Rogers and Noah Young.

Synopsis Will Rogers spoofs the Little Theater Movement and the uplifting of dramatic "Art" with his portrayal of a famous Russian little-theater actor signed to a movie contract at the urging of the film magnate's wife. The director rejects the little-theater actor and does everything possible, including pasting him with pies, to encourage him to quit.

Reviews The *Moving Picture World* reviewer said, "Will Rogers picked out what will doubtless prove a sure winner in practically any theatre, when he chose *High Brow Stuff*, which cleverly burlesques...the so-called uplift of dramatic arts.... Its series of thrills winds up in a mudhole with a big splash of a laugh."

Going to Congress

Release Date: May 25, 1924. Hal Roach Studios, Inc. Distributed by Pathé Exchange, Inc. 2 reels.

Credits Producer: Hal E. Roach. Director: Rob Wagner. Camera: Robert Doran. Titles: Will Rogers. Editor: T. J. Crizer.

Cast Jack Ackroyd (Advisor), Marie Mosquini (Alfalfa's Daughter), Will Rogers (Alfalfa Doolittle), Mollie Thompson (Mrs. Doolittle) and Noah Young.

Synopsis *Going to Congress* begins the Alfalfa Doolittle saga of political satire. This comedy short follows the route of an unknown, unqualified party faithful, Alfalfa Doolittle (Rogers), who becomes a political candidate and wins the election by promising the farmers rain. The movie ends with Doolittle arriving in Washington to set the scene for more hilarious situations in future Rogers comedy shorts.

Reviews "This two-reeler featuring Will Rogers is full of good laughable situations, and is up to the standard of Will Rogers always amusing his audience.... Will Rogers' wit is outstanding in every foot of film and is a big laugh from beginning to end," proclaimed *Exhibitors Trade Review.*

Don't Park There

Release Date: June 22, 1924. Hal Roach Studios, Inc. Distributed by Pathé Exchange, Inc. 2 reels.

Credits Producer: Hal E. Roach. Director: Fred L. Guiol with Rob Wagner. Scenario: Hal E. Roach. Titles: Will Rogers.

Cast Marie Mosquini, Will Rogers and Noah Young.

Synopsis White Horse Ranch owner (Rogers) follows his wife's orders to go to town to purchase a bottle of horse liniment. He and his pet rooster start from the ranch in Kansas with his horse and wagon and encounter a series of difficulties along the way. He is arrested for interfering with motor traffic and thereafter decides to trade in his rig for one of the new-fashioned vehicles, despite not knowing how to drive. Unable to find a parking space in town, he travels to Utah and California in a rather roundabout way. By the time he returns home, his tour has included New Orleans and Seattle and the liniment has been off the market for twenty years.

Reviews The *Moving Picture World* reviewer commented, "Typical Will Rogers humor pervades this subject."

Jubilo, Jr.

Release Date: June 29, 1924. Hal Roach Studios, Inc. Distributed by Pathé Exchange, Inc. 2 reels.

Credits Producer: Hal E. Roach. Director: Robert F. McGowan with Rob Wagner. Scenario: Hal E. Roach. Titles: H. M. Walker.

Cast Allen Cavan, Charlie Chase, Joe "Fatty" Cobb, Jackie Condon, Mickey Daniels (Jubilo, Jr.), Richard Daniels, Otto Himm, Allen "Farina" Hoskins, Mary Kornman, Will Rogers (Jubilo), Andy Samuels, Lyle Tayo (Jubilo's Mother), Leo Willis, Joy Winthrup and Noah Young (Jubilo's Father).

Synopsis Jubilo (Rogers) reminisces about a hat he once purchased for his mother. Jubilo used a variety of means to get the $3 to buy the birthday present, including a Mark Twain–like duping of "Our Gang" into paying him to fill a hole.

Reviews *Exhibitors Trade Review* remarked, "The picture is very good but we do not like to see Director McGowan wander from his straight gang stuff."

Photoplay wrote, "Each scene is enacted by 'Our Gang' and the combination is one of the cleverest things seen on the screen."

Our Congressman

Release Date: July 20, 1924. Hal Roach Studios, Inc. Distributed by Pathé Exchange, Inc. 2 reels.

Credits Producer: Hal E. Roach. Director: Rob Wagner with Hampton Del Ruth. Scenario: Hal E. Roach. Titles: Will Rogers.

Cast Chet Brandberg, Sammy Brooks, Helen Dale, Beth Darlington, Jules Mendell, Marie Mosquini, Will Rogers (Alfalfa Doolittle), Mollie Thompson (Mrs. Doolittle), Quida Wildman and Noah Young.

Synopsis The continued adventures and political satire of Congressman Alfalfa Doolittle (Rogers) after he arrives in Washington to assume his position in Congress. The congressman and his family embark on fulfilling the roles of their newly achieved social status, creating hilarious scenes while learning to play golf, proper dining techniques and other antics. The new congressman feels the weight of his own importance and admits that he conducts the destiny of the nation.

Will Rogers learns to golf in *Our Congressman* (1924) (courtesy Will Rogers Memorial).

A Truthful Liar

Release Date: August 19, 1924. Hal Roach Studios, Inc. Distributed by Pathé Exchange, Inc. 2 reels.

Credits Producer: Hal E. Roach. Director: Hampton Del Ruth with Rob Wagner. Scenario: Hal E. Roach. Camera: Robert Doran. Titles: H. M. Walker. Editor: T. J. Crizer.

Cast Jack Ackroyd (Flunkie), Baldy Bremont, Jack Cooper, Helen Dale, Beth Darlington, Madge Hunt, Jules Mendell, Marie Mosquini, Will Rogers (Alfalfa Doolittle), Richard Pennell (King), Mollie Thompson (Mrs. Doolittle), Quida Wildman and Noah Young.

Synopsis Congressman Doolittle (Rogers) returns home to mingle with the hometown folks and regale them with stories of his days as an ambassador. Congressman Doolittle tells many far-fetched stories such as slapping the king on the back and saving him from an assassination attempt. To prove his truthfulness, he declares that if he is lying may the chimney of the country store topple down. It does. *A Truthful Liar* concludes the three-movie political satire series starring Will Rogers as Alfalfa Doolittle.

Reviews *Exhibitors Trade Review* found *A Truthful Liar* "a good laugh throughout, and Will sure has the knack of looking silly when he is 'doing his stuff' and making them laugh.... There is a lot of humor in this comedy and it should fill the house, for Will Rogers' name is synonymous with laughter and people everywhere like to be amused."

Richard Pennell as the king and Will Rogers as Ambassador Doolittle in *A Truthful Liar* (1924) (courtesy Will Rogers Memorial).

Gee Whiz, Genevieve

Release Date: September 28, 1924. Hal Roach Studios, Inc. Distributed by Pathé Exchange, Inc. 2 reels.

Credits Producer: Hal E. Roach. Director: Jay A. Howe with Roy Clements, Percy Pembroke and Rob Wagner. Scenario: Hal E. Roach.

Cast Ed Baker, Billy Engle, May Foster, Ena Gregory, Don Maines, Earl Mohan, Marie Mosquini, Will Rogers (Jubilo), Laura Roessing, Mary Tansay, Leo Willis and Noah Young.

Synopsis Health authorities quarantine tramp Jubilo (Rogers) because he has been in contact with a smallpox virus. The health scare creates some amusing town situations. He meets another hobo who convinces him to visit his sister after he gets released by the health authorities. Jubilo is told that the sister is a former circus performer, and he envisions a lithe, beautiful young woman. Instead he finds a buxom older woman. The sister, Genevieve, owns a restaurant and is a widow three times over. She considers Jubilo a good fourth wedding prospect, and more fun ensues.

With Will Rogers in Dublin

Release Date: Week of March 6, 1927. A Carl Stearns Clancy Production. Distributed by Pathé Exchange, Inc. 1 reel, 10 minutes running time.

Credits Producer: Carl Stearns Clancy. Director: Carl Stearns Clancy. Scenario: Will Rogers. Camera: John LaMond. Titles: Will Rogers.

Cast Will Rogers.

Synopsis Will humorously interprets Irish sites while on tour as an unofficial ambassador. Shots include the capital buildings, a military review in Phoenix Park, the home of Guinness stout, Trinity College, statues of Irish presidents, William T. Cosgrave welcoming Will Rogers, Vice President O'Higgins and various street scenes.

Will delivers a number of quips: "The Irish Free State has an army of 15,000 men — that gives them a fighting force of 60,000."

"Ireland welcomes you even if you don't buy something every minute."

"I like Ireland perhaps better than any other foreign country. They got humor, and while they think they take life serious, they don't. They will joke with you, sing with you, drink with you, and, if you want, fight with you — or against you, whichever you want."

Reviews *Exhibitors Trade Review* called *With Will Rogers in Dublin* "a right smart little feature, with Rogers photographed in various interesting precincts of the Irish capital made much more interesting by his characteristic captions. The Chicago audience thought the world of it."

Variety found the short travelogue "breezy and easy to look at.... It should be a valuable link on any program, big or small."

Hiking through Holland with Will Rogers

Release Date: Week of April 3, 1927. A Carl Stearns Clancy Production. Distributed by Pathé Exchange, Inc. 1 reel.

Credits Producer: Carl Stearns Clancy. Director: Carl Stearns Clancy. Scenario: Will Rogers. Camera: John LaMond. Titles: Will Rogers.

Cast Will Rogers.

Synopsis Will continues his tour of Europe with a stop in Holland. Scenes include Volendam, a boat trip along the Amsterdam canals, Will Rogers ambling about in wooden shoes, Hollanders in traditional costumes and Will describing Dutch customs and manners.

"Although Holland is the lowest country in the world it comes nearer to being on the level than any of them."

"In 1913 they christened the Peace Palace—just prior to the World War."

"I had always thought those windmills were located by a little white house. Say, there's not a little white house in Holland. There's not even a big white house there. It's the only country in the world where there is absolutely only one color and a paintman would starve to death trying to sell any other."

"They got hundreds of canals and boats going along all of them. Your farm is not fenced off from your neighbor's, there is just a canal between you and him. You either visit by boat or holler over. If your next-farm neighbor starts to walk over to you some night, he may get there but he will arrive wet."

With Will Rogers in Paris

Release Date: Week of May 1, 1927. A Carl Stearns Clancy Production. Distributed by Pathé Exchange, Inc. 1 reel.

Credits Producer: Carl Stearns Clancy. Director: Carl Stearns Clancy. Scenario: Will Rogers. Camera: John LaMond. Titles: Will Rogers.

Cast Will Rogers.

Synopsis Paris scenes include the Eiffel Tower, the Latin Quarter, the Louvre, the American Express Company office, Place de l'Opéra, Café de la Paix, Maxim's sidewalk café, the Trocadero and Les Grands Boulevards.

"They call this the Latin Quarter because no one can speak Latin and no one has a quarter."

"This is the Chamber of Deputies where they throw a Prime Minister out every day at twelve o'clock."

"See where they captured an American spy in France. He must have been working on his own, for we already know all we want to know about 'em."

"The Louvre has more art—but Hollywood has more excitement."

"Here's the Eiffel Tower. Charley Schwab sold them the steel. Otis put in the elevators and the Americans go up and look."

"That's the Trocadero, Paris' largest auditorium. A name we use for burlesque houses."

"These saloons are so full, half the people can't fit in—so they set them on the sidewalk."

"The French women in here either wear everything they can get on—or nothing at all."

"A bunch of American tourists were hissed and stoned yesterday in France — but not until they had finished buying."

Hunting for Germans in Berlin with Will Rogers

Release Date: Week of May 29, 1927. A Carl Stearns Clancy Production. Distributed by Pathé Exchange, Inc. 1 reel.

Credits Producer: Carl Stearns Clancy. Director: Carl Stearns Clancy. Scenario: Will Rogers. Camera: John LaMond. Titles: Will Rogers.

Cast Will Rogers.

Synopsis German scenes on Will's tour include the Reichstag, the Winter Palace of the kaiser, the Schauspielhaus (state theater), Potsdam and the Palace Gardens, the Palace of San Souci, boating on the River Spree and night shots of Berlin.

"Here's to the German Republic — may it never be afflicted with senators."

"Germany has banned that splendid film, *All Quiet on the Western Front,* on account of it showing Germany losing the war. I guess Hollywood is going to take it back and make it with a different ending."

"Germany has some sort of a custom where they allow you to commit suicide in case you have been found to be against the government. In America we just let you go on making speeches, and it amounts to about the same in the end."

"Germany had an election to see if they approved leaving the League of Nations. There was one fellow voted against it, but they are on the track of him."

Tip Toes

Release Date: June 19, 1927. British National Pictures, Ltd. Distributed by Paramount–Famous Players–Lasky Corporation. 6 reels, 6,286 feet. Based on the play by Guy Bolton and Fred Thompson. Filmed at Elstree Studios in London.

Credits Producer: J. D. Williams. Director: Herbert Wilcox. Scenario: Herbert Wilcox. Camera: Roy Overbaugh.

Cast Hubert Carter, Ivy Ellison (Lord William's Sister), Annie Esmond (Lord William's Aunt), Dorothy Gish (Tip Toes), Judd Green, Dennis Hoey (Hotelier), Nelson Keys ("Uncle" Al Kaye), Miles Mander (Rollo Stevens), John Manners (Lord William Montgomery), Fred Rains, Jerrold Robertshaw and Will Rogers ("Uncle" Hen Kaye).

Synopsis An American dance team of Al Kaye (Keys), Hen Kaye (Rogers) and Tip Toes (Gish) gets stranded in London. Tip Toes poses as an American heiress in order to attract the attentions of Lord William Montgomery (Manners). Lord William uncovers her fraud, and Tip Toes is forced to work as a cabaret dancer to make ends meet and pay their hotel bill. Lord William discovers her at the cabaret and falls in love with her.

Reviews *Photoplay* found favor with Will Rogers' performance but panned the picture: "This is the third picture that Dorothy Gish has done abroad. Like its immediate predecessor, this one must be dubbed 'a cheater.' It will serve well enough to kill an hour if you have nothing better to do.... Will Rogers plays one of the two hoofers in the act with her. He is as funny as Will Rogers can be.... A brief moment of Will Rogers makes it worth your money."

Through Switzerland and Bavaria with Will Rogers

Release Date: Week of June 26, 1927. A Carl Stearns Clancy Production. Distributed by Pathé Exchange, Inc. 1 reel.

Credits Producer: Carl Stearns Clancy. Director: Carl Stearns Clancy. Scenario: Will Rogers. Camera: John LaMond. Titles: Will Rogers.

Cast Will Rogers.

Synopsis Will explores Switzerland and Bavaria with scenes of the Swiss mountains, the town of Grindelwald, old Munich, the Munich municipal brewery and a lake at Zurich.

"Switzerland, my friends, apparently the fairest of lands is not on the level."

"I've been away up in the mountains of Switzerland and couldn't get any news at all, if you didn't yodel it, they wouldn't read it."

"The League of Nations to perpetuate peace is in session in Geneva, Switzerland. On account of Spain being in the last war, they won't let her in. If you want to help make peace, you have to fight for it."

With Will Rogers in London

Release Date: Week of July 24, 1927. A Carl Stearns Clancy Production. Distributed by Pathé Exchange, Inc. 1 reel.

Credits Producer: Carl Stearns Clancy. Director: Carl Stearns Clancy. Scenario: Will Rogers. Camera: John LaMond. Titles: Will Rogers.

Cast Will Rogers.

Synopsis Will shows off Buckingham Palace, Saint James Palace, London Bridge, the Tower of London, Piccadilly Circus, Regent Street, the American embassy, Westminster Abbey, Scotland Yard, the statue of Peter Pan, a dog cemetery in Hyde Park and the Grenadier Guards.

"This is the Tower of London folks where Lords and Ladies have lost their heads—ain't no place for a new Mayor."

"In England politics is an obligation; at home it's a business."

"These Englishmen are just about the smartest folks there is. It's one place where fascism, communism, or nudism will never get anywhere. They got a park over here in London—Hyde Park—that's all built for folks that are *agin* something."

"England elected a Labour government, but nobody has ever accused ours of doing a tap of work. When a man goes in for politics over home, he has no time to labor, and any man that labors, has no time to fool with politics."

Roaming the Emerald Isle with Will Rogers

Release Date: Week of August 21, 1927. A Carl Stearns Clancy Production. Distributed by Pathé Exchange, Inc. 1 reel.

Credits Producer: Carl Stearns Clancy. Director: Carl Stearns Clancy. Scenario: Will Rogers. Camera: John LaMond. Titles: Will Rogers.

Cast Will Rogers.

Synopsis Will returns to Ireland with scenes of the home of Richard Croker (boss of Tammany Hall), Croker's Tomb, Croker's famous race horse, the lakes of Killarney, Ross Castle, the earl of Killarney and village life in the Vale of Glendalough.

"It keeps a small nation busy raising the Police Force of the world."

"Deer season opened; that's for those who can't hit grouse."

"If I were England, I would give Ireland home rule but reserve the motion picture rights for what follows."

Prowling Around France with Will Rogers

Release Date: Week of September 18, 1927. A Carl Stearns Clancy Production. Distributed by Pathé Exchange, Inc. 1 reel.

Credits Producer: Carl Stearns Clancy. Director: Carl Stearns Clancy. Scenario: Will Rogers. Camera: John LaMond. Titles: Will Rogers.

Cast Will Rogers.

Synopsis Will's tour of France includes stops at the French senate, the Bois de Bologne, the Cathedral of Notre Dame, the Folies Bergère, Longchamps Race Track, the Moulin Rouge, Le Rat Mort, Fontainebleau, Victor Hugo's house, the Claridge Hotel, the Ritz Hotel and night shots of Paris.

"Nice, France, is pronounced "neece" not "nice." They have no word for nice in French."

"It's a great kick to sit and hear somebody say, 'Well, I lived in France for years, I know what France will do! I know the heart of the real France.' Well, the poor fellow is not purposely lying. He really thinks he knows."

"We're off the coast of France. I hear a noise. I think it's the franc dropping."

Winging Round Europe with Will Rogers

Release Date: Week of November 20, 1927. A Carl Stearns Clancy Production. Distributed by Pathé Exchange, Inc. 1 reel.

Credits Producer: Carl Stearns Clancy. Director: Carl Stearns Clancy. Scenario: Will Rogers. Camera: John LaMond. Titles: Will Rogers.

Cast Will Rogers.

Synopsis Will starts out the tour at Imperal Airways at Croyden Field in London with flights over the White Cliffs of Dover, the English Channel, the Alps and the Arc de Triomphe. Along the way, Will stops at Oostende, Amsterdam, Zurich and Paris.

"Channel swimming is so popular they have to have traffic cops."

"You can't find a piece of ground in Europe that hasn't been taken at least a dozen times from somebody or other that really think they have an original claim to it."

"In Europe, public men do resign. But here it's a lost art. You have to impeach 'em."

"There is one good thing about European nations. They can't hate you so badly they wouldn't use you."

"There ought to be a law against anybody going to Europe till they had seen the things we have in this country."

A Texas Steer

Release Date: December 4, 1927. Sam E. Rork Productions. Distributed by First National Picture Company, Inc. 8 reels, 7,419 feet. Based on the musical comedy by Charles Hale Hoyt.

Credits Producer: Sam E. Rork. Director: Richard Wallace. Assistant Director: James F. O'Shea. Scenario: Bernard McConville. Adaptation: Paul Schofield. Camera: Jack MacKenzie. Production Manager: Ben Singer. Comedy Construction: Jack Wagner. Film Editor: Frank Lawrence. Titles: Will Rogers and Garrett Graham. In an early press release, the director was listed as Jack Dillon, but by the time the movie went into production Richard Wallace provided the direction.

Cast Douglas Fairbanks, Jr. (Fairleigh Bright), Louise Fazenda (Mrs. "Ma" Brander), Sam Hardy (Brassy Gall), Arthur Hoyt (Knott Innitt), Bud Jamieson (Othello), Lucien Littlefield (Yell), George Marion, Sr. (Fishback), William Orlamond (Blow), Will Rogers (Maverick Brander), Ann Rork (Bossy Brander), Mark Swain (Bragg) and Lilyan Tashman (Dixie Style). This was a remake of the 1915 film starring Tyrone Power as Maverick Brander.

Synopsis Maverick Brander (Rogers), a cattleman on the plains of Texas, unwittingly gets elected to Congress through the behind-the-scenes actions of his wife, Mrs. "Ma" Brander (Fazenda). Not sure of this dubious honor, he tells his constituency not to tell anyone where he is going for fear it might reflect badly on his reputation as a cowboy. He leaves Red Dog, Texas (where men are men and the plumbing is improving), to journey to Washington, D.C. Once in Washington, Brander trys to ride herd on the Washington bunch who are on the opposite side of key legislation. Brander is kidnapped and left without his outer clothes in order to stop him from voting on the Eagle Rock Dam bill. Of course, this starts a chain of amusing incidents. Fairleigh Bright (Fairbanks) and Bossy Brander (Rork) provide the love interest as the juvenile leads.

Reviews The *New York Times* raved:

> That versatile genius, Will Rogers, who pals with princes and Presidents and wings his way across continents, is to be seen this week in the pictorial version of Charles Hoyt's old-time play, *A Texas Steer*.... Not only does Mr. Rogers as Maverick Brander succeed in making this subject entertaining, but those who have beheld him on the *Follies* stage, or have sat at a table with him, will undoubtedly wriggle with laughter at the sight of this writer, rope-thrower, gum chewer, juggler of words and phrases, dashing about in a

woman's nightgown, which, even when he appears in the House of Representatives to make the memorable address in favor of the Eagle Rock Dam bill, is only covered by an unbuttoned overcoat.... Mr. Rogers furnished most of the titles for this film, and, that in itself, is a relief.... Mr. Rogers is a refreshing sight in a picture, for he not only succeeds in being comic, but he devotes a good deal of time to "acting naturally."... Louise Fazenda is capital as Brander's persistent wife.... Miss Tashman gives a good performance. Douglas Fairbanks, Jr. does very well in a juvenile role.

Harrison's Reports concluded, "While it is not an extraordinary picture, it is, nevertheless, entertaining. The presence of Mr. Will Rogers, the famous humorist, in the principal part assures one a good evening's entertainment. He is a good actor, as he proved when he appeared in Goldwyn pictures.... The sight of Mr. Rogers speeding on horseback towards the Capitol without any outer clothes will naturally cause many laughs. There are other laughs, too, in the sub-titles as well as the situations."

Exploring England with Will Rogers

Release Date: Week of December 18, 1927. A Carl Stearns Clancy Production. Distributed by Pathé Exchange, Inc. 1 reel.

Credits Producer: Carl Stearns Clancy. Director: Carl Stearns Clancy. Scenario: Will Rogers. Camera: John LaMond. Titles: Will Rogers.

Cast Will Rogers.

Synopsis Will revisits England and tours Windsor Castle (the dungeon, castle grounds, the king's life guards and the king's riding park) and continues on to enjoy Eton College, Ascot Race Track, Hampton Court Palace of Henry VIII, a boat ride down the Thames and motoring through the English countryside.

"This is Windsor Castle, the King's summer bungalow."

"England has the best statesmen and the rottenest coffee of any country in the world."

"Poor coffee and no bathtubs have drove more Americans out of England than unfamiliarity with their language."

"I told you how bad it's getting with the tourists over here. Some of them are getting almost what they deserve."

"You know, that's one thing about an Englishman. He can insult you, but he can do it so slick and polite that he will have you guessing until away after he leaves you just whether he was friend or foe."

Reeling Down the Rhine with Will Rogers

Release Date: Week of January 15, 1928. A Carl Stearns Clancy Production. Distributed by Pathé Exchange, Inc. 1 reel.

Credits Producer: Carl Stearns Clancy. Director: Carl Stearns Clancy. Scenario: Will Rogers. Camera: John LaMond. Titles: Will Rogers.

Cast: Jimmy Rogers, Mary Rogers and Will Rogers.

Synopsis Will and his family take a number of trips in Germany from Mainz to Cologne. Sights include vineyards, Mause Tower, Schloss Ehrenfels Castle, Die Katz Castle, Die Maus Castle, Lorelie Rock, the Baccarach wine distillery, the Cologne marketplace and the Kaiser's statue at Koblenz.

Reviews Chester J. Smith of *Motion Picture News* commented, "Will Rogers takes his audience for a trip down the Rhine in this travelogue, which is not so humorous in its titles as most of the series. Some beautiful scenery is the main attraction of the picture, which depicts the numerous castles overhanging the Rhine. The large and well-kept vineyards are also a feature. Young Miss Rogers and the Rogers boy lend a novel note when they relieve their famous father in announcing some of the attractions along the scenic route."

"The Rhine is Germany's wettest river—even the boat runs on Rhine Wine."

"I am going into Germany. I want to see what reason they had wanting to try and get into the next war by way of the League of Nations."

"England, France and Germany have diplomats that have had the honor of starting every war they have ever had in their lifetime. Ours are not so good—they are amateurs—they have only talked us into one."

Over the Bounding Blue with Will Rogers

Release Date: Week of February 12, 1928. A Carl Stearns Clancy Production. Distributed by Pathé Exchange, Inc. 1 reel.

Credits Producer: Carl Stearns Clancy. Director: Carl Stearns Clancy. Scenario: Will Rogers. Camera: John LaMond. Titles: Will Rogers.

Cast Will Rogers.

Synopsis Will wraps up his European trip aboard the *Leviathan,* which disembarks Southampton, England, bound for the United States. On board ship, Will introduces the audience to Captain Hartley and a number of distinguished passengers, including William Phillips, the US ambassador to Canada; actor Jimmy Gleason; Ethelind, star of *Rio Rita*; Charles Evans Hughes and all the dogs he could find. Other interesting sights include a woman boxing a man, women diving into the swimming pool in slow motion and passengers playing deck golf. The series ends with the luggage being carted off the dock.

Reviews *Motion Picture News* reviewer Chester J. Smith said, "Will Rogers turns in his final page of the picture diary in which he concludes the last lap of Europe and the Continent and in which he reveals some splendid scenic shots and the usual abundance of Rogers' humor. It proved an interesting and instructive series of pictures and he winds it up in a blaze of glory with the trip back on the *Leviathan,* the final page of this picture story and humorous commentary aboard this mammoth, floating palace. The Rogers subtitles are more humorous in this one than in some of the preceding pictures of the series, all of which, however, have provided good entertainment."

"If all the hundred percent Americans would quit riding on ships with wine cellars maybe we could keep our merchant marine a year longer."

"Will you kindly find out for me through our intelligence department who the fellow is that said a big boat don't rock? Hold him till I return."

"You know I am the champion of the world getting seasick, and I know that is just the lack of nerve. If you will just keep up there and battle with it, and keep going, why you are okay. But I am kinder yellow, anyhow, and when I feel a little squirmish, why, I start hitting for the hay, and when once I get down on the bunk, why, I am a dead dog from then on, no matter if we are out for a week or a month."

They Had to See Paris

Release Date: September 8, 1929. Fox Movietone. 9 reels, 8,602 feet. Based on the novel by Homer Croy.

Credits Producer: William Fox. Director: Frank Borzage. Assistant Director: Lew Borzage. Scenario: Sonya Levien. Choreography: Bernard Steele. Dialogue: Owen Davis, Sr. Titles: Wilbur J. Morse, Jr. Camera: Chester Lyons, Al Brick. Music Composer: Con Conrad, Sidney Mitchell and Archie Gottler. Art Director: Harry Oliver. Film Editor: Margaret V. Clancey. Costuming: Sophie Wachner. *They Had to See Paris* was also released in a silent version, with titles by Wilbur J. Morse, Jr., for theatres which had not yet converted to talking pictures.

Cast Rex Bell (Clark McCurdy), Andre Cheron (Valet), Marguerite Churchill (Opal Peters, Daughter), Marcelle Corday (Marquise de Brissac), Owen Davis, Jr. (Ross Peters, Son), Fifi D'Orsay (Claudine), Gregory Gaye (Prince Ordinsky), Edward Kennedy (Ed Eggers), Bob Kerr (Tupper), Ivan Lebedeff (Marquis de Brissac), Theodore Lodi (Grand Duke Makiall), Marcia Manon (Miss Mason), Mr. Persian Pussy (Claudine's Kitty), Irene Rich (Mrs. Peters), Will Rogers (Pike Peters) and Christine Yves (Fleurie).

Synopsis Garage owner Pike Peters (Rogers) strikes oil on his property in Oklahoma, and he and his wife go to Paris to expose their children to culture. While Mrs. Peters (Rich) maneuvers to interest a French nobleman in their daughter, Opal (Churchill), their son, Ross (Davis), develops an interest in an artist's model, Fleurie (Yves). Pike tries to bring his family back to their senses by faking a fling with French cabaret singer Claudine (D'Orsay).

Reviews A number of movie critics rated the film one of the top ten movies of 1929, and *Photoplay* honored Will Rogers with one of the Best Performances of the Month in its November 1929 issue.

Happy Days

Release Date: February 13, 1930. Fox Movietone. 9 reels, 7,526 feet.

Credits Producer: William Fox. Director: Benjamin Stoloff. Assistant Director: Ad Schaumer, Michael Farley and Lew Breslow. Scenario: Sidney Lanfield. Camera: Lucien Andriott, John Schmitz. Grandeur Camera: J. O. Taylor. Songs: Abel Baer, James Brockman, Con Conrad, L. Wolfe Gilbert, Archie Gottler, James Hanley, Marcy Klauber, Joseph McCarthy, Sidney Mitchell, and Harry Stoddard. Choreography: Walter Catlett. Sound Engineer: Samuel Waite. Dialogue: Edwin Burke. Art Director: Jack Schultze. Film Editor: Clyde Carruth. Dance Director: Earl Lindsay. Recording Engineer: Samuel Waite. Costuming: Sophie Wachner. Production began under the working title of *New Orleans Frolic.*

Cast Frank Albertson, Warner Baxter, Rex Bell, Flo Bert, Ed Brendel, Lew Brice, Walter Catlett, Choral Ensemble, William Collier, Sr., James J. Corbett (Interlocutor), Dancing Ensemble, Clifford Dempsey (Sheriff Benton), Stuart Erwin (Jig), Charles E. Evans (Colonel Billy Batcher), Charles Farrell, Janet Gaynor, George Jessel, Richard Keene (Dick), Dixie Lee, Edmund Lowe, Sharon Lynn, Farrell MacDonald, George MacFarlane (Interlocutor), Victor McLaglen, J. Harold Murray, George Olsen and His Orchestra, Paul Page, Tom Patricola, Ann Pennington, Frank Richardson, Will Rogers, David Rollins, the Slate Brothers, "Whispering" Jack Smith, Martha Lee Sparks (Nancy Lee), Nick Stuart and Marjorie White (Margie).

Happy Days was the first Fox production to be filmed and released exclusively using the large-film Grandeur process. The film premiered at the Roxy Theatre in New York City on a Grandeur screen measuring 42 feet by 20 feet compared with a regular-size screen of 24 feet by 18 feet. The film's soundtrack measured more than three times that of older-style films.

Synopsis Despite the thin storyline and Will's brief cameo role, the film itself delivered some enjoyable moments due to its all-star cast and musical revue numbers. Margie (White) sends out the distress call to previous performers to come to New Orleans and help Colonel Billy Batcher (Evans) save his failing showboat revue. Of course, the troupes rally around the old colonel and present a rousing display of talent in various skits and singing and dancing numbers. Interestingly, Betty Grable performed as a member of the choral and dance ensemble.

One bright moment is Janet Gaynor and Charles Farrell singing *We'll Build a World All Our Own*, first dressed as lovers and later as their own children, dressed in bonnets and lying in a baby carriage. The "Crazy Feet" bit ranks as a clever piece of entertainment that would make Busby Berkeley envious as the choral and dancing ensembles emerge from a huge pair of pants legs suspended from the ceiling and travel down shoelace staircases. The grand finale gets everybody onstage for a successful fadeout.

Reviews *Harrison's Reports* found that the Grandeur screen did nothing to improve the quality of the movie: "It is mediocre. There is nothing in it that has not been shown before on the regular screen. It is a minstrel show in which all the worthwhile Fox stars are given a chance to appear and to say or to do something."

The *New Yorker* concurred: "The screen reaches all the way across Roxy's big stage, and it is very effective especially for landscape scenes or for big musical ensembles ... but its size is the chief interest of this opus. This is another case where a hundred entertainers, including a number of celebrities are corralled for a moment's appearance. It has its bright moments."

So This Is London

Release Date: May 23, 1930. Fox Movietone. 10 reels, 8,300 feet. Based on the international hit George M. Cohan stage play written by Arthur Goodrich.

Credits Producer: William Fox. Director: John Blystone. Assistant Director: Jasper Blystone. Scenario: Sonya Levien. Adaptation/Dialogue: Owen Davis, Sr. Camera: Charles G. Clarke. Music/Lyrics: James F. Hanley, Joseph McCarthy. Sound Engineer: Frank

Will Rogers and Mary Forbes in *So This Is London* (1930) (courtesy Will Rogers Memorial).

MacKenzie. Set Director: Jack Schultze. Film Editor: Jack Dennis. Costuming: Sophie Wachner. The pre-production announcement mentioned Benjamin Stoloff as the director. *So This Is London* was remade in 1940 starring Berton Churchill, Lily Cahill and Stewart Granger.

Cast Frank Albertson (Junior Draper), Dorothy Christy (Lady Amy Ducksworth), Bramwell Fletcher (Alfred Honeycutt), Mary Forbes (Lady Worthing), Lumsden Hare (Lord Percy Worthing), Maureen O'Sullivan (Elinor Worthing), Irene Rich (Mrs. Hiram Draper), Will Rogers (Hiram Draper), Martha Lee Sparks (Little Girl) and Ellen Woodston (Nurse).

Synopsis Cottonmill-owner Hiram Draper (Rogers) travels to England on business with his wife and children. Junior (Albertson) falls in love with an English girl, Elinor (O'Sullivan), aboard ship and conspires to have his parents meet her English parents. Hiram despises the English, and a series of humorous events unfold as he plays the buffoon. In the end, the Americans and English call a truce and become friends for the benefit of their marrying children.

LIGHTNIN'

Release Date: November 28, 1930. Fox Movietone. 10 reels, 8,500 feet. Based on the stage play produced by John Golden and written by Winchell Smith and Frank Bacon.

Credits Producer: William Fox. Director: Henry King. Scenario: S. N. Behrman, Sonya Levien. Camera: Chester Lyons. Music/Lyrics: Joseph McCarthy, James F. Hanley. Art Director: Harry Oliver. Film Editor: Louis Loeffler. Costuming: Sophie Wachner. Fox previously filmed *Lightnin'* as a silent production in 1925 under the direction of John Ford and starring Edythe Chapman, Jay Hunt and Otis Harlan.

Cast Betty Alden (Mrs. Graham), Rex Bell (Ronald, Diana's Husband), Frank Campeau (Sheriff Brooks), Moon Carroll (Mrs. Blue), Helen Cohan (Milly Jones), Joyce Compton (Diana, a Divorcée), Luke Cosgrave (Zeb), Roxanne Curtis (Flapper Divorcée), Eva Dennison (Mrs. George), Louise Dresser (Mrs. Mary Jones), Gwendolyn Faye (Mrs. Starr), Bess Flowers (Mrs. Weeks), Thomas Jefferson (Walter Lannon, Clerk of Court), J. M. Kerrigan (Judge Lem Townsend), Blanche Le Clair (Mrs. Leonard), Sharon Lynn (Mrs. Lower, the Chiseler), Joel McCrea (John Marvin), Goodee Montgomery (Mrs. Brooks), Antica Nast (Mrs. Lord, a Divorcée), Walter Percival (Everett Hammond), Jason Robards, Sr. (Lawyer Thomas), Will Rogers (Lightnin' Bill Jones), Betty Sinclair (Mrs. Bigg), Philip Tead (Monte Winslow), Charlotte Walker (Mrs. Thatcher), Bruce Warren (Mr. Leonard), Ruth Warren (Margaret Davis) and Lucille Young (Mrs. Young). George M. Cohan's daughter, Helen, made her film debut in *Lightnin'* in the role of Milly Jones.

Synopsis Lightnin' Bill Jones (Rogers) and his wife (Dresser) operate a hotel situated on the California/Nevada border and cater to the divorce trade. A shyster lawyer (Robards) tries to get Mrs. Jones to sell the valuable property, but Lightnin' won't sign the deed and leaves the area. The lawyer convinces Mrs. Jones to file for divorce in order

Helen Cohan and Will Rogers in *Lightnin'* (1930) (authors' collection).

to finalize the land deal. A subplot involves the love interest of Milly Jones (Cohan) and John Marvin (McCrea), who deftly escapes capture by Sheriff Brooks (Campeau) by crisscrossing state borders throughout the movie. The court proceedings backfire on the villains as Lightnin' tries his own case. Lightnin' and his wife are reunited, and Milly and John Marvin are free to marry.

A Connecticut Yankee

Release Date: April 6, 1931. Fox Film Corporation. 11 reels, 8,700 feet. Based on the novel *A Connecticut Yankee in King Arthur's Court* by Mark Twain. Adapted by William Conselman.

Credits Producer: William Fox. Director: David Butler. Assistant Director: Ad Schaumer. Camera: Ernest Palmer. Sound Engineer: Joseph Aiken. Art Director: William Darling. Set Design: Joseph Urban. Film Editor: Irene Morra. Special Effects: Fred Sersen, Ralph Hammeras. Costuming: Sophie Wachner.

Cast Frank Albertson (Clarence), William Farnum (King Arthur), Mitchell Harris (Sir Sagramor), Brandon Hurst (Merlin the Magician), Myrna Loy (Queen Morgan Le Fay), Maureen O'Sullivan (Princess Alisande) and Will Rogers (Hank Martin/Sir Boss).

Brandon Hurst, William Farnum and Will Rogers in *A Connecticut Yankee* (1931) (courtesy Will Rogers Memorial).

Synopsis Hank Martin (Rogers) is summoned on a radio repair call to a foreboding mansion during a terrific storm. After he arrives, he is accidentally struck on the head by a falling suit of armor and transported back through time to the era of King Arthur and the Knights of the Round Table. King Arthur (Farnum) sentences him to death, but Will escapes this fate by using an eclipse to overshadow Merlin the Magician's (Hurst) magic. Clarence (Albertson) desires to marry Princess Alisande (O'Sullivan) but is prevented because he is a commoner. Sir Boss (Rogers) and King Arthur attempt to rescue the princess from the wicked Queen Morgan Le Fay (Loy) but are captured. Clarence comes to the rescue leading an army of tanks, armored vehicles, helicopters and planes and is rewarded with the hand of the princess in marriage. Martin awakens to find himself in the present day, lying on the floor next to a suit of armor.

Young as You Feel

Release Date: August 7, 1931. Fox Film Corporation. 9 reels, 7,000 feet. Based on the stageplay *Father and the Boys* by George Ade. Adapted by Edwin Burke.

Credits Producer: William Fox. Director: Frank Borzage. Assistant Director: Lew Borzage. Camera: Chester Lyons. Music/Lyrics: James F. Hanley. Sound Engineer: George P. Costello. Art Director: Jack Schultze. Film Editor: Margaret V. Clancey. Production took place under the working titles of *Father and the Boys* and *Cure for the Blues.*

Cast Lucille Browne (Dorothy Gregson), Donald Dillaway (Billy Morehouse), Fifi D'Orsay (Fleurette), Gregory Gaye (Pierre, Fleurette's Husband), C. Henry Gordon (Lamson), Brandon Hurst (Robbins), Marcia Hurst (Mrs. Denton), Lucien Littlefield (Mr. Marley), John T. Murray (Colonel Stanhope), Terrance Ray (Tom Morehouse), Will Rogers (Lemuel Morehouse), Rosalie Roy (Rose Gregson) and Joan Standing (Lemuel's Secretary).

Synopsis Meat-packing company owner Lemuel Morehouse (Rogers) changes his ways from requiring a strict routine and tending to his business in order to drum some sense into his two playboy sons. After indulging in a drink of champagne, he takes up with a cabaret singer, Fleurette (D'Orsay), and starts acting young again. He begins dressing dapper, visiting the racetrack and going out on the town with Fleurette. While Lemuel is tripping the light fantastic, the two sons are forced to take care of the meat-packing business matters. When Lemuel and Fleurette fly to Colorado to clear up a land deal in which shyster Colonel Stanhope (Murray) tries to swindle Fleurette, the two sons, Billy (Dillaway) and Tom (Ray), follow, believing their father is the target of a con game being perpetrated by Fleurette. All ends well when Fleurette regains her land and the boys find out she is innocent of any con concerning their father. The boys find their own love interests in the now grown-up daughters, Rose Gregson (Roy) and Dorothy Gregson (Browne), of old family friends.

Ambassador Bill

Release Date: November 13, 1931. Fox Film Corporation. 8 reels, 6,300 feet. Based on the novel *Ambassador from the United States* by Vincent Sheean.

Credits Producer: William Fox. Director: Sam Taylor. Assistant Director: Walter Mayo. Scenario/Dialogue: Guy Bolton. Camera: John Mescal. Sound Engineer: Alfred Bruzlin. Art Director: Duncan Cramer. Film Editor: Harold Schuster. Costuming: Guy Duty. The working title for this film was *Dollar Bill.*

Cast Tad Alexander (Young King Paul), Herbert Bunston (British Ambassador), Marguerite Churchill (The Queen), Arnold Korff (The General), Theodore Lodi (French Ambassador), Edwin Maxwell (Monte), Ray Milland (Lothar), Ferdinand Munier (Senator Pillsbury), Greta Nissen (Countess Lika), Russ Powell (Drunk), Tom Ricketts (Littleton), Will Rogers (Bill Harper), Gustav von Seyffertitz (Prince de Polikoff), Ben Turpin (Butcher) and Ernest Wood (Northfield Slater).

Synopsis Oklahoman Bill Harper (Rogers) receives appointment as ambassador to the country of Sylvania, which experiences weekly revolutions. Harper becomes advisor to the queen (Churchill) and playmate of Young King Paul (Alexander) when he teaches the king how to play baseball and use a lariat and engages other members of the royal family in a friendly poker game. Harper's run-ins with pompous Senator Pillsbury (Munier) creates a number of humorous situations and allows Rogers to expound on politics. Harper helps restore the crown to King Paul's exiled father.

Ernest Wood, Will Rogers and Edwin Maxwell in ***Ambassador Bill*** (1931) (authors' collection).

Business and Pleasure

Release Date: February 12, 1932. Fox Film Corporation. 8 reels, 6,975 feet. Based on the novel *The Plutocrat* by Booth Tarkington and the play of the same name by Arthur Goodrich.

Credits Producer: William Fox. Associate Producer: A. L. Rockett. Director: David Butler. Assistant Director: Ad Schaumer. Scenario: William Conselman, Gene Towne. Camera: Ernest Palmer. Sound Engineer : Joseph Aiken. Art Director: Joseph Wright. Film Editor: Irene Morra. Costuming: Dolly Tree. Production began under the working title of *The Plutocrat.*

Cast Oscar Apfel (P. D. Weatheright), Vernon Dent (Charlie Turner), Jetta Goudal (Madame Momora), Boris Karloff (Sheikh), Joel McCrea (Lawrence Ogle), Dorothy Peterson (Mrs. Tinker), Jed Prouty (Ben Wackstle), Cyril Ring (Arthur Jones), Will Rogers (Earl Tinker) and Peggy Ross (Olivia Tinker).

Synopsis Razor-blade manufacturer Earl Tinker (Rogers) journeys to the Middle East in order to acquire the secret process for making the Damascus steel he uses in production. On board ship, Madame Momora (Goudal) warns him of danger but in reality she is in the employ of his competitor. Playwright Lawrence Ogle (McCrea) and Tinker's daughter Olivia (Ross) supply the young love angle. Tinker discovers that Madame Momora works for his competitor and goes underground as a swami to lead her astray. Tinker is subsequently captured and led away to be beheaded by a blade of Damascus steel at the order of the sheikh (Karloff). Ogle and Tinker's wife and daughter follow in pursuit. Tinker works a bit of magic using a radio receiver, gaining the sheikh's confidence and his steel business.

Down to Earth

Release Date: September 1, 1932. Fox Film Corporation. 9 reels, 7,150 feet. Based on the story by Homer Croy.

Credits Producer: William Fox. Director: David Butler. Assistant Director: Ad Schaumer. Scenario/Dialogue: Edwin Burke. Camera: Ernest Palmer. Music: George Lipschultz. Sound Engineer: George Leverett. Art Director: William Darling. Film Editor: Irene Morra. Costuming: Earl Luick.

Cast Mary Carlisle (Jackie Harper), Harvey Clark (Cameron), Brandon Hurst (Jeffrey, the Butler), Dorothy Jordan (Julia Pearson), Matty Kemp (Ross Peters), Henry Kolker (Randolph), Theodore Lodi (Grand Duke Michael), Louise Mackintosh (Mrs. Phillips), Irene Rich (Idy Peters), Will Rogers (Pike Peters) and Clarence Wilson (Ed Eggers).

Synopsis Homer Croy's *Down to Earth* takes off from the premise established in *They Had to See Paris.* The stock market crash and bank failures destroy the business of newly wealthy Pike Peters (Rogers). His high-living wife, Idy (Rich), finds it hard to give up the "necessities" like servants. The depth of the depression is illustrated by Peters meeting his friend, the Russian Grand Duke Michael (Lodi), working as a doorman at a Chicago hotel. After a series of humorous incidents involving bankers and snooty neighbors, the Peters family's lifestyle is restored to its roots — back down to earth.

Will Rogers, Matty Kemp, Dorothy Jordan and Mary Carlisle in *Down to Earth* (1932) (courtesy Will Rogers Memorial).

Too Busy to Work

Release Date: December 2, 1932. Fox Film Corporation. 8 reels, 6,900 feet. Based on the *Saturday Evening Post* story *Jubilo* by Ben Ames Williams.

Credits Producer: William Fox. Director: John G. Blystone. Assistant Director: Jasper Blystone. Scenario/Dialogue: Barry Conners, Philip Klein. Camera: Charles Clarke. Sound Engineer: Eugene Grossman. Art Director: Max Parker. Film Editor: Alexander Troffey. Costuming: Earl Luick.

Cast Louise Beavers (Mammy), Frederick Burton (Judge Hardy), Douglas Cosgrove (Sheriff), Bert Hanlon (Pete), Charles B. Middleton (Chief of Police), Marian Nixon (Rose), Jack O'Hara (Under Sheriff), Dick Powell (Dan Hardy), Will Rogers (Jubilo) and Constantine Romanoff (Axel).

Synopsis Jubilo (Rogers) shuns any notion of work or gainful employment but for good reason. He travels the country trying to find the man who made off with his wife and daughter, Rose (Nixon), while Jubilo was away at war. Because of his search, he is "too busy to work." He arrives in town and witnesses a bank robbery in which Judge Hardy's (Burton) son, Dan (Powell), is later implicated. In the meantime, Jubilo finds work at the Hardy ranch and discovers Judge Hardy is the man who stole his wife, who has since died.

Jubilo clears the judge's son and shoots the remaining bank robber who tries to rob the judge's safe. He has an opportunity to have the judge arrested but realizes that the judge truly loves Rose and has done a good job of raising her. Rose and Dan provide the love interest, and the movie ends with Jubilo resuming his wanderings but now at peace.

State Fair

Release Date: January 26, 1933. Fox Film Corporation. 10 reels, 8,894 feet. Based on the Literary Guild Prize–winning novel by Philip Dunfield Stong.

Credits Producer: Winfield R. Sheehan. Director: Henry King. Assistant Director: Ray Flynn. Scenario: Paul Green, Sonya Levien. Camera: Hal Mohr. Music: Louis DeFrancesco. Sound Engineer: A. L. von Kirbach. Art Director: Duncan Cramer. Film Editor: R.W. Boschoff. Costuming: Rita Kaufman.

Cast Erville Alderson (Hog Owner), Lew Ayres (Pat Gilbert, Reporter), Blue Boy the Hog (Himself), Hobart Cavanaugh (Hog Judge), Frank Craven (Storekeeper), Louise Dresser (Melissa Frake, Wife), Sally Eilers (Emily Joyce, Girl at the Fair), Norman Foster (Wayne Frake, Son), Janet Gaynor (Marguerita "Margy" Frake, Daughter), Harry Holman (Hog Judge), Victor Jory (Hoopla Stand Barker), Frank Melton (Neighbor Harry Ware), Doro Merande (Food Contest Lady), Will Rogers (Abel Frake, Farmer and Hog Raiser), John Sheehan (Aerial Act Barker) and Ruth Warren (Mrs. Edwin Metcalfe).

Synopsis The Frake family travels to the state fair where Abel (Rogers) plans to exhibit his prize Hampshire boar, Blue Boy (Himself). Unbeknownst to Mrs. Frake (Dresser), Abel spiked her mincemeat recipe, and she wins the contest hands down after the judges help themselves to several servings. Margy Frake (Gaynor) meets a newsman, Pat Gilbert (Ayres), and falls madly in love while her brother, Wayne (Foster), is seduced by a trapeze artist.

The climax comes when Blue Boy, who has been listless since arriving at the fair and through the first part of the judging, spies a frisky sow, regains his exuberance and captures the admiration of the judges. Blue Boy earns the blue ribbon, Margy ends up with Gilbert, and Wayne has his memories. Blue Boy's performance gained such notoriety that the prize hog earned a mention in the January 1934 issue of *Time* after he passed away.

This picture was so successful for Fox that the company remade it two more times. In 1945, an all-star cast, including Dana Andrews, Fay Bainter, Jeanne Crain and Charles Winniger, did the honors while Pat Boone, Bobby Darin, Tom Ewell, Ann-Margret and Pamela Tiffin took over the roles of the lead characters in the 1962 release. The later versions featured a number of Rogers and Hammerstein songs.

Doctor Bull

Release Date: August 5, 1933. Fox Film Corporation. 8 reels, 7,000 feet. Based on the novel *The Last Adam* by James Gould Cozzens.

Credits Producer: William Fox. Director: John Ford. Assistant Director: E. O'Fearna. Scenario: Paul Green, Jane Storm. Camera: George Schneiderman. Music: Samuel Kaylin. Sound Engineer: Eugene Grossman. Art Director: William Darling. Costuming: Rita Kaufman. The working title for this film was *Life's Worth Living*.

Cast Vera Allen (Janet Cardmaker), Vera Buckland (Mary), Nora Cecil (Aunt Emily), Berton Churchill (Herbert Banning), Andy Devine (Larry Ward), Louise Dresser (Mrs. Banning), Effie Ellsler (Aunt Myra), Francis Ford, Helen Freeman (Helen Upjohn), Rochelle Hudson (Virginia Banning), Howard Lally (Joe Tupping), Charles Middleton, Ralph Morgan (Dr. Verney), Marian Nixon (May Tupping), Patsy O'Byrne (Susan), Robert Parrish, Elizabeth Patterson (Aunt Patricia), Tempe Pigott (Grandma) and Will Rogers (Dr. Bull).

Synopsis Dr. Bull (Rogers) keeps the town's wags gossiping with his frequent evening visits to widow Cardmaker's (Allen) home. However, he goes on about his business of delivering babies, healing the sick, tending to a man paralyzed by a work accident, playing nursemaid to sick cows and treating patients stricken with an outbreak of typhoid fever. The powerful Banning family puts pressure on the townfolks to have Dr. Bull voted out as health officer because he failed in his duties to protect the town of New Winton, Connecticut, from typhoid. Dr. Bull vindicates himself by tracking down the

Berton Churchill, Will Rogers and Louise Dresser in *Doctor Bull* (1933) (courtesy Will Rogers Memorial).

source of the typhoid fever to Banning's construction camp and discovering a cure for the paralyzed man.

Mr. Skitch

Release Date: December 22, 1933. Fox Film Corporation. 7 reels, 6,150 feet. Based on the *Saturday Evening Post* story *Green Dice* by Anne Cameron.

Credits Producer: William Fox. Director: James Cruze. Scenario: Ralph Spence, Sonya Levien. Camera: John Seitz. Music: Louis DeFrancesco. Sound Engineer: W. D. Flick. Art Director: William Darling. Costuming: Rita Kaufman. *Green Dice, America's Guest* and *There's Always Tomorrow* all served as working titles for this film.

Cast Florence Desmond (Flo), Harry Green (Cohen), Rochelle Hudson (Emily Skitch), ZaSu Pitts (Mrs. Skitch), Eugene Pallette (Cliff Merriweather), Cleora Joan Robb (Twin), Gloria Jean Robb (Twin), Will Rogers (Mr. Skitch) and Charles Starrett (Harvey Denby).

Synopsis Mr. Skitch (Rogers) loses his Flat River, Missouri, homestead during a bank failure and takes to the open road with Mrs. Skitch (Pitts), daughter Emily (Hudson), the twins (the Robbs) and the family dog. A series of humorous adventures await the family as they head west through Yellowstone and the Grand Canyon. The love interest is provided by West Point cadet Harvey Denby (Starrett), who rescues Emily from a river undertow. The family stops at an auto camp, and Mr. Skitch gets a job waiting tables in a gambling casino. He wins $3,000 playing roulette and decks out the family in new clothes and orders a new car. He returns to the gambling tables once more to win just $500 more and loses it all. All ends well when Denby marries Emily and sets up Mr. Skitch in an auto camp of his own back in Missouri.

David Harum

Release Date: March 1, 1934. Fox Film Corporation. 9 reels, 7,525 feet. Based on the novel by Edward Noyes Westcott.

Credits Producer: Winfield R. Sheehan. Director: James Cruze. Assistant Director: Eli Dunn. Scenario: Walter Woods. Camera: Hal Mohr. Music: Louis DeFrancesco. Sound Engineer: W. D. Flick. Art Director: William Darling. Film Editor: Jack Murray. Costuming: Russell Patterson. Famous Players produced a silent version of this film in 1915.

Cast William Arnold, William Norton Bailey, Connie Baker (Guest), Noah Beery, Sr. (General Woolsey), Arthur Belasco (Crocker), Willie Best (Sleep 'n' Eat), Mary Blackwood (Guest), Hugh Boswell (Business Man), Clifford Carling (Steve), Jack Clark (Traveler), Charles Colman (Flowers, the Butler), Luke Cosgrave, Thomas Curran (Banker), Jane Darwell (Mrs. Woolsey), Wally Dean (Guest), Louise Dresser (Polly Harum), Harry Dunkinson, Stepin Fetchit (Sylvester), Larry Fisher, Edward Gargan (Bill Montague), Ruth Gillette (Lillian Russell), Harrison Greene (Barber), Roger Imhof (Edwards), George Irving (Father), Frank La Rue (Politician), The Leading Man (Horse, Himself), Eric Mayne (Doctor), Walter McGrail, Frank Melton (Caruthers Elwin), Charles Middleton

Will Rogers and Evelyn Venable in *David Harum* (1934) (authors' collection).

(Deacon Perkins), Jack Mower (Guest), Harold Nelson (Jeff), Ned Norton, Spec O'Donnell (Tim, Office Boy), Sarah Padden (Widow), Gus Reed, Frank Rice (Robinson), Ky Robinson (Steve Willis), Will Rogers (David Harum), Jerry Stewart (Chet Timson), Lillian Stuart (Sairy Harum), Kent Taylor (John Lennox), Harry Todd (Elmer), Evelyn Venable (Ann Madison), Morgan Wallace (Mr. Blake) and John Westervelt (Singer).

Synopsis Small-town banker David Harum (Rogers) engages in a bit of horse-trading with anyone who thinks they are savvy enough to outsmart him. Deacon Perkins (Middleton) appears to have bested Harum by selling him a blind horse, but Harum counters by sticking the deacon with a horse that balks right in front of Harum's house with the deacon getting drenched in the rain. Harum repurchases the horse and sends Ann Madison (Venable) and her suitor, John Lennox (Taylor), out on a Sunday afternoon ride. Madison then purchases the horse in an effort to further her romantic interests. She enters the balker, with David Harum at the harness, in a race against the deacon's prize horse after she discovers that her horse will continue to run as long as it is sung to. The film climax comes with Harum winning the race by singing "ta-ra-ra-boom-de-ay" to the horse in an exciting finish.

Handy Andy

Release Date: August 3, 1934. Fox Film Corporation. 9 reels, 7,600 feet. Based on the stageplay *Merry Andrew* by Lewis Beach.

Credits Producer: Sol M. Wurtzel. Director: David Butler. Scenario: William M. Conselman, Henry Johnson. Adaptation: Kubec Glason. Camera: Arthur Miller. Music: Richard Whiting. Lyrics: William M. Conselman. Music Director: Samuel Kaylin. Sound Engineer: F. C. Chapman. Art Director: Duncan Cramer. Costuming: Royer. This film began production under the working title of *Merry Andrew.*

Cast August Aguirre (Will Rogers' Double), Mary Carlisle (Janice Yates), James Conlin (Henry), Ann Doran (Peggy Wood's Double), Helen Flint (Mrs. Beauregard), Clara Fontaine (Party Guest), Gregory Gaye (Pierre Martel), Grace Goodall (Mattie Norcross), Charles Gregg (Carpenter), Paul Harvey (Charlie Norcross), Roger Imhof (Doc Burmeister), Eddie Lee (Japanese Cook), Patsy Lehigh (Conchita Montenegro's Double), Al Logan (Williams), Ella McKenzie (Young Mother), Frank Melton (Howard Norcross), Conchita Montenegro (Fleurette), Jessie Pringle (Jennie), Addison Richards (Golf Professional), Bert Roach (Phil), Will Rogers (Andrew Yates), Adrian Rosley, Gloria Roy (Party Guest), Robert Taylor (Lloyd Burmeister), Charles Teske (Rogers' Dancer Double), Fred "Snowflake" Toome (Darky), Richard Tucker (Mr. Beauregard), William Wagner (Music Teacher), Gertrude Weber (Bridge Party Guest) and Peggy Wood (Ernestine Yates). *Handy Andy* marks the film acting debut of Robert Taylor as a leading man and the final American film appearance of Conchita Montenegro.

Synopsis Andrew Yates (Rogers) sells his small drugstore business after much urging by his wife, Ernestine (Wood), who aspires to high social status and a music career. Andrew busies himself with disastrous and humorous hobbies ranging from learning to play golf to harboring pigeons. Ernestine convinces Andrew to travel to New Orleans where the fun escalates. She becomes involved with a gigolo at a Mardi Gras costume ball, and Andrew rescues his wife by arriving in a Tarzan costume and dancing an adagio dance with Fleurette (Montenegro). The chain drugstore that bought out Andrew fails, and he regains his store. Lloyd Burmeister (Taylor) and Andrew's daughter, Janice (Carlisle), wed, and Burmeister becomes Andrew's partner.

Judge Priest

Release Date: October 11, 1934. Fox Film Corporation. 9 reels, 7,400 feet. Based on short stories by Irvin S. Cobb.

Credits Producer: Sol. M. Wurtzel. Director: John Ford. Scenario: Dudley Nichols, Lamar Trotti. Camera: George Schneiderman. Music: Cyril J. Mockridge. Lyrics: Dudley Nichols, Lamar Trotti. Music Director: Samuel Kaylin. Sound Engineer: Albert Protzman. Art Director: William Darling. Costuming: Royer. John Ford revisited this material and the Judge Priest character for the 1953 Republic production entitled *The Sun Shines Bright.* Leonard Traynor, a one-eighth Cherokee Indian from Oklahoma, stood in for Will in this picture as well as the 1935 films *The County Chairman* and *Life Beings at Forty.*

Cast Melba Brown (Singer), Thelma Brown (Singer), Tom Brown (Jerome Priest), Vera Brown (Singer), Berton Churchill (Senator Horace "Hod" K. Maydew), Stepin Fetchit (Jeff Poindexter), Francis Ford (Juror No. 12), Brenda Fowler (Mrs. Caroline Priest), Grace Goodall (Mrs. Maydew), Charley Grapewin (Sergeant Jimmy Bagby), Winter Hall (Judge Fairleigh), Pat Hartigan (Saloon Patron), Rochelle Hudson (Virginia May-

Brenda Fowler, Will Rogers, Anita Louise and Tom Brown in *Judge Priest* (1934) (authors' collection).

dew), Roger Imhof (Billy Gaynor), Beulah Hall Jones (Singer), David Landau (Bob Gillis), Duke Lee (Deputy), Anita Louise (Ellie May Gillespie), Margaret Mann (Governess), Louis Mason (Sheriff Birdsong), Paul McAllister (Doc Lake), Hattie McDaniel (Aunt Dilsey), Matt McHugh (Gabby Rives), Paul McVey (Trimble), Frank Melton (Flem Tally), Hyman Meyer (Hean Feldsburg), Frank Moran (Saloon Patron), Robert Parrish, Vester Pegg (Herringer), George H. Reed (Servant), Will Rogers (Judge William Pitman Priest), Constantine Romanoff (Saloon Patron), Mary Rousseau (Guitar Player), Ernest Shields (Milan), Harry Tenbrook (Saloon Patron), Leonard Traynor (Will Rogers' Stand-in), Henry B. Walthall (Reverend Ashby Brand), Gladys Wells (Singer) and Harry Wilson (Saloon Patron).

Synopsis Irvin S. Cobb's story serves as a perfect vehicle for John Ford's trademark American characters striving to do what is right in spite of the odds. Set in the Kentucky post–Civil War period of the 1890s, *Judge Priest* captures the feeling of a bygone era. Judge Priest (Rogers) sits on the bench where he presides over the mundane goings-on of a small Kentucky town. His cases include trying a chicken thief, Jeff Poindexter (Fetchit), whom he takes into his personal custody when he discovers Jeff knows a special fishing hole.

Jerome "Rome" Priest (Brown) arrives to start his law practice and romance Ellie May Gillespie (Louise). The true character of the town is tested when Bob Gillis (Landau) strikes barber Flem Tally (Melton) over a crude remark Flem made about Ellie May.

A later confrontation leads to Tally being knifed, and Gillis is brought to trial. Senator Hod Maydew (Churchill) prosecutes Gillis and appears to be winning the case until Judge Priest interferes and proves that Gillis is a Confederate war hero and the father of Ellie May.

The Reverend Ashby Brand (Walthall) delivers emotion-stirring testimony that swings the jury in Gillis' favor. Juror No. 12 (Ford) adds a bit of levity to the courtroom scene when he deftly hits the spittoon in front of Senator Maydew just as he finishes his eloquent oratory. The movie ends with the Confederate Reunion Parade on Main Street and Rome and Ellie May in love.

The County Chairman

Release Date: January 18, 1935. Fox Film Corporation. 9 reels, 6,950 feet. Based on the 1903 stageplay by George Ade.

Credits Producer: Edward W. Butcher. Director: John Blystone. Scenario: Sam Hellman, Gladys Lehman. Camera: Hal Mohr. Music: Arthur Lange. Sound Engineer: W. D. Flick. Art Director: William Darling. Costuming: William Lambert. Famous Players produced a silent version of this film in 1915 starring Maclyn Arbuckle and Harold Lockwood.

Cast Erville Alderson (Wilson Prewitt), Frank Austin (Delegate), William Burress (Doolittle), Berton Churchill (Elias Rigby), Walter Downing, Louise Dresser (Mrs. Mary Rigby), Jan Duggan (Abigail Teksbury), Harry Dunkinson, Stepin Fetchit (Sassafras), Sam Flint (Delegate), Francis Ford (Rancher), Frank Hammond, Alfred James (Ezra Gibbon), Carmencita Johnson, Lew Kelley (Station Agent), Harlan Knight (Sheep Herder), Paul Kruger (Bridegroom Delegate), Robert McWade (Tom Cruden), Frank Melton (Henry Cleaver), Charles Middleton (Riley Cleaver), William V. Mong (Uncle Eck), Lorraine Rivero, Will Rogers (Jim Hackler), Mickey Rooney (Freckles), Gay Seabrook (Lorna Cruden), Ernest Shields, Russell Simpson (Vance Jimmison), Carl Stockdale (Delegate), Kent Taylor (Ben Harvey), Leonard Traynor (Will Rogers' Stand-in), Anders Van Haden (Man in Bowling Alley), Evelyn Venable (Lucy Rigby) and Eleanor Wesselhaeft (Squatter's Wife).

Synopsis In Tomahawk County, Wyoming, Jim Hackler (Rogers) promotes his law partner, Ben Harvey (Taylor), in a political race against corrupt Elias Rigby (Churchill) for the position of public prosecutor. Complications set in because Rigby had stolen Hackler's girl twenty years ago, and Harvey is in love with his political opponent's daughter, Lucy Rigby (Venable).

An old hand at political campaigns, Hackler teaches Harvey how to win an election and provides plenty of laughs in the process. During a heated public meeting, Harvey questions Rigby's character. Lucy, in anger, retaliates by promising to marry newspaper man Henry Cleaver (Melton) if he helps her father get elected. Hackler uncovers some dirt on Rigby but decides not to use it after Mrs. Mary Rigby (Dresser), Hackler's old girlfriend, pleads with him that the story would shame Lucy and break Mary's heart. The political contest is down to the wire with returns from Hiawatha County providing the margin of victory. The telegraph wire goes down, and Sassafras (Fetchit) is sent to retrieve

Will Rogers, Berton Churchill and Kent Taylor in *The County Chairman* (1935) (authors' collection).

the last returns from the telegraph station. He mixes them up and incorrectly reports that Rigby has won the election. Cleaver takes Lucy to get married as per their bargain. The vote error is discovered. Hackler and Harvey lead the town in pursuit of Cleaver and Lucy to stop the marriage. In the end, justice prevails with Ben Harvey winning the election and marrying Lucy.

Life Begins at Forty

Release Date: April 4, 1935. Fox Film Corporation. 8 reels, 7,325 feet. Based on the novel by Walter B. Pitkin.

Credits Producer: Sol M. Wurtzel. Director: George Marshall. Scenario: Lamar Trotti, Robert Quillen, Dudley Nichols, William M. Conselman. Camera: Harry Jackson. Music: Samuel Kaylin. Choreography: Jack Donohue. Sound Engineer: Bernarr Fredricks. Art Director: Duncan Cramer. Assistant Art Director: Albert Hogsett. Film Editor: Alexander Troffey. Costuming: Lillian.

Cast Emily Baldwin (Hudson's Stand-In), George Barbier (Colonel Joseph Abercrombie), T. Roy Barnes (Simonds, Salesman), Barbara Barondess (Abercrombie's Maid),

Bill Baxter (Townsman), Thomas Beck (Joseph Abercrombie, Jr.), Billy Bletcher (Hog Caller), E. W. Borman (Townsman), John Bradford (Wally Stevens), William Burress (Abercrombie's Friend), Gordon Carveth (Stunts), Floyd Criswell (Stunts), Richard Cromwell (Lee Austin), Robert Dalton (Stevens' Henchman), Frank Darien (Abercrombie's Friend), Jane Darwell (Ida Harris), John Webb Dillon (Townsman), James Donlon (Farmer), Clair Du Brey (Mrs. T. Watterson Meriwether), Harry Dunkinson (Abercrombie's Friend), Larry Fisher (Townsman), Ruth Gillette (Mrs. Cotton), Creighton Hale (Drug Clerk), Rhody Hathaway (Townsman), Herbert Hayward (Rural Character), Jack Henderson (Townsman), Rodney Hildebrand (Townsman), Jac Hoffman (Townsman), Sterling Holloway (Chris), Rochelle Hudson (Adele Anderson), Roger Imhof ("Pappy" Smithers), John Ince (Storekeeper), J. B. Kenton (Townsman), Robert Kerr (Bank Teller), W. J. Kolberg (Rural Character), Edward Le Saint (Townsman), James Marcus (Townsman), Robert McKenzie (Townsman), Edward McWade (Doctor), Carl Miller (Townsman), Jed Prouty (Charles Beagle), Will Rogers (Kenesaw H. Clark), Gloria Roy (Girl), Allen Sears (Townsman), Charles Sellon (Tom Cotton), Ernest Shields (Townsman), Crete Sipple (Townswoman), Slim Summerville (T. Watterson Meriwether), William Sundholm (Stunts), Len Traynor (Rogers' Stand-in), Guy Usher (Sheriff), John

Will Rogers, Richard Cromwell and Rochelle Hudson in *Life Begins at Forty* (1935) (authors' collection).

Wallace (Peg-Leg Man), Katherine Clare Ward (Housewife), Jack Waters (Townsman) and the Watson Children (Meriwether Children).

Synopsis Publisher Kenesaw H. Clark (Rogers) is forced out of business by the local banker, Colonel Joseph Abercrombie (Barbier), when Clark hires a young man, Lee Austin (Cromwell), who had been framed on bank robbery charges. Clark retaliates by starting a rival paper, running the town ne'er-do-well, T. Watterson Meriwether (Summerville), against Abercrombie for the office of mayor and eventually proving that the banker's own son had misappropriated the money. All ends well with Austin cleared of the crime and he and Adele Anderson (Hudson) becoming romantically involved.

Doubting Thomas

Release Date: July 10, 1935. Fox Film Corporation. 8 reels, 6,500 feet. Based on the stageplay *The Torch Bearers* by George Edward Kelly.

Credits Producer: B. G. DeSylva. Director: David Butler. Scenario: William M. Conselman, Bartlett Cormack. Camera: Joseph Valentine. Music: Arthur Lange. Sound Engineer: Joseph E. Aiken. Art Director: Jack Otterson. Costuming: René Hubert. This film followed the 1922 silent version of *The Torch Bearers.*

Cast Frank Albertson (Jimmy Brown), Johnny Arthur (Ralph Twiller), Lynn Bari (Girl), T. Roy Barnes (LaMaze), William Benedict (Caddie), Billie Burke (Paula Brown), Ray Cook (Cameraman), George Cooper (Stage Hand), Helen Flint (Nelly Fell), Helen Freeman (Mrs. Sheppard), Frances Grant (Peggy Burns), Sterling Holloway (Spindler), Gail Patrick (Florence McCrickett), John Qualen (Von Blitzen), Will Rogers (Thomas Brown), Alison Skipworth (Mrs. Pampinelli), Kay Thiel (Beauty Operator), Andy Tombes (Huxley Hossefrosse), Fred Wallace (Teffy) and Ruth Warren (Jenny).

Synopsis Thomas Brown (Rogers), owner of a sausage-manufacturing company, doubts his wife Paula's (Burke) acting ability and is frustrated by her spending so much time with the local theater group. The action leads to many amusing situations with falling scenery, muffed lines and wardrobe mishaps on the part of the amateur production. To teach her a lesson, Brown convinces a friend to masquerade as a Hollywood director seeking new talent. The "director" pans all of the applicants but finds favor with Thomas Brown's acting ability. Brown feigns interest and announces that he is forsaking all and going to Hollywood to seek his fame and fortune. His plot is uncovered, but Mrs. Brown forgives him because "Mr. Thomas must love me a great deal to go through all that trouble."

Steamboat Round the Bend

Release Date: September 19, 1935. Twentieth Century–Fox Film Production. 9 reels, 7,350 feet. Based on a novel by Ben Lucien Burman.

Credits Producer: Winfield R. Sheehan. Supervisor: Sol M. Wurtzel. Director: John Ford. Assistant Director: Edward O'Fearna. Scenario: Dudley Nichols, Lamar Trotti. Camera: George Schneiderman. Music: Samuel Kaylin. Sound Engineer: Albert Protz-

Will Rogers and Irvin S. Cobb (Captain Eli) in *Steamboat Round the Bend* (1935) (authors' collection).

man. Art Director: William Darling. Set Director: Albert Hogsett. Film Editor: Al De Gaetano. The working title for this film was *Steamboat Bill.*

Cast Captain Anderson (Jailer), Sam Baker, William Benedict (Breck), Hobart Bosworth (Chaplain), Hobart Cavanaugh (A Listener), Berton Churchill (New Moses), Irvin S. Cobb (Captain Eli), Heinie Conklin (Tattoo Artist), D'Arcy Corrigan (Hangman), Luke Cosgrave (Labor Boss), Stepin Fetchit (George Lincoln Washington/Jonah), Francis Ford (Efe), Grace Goodall (Sheriff's Wife), Ben Hall (Fleety Belle's Brother), Raymond Hatton (Matt Abel), Del Henderson (Salesman), Robert E. Homans (Race Official), Roger Imhof (Pappy), Si Jenks (Farmer) John Lester Johnson (Uncle Jeff), Pardner Jones (New Elijah), Fred Kohler, Jr. (Popkins, Fleety Belle's Suitor), James Marcus (Warden), Louis Mason (Boat Race Organizer), John McGuire (Duke), Charles B. Middleton (Fleety Belle's Father), Ferdinand Munier (Governor), Eugene Pallette (Sheriff Rufe Jeffers), Vester Pegg, Jack Pennick (Ringleader of the Boat Attack), Otto Richards (Prisoner), Will Rogers ("Doc" John Pearly), Anne Shirley (Fleety Belle), Wingate Smith, John Tyke, Lois Verner (Addie May, Sheriff's Daughter) and John Wallace.

Synopsis The film opens with snake-oil peddler "Doc" John Pearly (Rogers) promising that his Pocahontas Remedies cure-all ailments. Pearly and his nephew, Duke (McGuire), have purchased the rundown *Claremore Queen* with hopes of restoring her to her former glory. Duke falls in love with a "swamp girl," Fleety Belle (Shirley), and gets himself into trouble by killing a man. Pearly and Fleety Belle take over a floating museum to raise money for Duke's defense. Pearly wagers his boat against Captain Eli (Cobb) and enters a race both against Captain Eli's *Pride of Paducah* and against time to reach the governor (Munier) and obtain a pardon for Duke before he is hanged. The climactic race scene finds Doc's *Claremore Queen* running out of steam as its supply of wood fuel gets depleted. The crew stokes the boiler with everything in sight, including a supply of potent "hootch," which supplies a burst of energy enabling the *Claremore Queen* to win the race and save the day for Duke and Fleety Belle.

In Old Kentucky

Release Date: November 22, 1935. Fox Film Corporation. 9 Reels, 7,649 feet. Based on the stageplay by Charles Turner Dazey.

Credits Producer: Edward W. Butcher. Director: George Marshall. Assistant Director: Ray Flynn. Scenario: Sam Hellman, Gladys Lehman, Henry Johnson. Camera: Lewis William O'Connell. Music: Arthur Lange. Sound Engineer: W. D. Flick. Art Director: William S. Darling. Film Editor: Jack Murray. Costuming: William Lambert. This is the third film production of *In Old Kentucky.* Up-and-coming producer Louis B. Mayer made the silent film for Associated Producers in 1920, and Fox Film Corporation followed that

Bill "Bojangles" Robinson, Will Rogers and Dorothy Wilson *In Old Kentucky* (1935) (courtesy Will Rogers Memorial).

with a 1927 version starring Wesley Barry, Helene Costello, Stepin Fetchit and James Murray.

Cast Stanley Andrews (Steward), Allen Caven (Steward), Dora Clement (Saleslady), Esther Dale (Dolly Breckenridge), Alan Dinehart (Slick Doherty), Etienne Girardot (Rainmaker Pluvius J. Aspinwall), Greyboy (Horse, Self), Russell Hardie (Lee Andrews), Louise Henry (Arlene Shattuck), John Ince (Sheriff), Fritz Johannet (Jockey), Edward Le Saint (Steward), Ned Norton (Bookie), G. Raymond "Bill" Nye (Deputy Officer), Charles Richman (Pole Shattuck), Bill "Bojangles" Robinson (Wash Jackson), Will Rogers (Steve Tapley), Bobby Rose (Jockey), Charles Sellon (Ezra Martingale), Everett Sullivan (Jailer), Eddie Tamblyn (Jockey), Dorothy Wilson (Nancy Martingale) and William J. Worthington.

Synopsis Horse trainer Steve Tapley (Rogers) is caught in the middle of a longstanding feud between rival horse racing families and star-crossed lovers Nancy Martingale (Wilson) and Lee Andrews (Hardie). A number of humorous situations take place. Wash Jackson (Robinson) teaches Tapley to tap dance. More laughs ensue when Tapley escapes from jail by impersonating Jackson in blackface and dancing for the sheriff (Ince). Pluvius J. Aspinwall (Girardot) tries to make rain over the racetrack so Greyboy, a mudder, can win the race. As in every Kentucky horse flick, the finale comes down to an exciting horse race between the two rivals. Greyboy wins, and Tapley's efforts to unite Nancy and Lee succeed.

Bibliography

Books

American Film Institute. *The American Film Institute Catalog of Motion Pictures Produced in the United States: Feature Films 1911–1920.* Berkeley: University of California Press, 1988.

_____. *The American Film Institute Catalog of Motion Pictures Produced in the United States: Feature Films 1921–1930.* Berkeley: University of California Press, 1988.

_____. *The American Film Institute Catalog of Motion Pictures Produced in the United States: Feature Films 1931–1940.* Berkeley: University of California Press, 1993.

Atkins, Irene Kahn. *David Butler.* Metuchen, NJ: Directors Guild of America and Scarecrow, 1993.

Ayres, Alex. *The Wit and Wisdom of Will Rogers.* New York: Meridian, 1993.

Beardsley, Charles. *Hollywood's Master Showman: The Legendary Sid Grauman.* New York: Cornwall, 1983.

Berg, A. Scott. *Goldwyn: A Biography.* New York: Alfred A. Knopf, 1989.

Billips, Connie. *Janet Gaynor: A Bio–Bibliography.* Westport, CT: Greenwood, 1992.

Blum, Daniel. *A Pictorial History of the Silent Screen.* New York: Grosset & Dunlap, 1953.

Bolio, Tino. *History of the American Cinema: Volume 5.* New York: Scribner, 1993.

Bradley, Edwin M. *The First Hollywood Musicals: A Critical Filmography of 171 Features, 1927 through 1932.* Jefferson, NC: McFarland, 1996.

Brady, Anna, and Richard Wall. *Union List of Film Periodicals: Holdings of Selected American Collections.* Westport, CT: Greenwood, 1984.

Buxton, Frank, and Bill Owen. *The Big Broadcast 1920–1950.* New York: Viking, 1972.

Byers, Chester. *Roping: Trick and Fancy Rope Spinning.* New York: Putnam, 1928.

Cantor, Eddie. *As I Remember Them.* New York: Duell, Sloan and Pearce, 1963.

Carter, Joseph H. *Never Met a Man I Didn't Like.* New York: Avon, 1991.

Corey, Melinda, and George Ochoa. *A Cast of Thousands: A Compendium of Who Played What in Film.* New York: Facts on File, 1992.

D'Agostino, Annette M. (comp.). *An Index to Short and Feature Film Reviews in the Moving Picture World: The Early Years 1907–1915.* Westport, CT: Greenwood, 1995.

_____. *Filmmakers in* The Moving Picture World*: An Index of Articles, 1907–1927.* Jefferson, NC: McFarland, 1997.

Day, Donald. *The Autobiography of Will Rogers.* Boston: Houghton Mifflin, 1949.

DeLong, Thomas A. *Radio Stars: An Illustrated*

Biographical Dictionary of 953 Performers, 1920 through 1960. Jefferson, NC: McFarland, 1996.

Dimmitt, Richard B. *A Title Guide to the Talkies*. Metuchen, NJ: Scarecrow, 1965.

Douglas, George H. *The Early Days of Radio Broadcasting*. Jefferson, NC: McFarland, 1987.

Dressler, Marie, as told to Mildred Harrington. *Marie Dressler: My Own Story*. Boston: Little, Brown, 1934.

Easton, Carol. *The Search for Sam Goldwyn*. New York: William Morrow, 1976.

Ellrod, J. G. *Hollywood Greats of the Golden Years: The Late Stars of the 1920s through the 1950s*. Jefferson, NC: McFarland, 1989.

Epstein, Lawrence J. *Samuel Goldwyn*. Boston: Twayne, 1981.

Everson, William K. *American Silent Films*. New York: Oxford University Press, 1978.

_____. *The Films of Hal Roach*. New York: Museum of Modern Art, 1971.

Falk, Byron A., Jr., and Valerie R. Falk. *Personal Name Index to the New York Times Index 1851–1974*. Succasunna, NJ: Roxbury Data Interface, 1981.

Fetrow, Alan. *Feature Films, 1940–1949: A United States Filmography*. Jefferson, NC: McFarland, 1994.

_____. *Sound Films, 1927–1939: A United States Filmography*. Jefferson, NC: McFarland, 1992.

Finler, Joel W. *The Hollywood Story*. New York: Crown, 1988.

Gallagher, Tag. *John Ford: The Man and His Films*. Berkeley: University of California Press, 1986.

Gifford, Denis. *The British Film Catalogue 1895–1970*. New York: McGraw-Hill, 1973.

Goldwyn, Samuel. *Behind the Screen*. New York: George H. Doran, 1923.

Gragert, Steven K. *Radio Broadcasts of Will Rogers*. Stillwater: Oklahoma State University Press, 1983.

Green, Abel, and Joe Laurie, Jr. *Show Biz: From Vaudeville to Video*. New York: Holt, 1951.

Greenfield, Thomas Allen. *Radio: A Reference Guide*. Westport, CT: Greenwood, 1989.

Griffith, Richard. *The Movie Stars*. Garden City, NY: Doubleday, 1970.

_____. *Samuel Goldwyn: The Producer and His Films*. New York: Museum of Modern Art, 1956.

Halliwell, Leslie. *The Filmgoer's Companion*. New York: Avon, 1977.

_____. *Halliwell's Film Guide*. New York: Scribner, 1985.

_____. *Halliwell's Filmgoer's Companion*. New York: Scribner, 1988.

Harrison, P. S. *Harrison's Reports and Film Reviews: 1919–1931*. Hollywood: Hollywood Film Archives, 1994.

Hirschorn, Clive. *The Hollywood Musical*. New York: Crown, 1981.

Hochman, Stanley. *From Quasimodo to Scarface*. New York: Frederick Ungar, 1982.

Hughes, Elinor. *Famous Stars of Filmdom*. Boston: L. C. Page, 1931.

Hurst, Walter E. *Film Superlist: 20,000 Motion Pictures in the U.S. Public Domain*. Hollywood: Seven Arts, 1986.

Johnson, Alva. *The Great Goldwyn*. New York: Random House, 1937.

Katchmer, George A. *Eighty Silent Film Stars*. Jefferson, NC: McFarland, 1991.

Katz, Ephriam. *The Film Encyclopedia*. New York: Putnam, 1979.

Kay, Karyn. *Myrna Loy*. New York: Pyramid, 1977.

Ketchum, Richard M. *Will Rogers: His Life and Times*. New York: American Heritage, 1973.

Koszaeski, Richard, and Charles Harpole (gen. eds.). *History of the American Cinema: Volume 3*. New York: Scribner, 1990.

Kotsilibas-Davis, James, and Myrna Loy. *Myrna Loy: Being and Becoming*. New York: Alfred A. Knopf, 1987.

Lackmann, Ron. *Same Time ... Same Station: An A–Z Guide to Radio from Jack Benny to Howard Stern*. New York: Facts On File, 1995.

Lahue, Kalton C. *Gentlemen to the Rescue: The Heroes of the Silent Screen*. New York: Castle, 1972.

Lait, Jack. *Our Will Rogers*. New York: Greenberg, 1935.

Lamparski, Richard. *Whatever Became of ...* New York: Crown, 1967.

_____. *Whatever Became of ... Second Series*. New York: Crown, 1968.

Langman, Larry. *Encyclopedia of American Film Comedy*. New York: Garland, 1987.

_____. *A Guide to Silent Westerns*. New York: Greenwood, 1992.

Lauritzen, Einar, and Gunnar Lundquist. *American Film-Index 1916–1920*. Stockholm: Film-Index, 1984.

Lieberman, Susan, and Frances Coble. *Memorable Film Characters: An Index to Roles and Performers, 1915–1983*. Westport, CT: Greenwood, 1984.

Lloyd, Ann (ed.). *Movies of the Silent Years*. London: Orbis, 1984.

Lodge, Jack. *Hollywood: 1930s*. New York: Gallery, 1985.

Magill, Frank N. (ed.). *Magill's Survey of Cinema — Silent Films*. Englewood Cliffs, NJ: Salem, 1982.

Magliozzi, Ronald S. (ed.). *Treasures from the Film Archives*. Metuchen, NJ: Scarecrow, 1988.

Marx, Arthur. *Goldwyn: A Biography of the Man behind the Myth*. New York: W. W. Norton, 1976.

Mix, Paul E. *The Life and Legend of Tom Mix*. New York: A. S. Barnes, 1972.

Montana, Montie. *Montie Montana: Not Without My Horse*. Agua Dulce, CA: Double M, 1993.

Nash, Jay Robert, and Stanley Ralph Ross. *The Motion Picture Guide*. Chicago: Cinebooks, 1987.

Neibaur, James L. *Movie Comedians: The Complete Guide*. Jefferson, NC: McFarland, 1986.

The New York Times Directory of the Film. New York: Arno, 1971.

The New York Times Film Encyclopedia: 1896–1979. New York: Times Books, 1984.

The New York Times Film Reviews: 1913–1958. New York: Arno, 1970.

The New York Times Index. New York: New York Times.

The New York Times Names Index. New York: New York Times.

The New York Times Theater Reviews. New York: Arno, 1971.

Nowlan, Gwendolyn Wright, and Robert A. Nowlan. *Cinema Sequels and Remakes, 1903–1987*. Jefferson, NC: McFarland, 1989.

O'Brien, P. J. *Will Rogers: Ambassador of Good Will, Prince of Wit and Wisdom*. Chicago: John C. Winston, 1935.

Pitts, Michael R. *Radio Soundtracks: A Reference Guide*. Metuchen, NJ: Scarecrow, 1986.

Place, J. A. *The Non-Western Films of John Ford*. Secaucus, NJ: Citadel, 1979.

Quinlan, David. *The Illustrated Directory of Film Stars*. New York: Hippocrene Books, 1981.

_____. *Quinlan's Illustrated Registry of Film Stars*. New York: Henry Holt, 1991.

Quirk, Lawrence J. *The Films of Myrna Loy*. Secaucus, NJ: Citadel Press, 1980.

Rainey, Buck. *The Reel Cowboy: Essays on the Myth in Movies and Literature*. Jefferson, NC: McFarland, 1996.

Robinson, David. *Hollywood in the Twenties*. New York: A. S. Barnes, 1968.

Robinson, Ray. *American Original: A Life of Will Rogers*. Oxford: Oxford University Press, 1996.

Rogers, Betty. *Will Rogers: His Wife's Story*. New York: Bobbs-Merrill, 1941.

Rogers, David. *Who's Who in Hollywood, 1900–1976*. New Rochelle, NY: Arlington House, 1977.

Rogers, Will. *The Illiterate Digest*. Stillwater: Oklahoma State University Press, 1974.

Rollins, Peter C. *Will Rogers: A Bio-Bibliography*. Westport, CT: Greenwood, 1984.

Shipman, David. *The Great Movie Stars: The Golden Years*. New York: Crown, 1970.

_____. *The Story of Cinema*. New York: St. Martin's, 1982.

Siegel, Barbara, and Scott Siegel. *The Encyclopedia of Hollywood*. New York: Avon, 1991.

Silverman, Stephen M. *The Fox That Got Away*. Secaucus, NJ: Lyle Stuart, 1988.

Slide, Anthony. *The Encyclopedia of Vaudeville*. Westport, CT: Greenwood, 1994.

_____. *Selected Film Criticism, 1912–1950*. Metuchen, NJ: Scarecrow, 1982.

_____. *The Vaudevillians: A Dictionary of Vaudeville Performers*. Westport, CT: Arlington House, 1981.

Smallwood, James M. (ed.), and Steven K. Gragert (asst. ed.). *Will Rogers' Daily Telegrams*. Stillwater: Oklahoma State University Press, 1978.

_____, and _____. *Will Rogers' Weekly Articles*. Stillwater: Oklahoma State University Press, 1980.

Smith, Ronald L. *Who's Who in Comedy: Comedians, Comics and Clowns from Vaudeville to Today's Stand-Ups*. New York: Facts on File, 1992.

Solomon, Aubrey. *Twentieth Century–Fox: A Corporate and Financial History*. Metuchen, NJ: Scarecrow, 1988.

Spehr, Paul C. *The Movies Begin: Making Movies in New Jersey, 1887–1920*. Newark, NJ: Newark Museum, 1977.

_____, with Gunnar Lundquist. *American Film Personnel and Company Credits, 1908–1920: Filmographies Reordered by Authoritative Organizational and Personal Names from Lauritzen and Lundquist's* American Film-Index. Jefferson, NC: McFarland, 1996.

Steinberg, Cobbett. *Reel Facts: The Movie Book of Records*. New York: Vintage, 1982.

Sterling, Bryan B. *The Best of Will Rogers*. New York: Crown, 1979.

_____. *The Will Rogers Scrapbook*. New York: Bonanza, 1976.

_____, and Frances N. Sterling. *Will Rogers in Hollywood.* New York: Crown, 1984.

_____, and _____. *A Will Rogers Treasury: Reflections and Observations.* New York: Bonanza, 1982.

Stine, Whitney. *Stars and Star Handlers: The Business of Show.* Santa Monica: Roundtable, 1985.

Stuart, Ray. *Immortals of the Screen.* Los Angeles: Sherbourne, 1965.

Terrace, Vincent. *Radio's Golden Years: The Encyclopedia of Radio Programs 1930–1960.* San Diego: A. S. Barnes, 1981.

Thomas, Anthony, and Aubrey Solomon. *The Films of Twentieth Century–Fox: A Pictorial History.* Secaucus, NJ: Citadel, 1985.

Thomson, David. *A Biographical Dictionary of Film.* New York: William Morrow, 1981.

Truitt, Evelyn Mack. *Who Was Who on Screen.* New York: R. R. Bowker, 1983.

Variety Film Reviews. New York: R. R. Bowker, 1983.

Variety Obituaries, 1905–1986. New York: Garland, 1988.

Vazzana, Eugene Michael. *Silent Film Necrology: Births and Deaths of Over 9,000 Performers, Directors, Producers and Other Filmmakers of the Silent Era, Through 1993.* Jef-ferson, NC: McFarland, 1995.

Vermilye, Jerry. *The Films of the Thirties.* Secaucus, NJ: Citadel, 1982.

Vinson, James. *The International Dictionary of Films and Filmmakers.* Chicago: St. James, 1986.

Ward, Richard Lewis. *A History of the Hal Roach Studios.* Austin: University of Texas at Austin, 1995.

Warren, Patricia. *Elstree: The British Hollywood.* London: Elm Tree, 1983.

Weaver, John T. (ed.). *Forty Years of Screen Credits 1929–1969.* Metuchen, NJ: Scarecrow, 1970.

Wertheim, Arthur Frank. *Will Rogers at the Ziegfeld Follies.* Norman: University of Oklahoma Press, 1992.

_____, and Barbara Blair. *The Papers of Will Rogers: The Early Years Volume 1.* Norman: University of Oklahoma Press, 1996.

Wilkerson, Ticki, and Marcia Borie. *The Hollywood Reporter: The Golden Years.* New York: Coward-McCann, 1984.

Yagoda, Ben. *Will Rogers: A Biography.* New York: HarperCollins West, 1993.

Magazines/Journals

The American Magazine
Better Homes & Gardens
Charm
Classic Film Collector/Classic Images
Collier's
Everybody's Magazine
Exceptional Photoplays
Exhibitors' Trade Review
Film Daily
Film Daily Yearbook of Motion Pictures
The Film Weekly
Film Year Book
Films in Review
Forbes
The Green Book Magazine
Hollywood
Hollywood Reporter
The Home Magazine
Keith's Theatre News
Liberty
Life
The Literary Digest
Modern Screen
Motion Picture Classic
Motion Picture Herald
Motion Picture Magazine
Motion Picture News
Motion Picture Story Magazine
Motion Pictures
Motography
Movie Classic
Movie Mirror
The Moving Picture World
Munsey Magazine
The Nation
The New Movie Magazine
Newsweek
The New Yorker
Omnibook
The Orange Disc
Photo-Play Journal
Photoplay Magazine
Picture Play Weekly
The Picture Show
Popular Science Monthly
Radioland
Saturday Evening Post
Screenland
Screenplay
Successful Farming

Theatre
Time
Vanity Fair
Variety
Vogue
Wid's Daily

Newspapers

Claremore Messenger
Claremore Weekly Progress
Dramatic Mirror
Los Angeles Examiner
Los Angeles Times Review
New York Evening Mail
New York Telegraph
New York Times
Toledo Blade
Vinita Daily Chieftain

Index

Will Rogers, Aviation Enthusiast

People wouldn't believe that man could fly, ***and Congress don't believe it yet.***

Will Rogers was an early and avid aviation enthusiast. He took his first airplane ride in 1915 and logged more than 500,000 miles in the air before his fatal crash with Wiley Post in Alaska twenty years later. Through the air, Will Rogers beat the Red Cross to the scene of every disaster. Will knew just about every aviation pioneer and personally flew with many of them. He commented on aviation regularly in his *Daily Telegrams* and weekly newspaper articles which were read by millions of people from 1922 until his death in 1935.

Will Rogers (seated) and pilot E. K. Jaquith readying for Will Rogers' first flight in the summer of 1915 at Atlantic City, New Jersey. The plane was built by Curtiss Aeroplane Company (courtesy Will Rogers Memorial Museum).

Will often took Congress to task. On January 27, 1924, Will commented, "They say hot air rises. And I guess it does. An airplane flying over the Capitol the other day caught fire from outside sources." He finished the year chastising Congress over its failure to recognize the importance of aviation in a military role. He titled his December 29, 1924, column, "Aviation is 20 years Old But Congress Never Heard of It." Will reported, "The anniversary of the Wrights' flight was celebrated all over the World yesterday, France launched their 54th Flying Squadron…England turned out two gross. Japan hatched a bunch. America celebrated by letting one aviator out…Our Air Service is waiting for Congress to make an appropriation to have the valves ground and carbon removed from the engines."

Will Rogers (l) and Brigadier General William (Billy) Mitchell (r), who took Will on an aerial tour of Washington, D.C. in April 1925 (courtesy Will Rogers Memorial Museum).

Will Rogers (l) and Brigadier General Billy Mitchell (r) preparing for flight (courtesy Will Rogers Memorial Museum).

Will Rogers (l) and Brigadier General Billy Mitchell (r) preparing for takeoff in April 1925. After landing, Mitchell informed Rogers that was his last flight as a brigadier general. He was soon demoted to colonel due to his public criticism of the Army's lack of aviation preparedness. He was court-martialed in 1926 for his vocal advocacy of airpower. Mitchell is enshrined in the World War I Section of the National Aviation Hall of Fame (courtesy Will Rogers Memorial Museum).

Will Rogers (r) and aviator Casey Jones (l) after Philadelphia to New York flight October 1, 1926. Charles "Casey" Jones was president of the Curtiss Aeroplane Company and early sponsor of air races. Jones was a pioneer aviator, test pilot and World War I Army Air Corps Instructor (courtesy Will Rogers Memorial Museum).

Will Rogers (r) and C. A. Beil (l), sculptor and friend of Charlie Russell in front of "Miss Dillon" aeroplane before Will's 1927 flight to Billings Montana (courtesy Will Rogers Memorial Museum).

In April 1927, Will heralded aviation's new flight record, "Hurrah for our aviators that broke the continuous flight record. Fifty-one hours! That breaks the Arizona Senators' continuous air record in the last Senate filibuster...No automobile ever went fifty hours without stopping or refueling or meeting a train at a grade crossing or something, yet we spend a billion dollars on good roads for them. Why not a subsidy to commercial aviation. Congress is waiting for two more wars to see if they are practical."

A month later, Colonel Charles A. Lindbergh electrified the world when he took off from Roosevelt Field near New York City early in the morning of May 20, 1927, and braved snow and sleet to land at Le Bourget Field near Paris thirty-three and a half hours later. A frenzied crowd of 100,000 people greeted him.

Will Rogers (r) with Colonel Charles Lindbergh (l) in September 1927 (courtesy Will Rogers Memorial Museum).

"All an American aviator has to do these days is to have a helmet, put in some extra gas and two chicken sandwiches and be met next day by the Mayor of Honolulu or Paris or Berlin or Shanghai. The tough part with aviation is to think up some place to go."

"I always told you we have the aviators. Just give them the planes. I have flown in the past years with at least a dozen boys whom I wouldn't be afraid to start to Siberia with."

—Will Rogers 6-30-1927

"We certainly are pulling for that lady aviator. Just because we can't pronounce either barrel of her name won't lesson our reception of her. She's the only titled person we ever heard of that did anything."

—Will Rogers 9-1-1927 on Princess Loewenstein-Wertheim, the first woman to fly the English Channel

"All the way across Wyoming we chased wolves and antelopes. If you left Los Angeles on the train at the same time I did you wouldn't even arrive there till Saturday morning, and, boy, what pilots those air mail babies are. Lindbergh came from a great school."

—Will Rogers 10-21-1927

"If you never take but one airplane trip in your life, make it the one where you fly over the Grand Canyon." —Will Rogers 8-24-1928

"If there is a safer mode of transportation I have never found it. Even horseback. I got bucked off the other day." —Will Rogers 10-31-1929

Will Rogers (r) and aviator Roscoe Turner (l). Turner, an early barnstormer, broke seven transcontinental speed records and served as a Lieutenant Colonel in the Nevada National Guard. He later worked as a stunt flier in aviation films, including Howard Hughes' classic *Hell's Angels*. In 1952, Congress awarded Turner the Distinguished Flying Cross for his contributions to aviation. Turner is enshrined in the Golden Age Section of the National Aviation Hall of Fame (courtesy Will Rogers Memorial Museum).

Will Rogers kissing his wife, Betty, goodbye before one of his frequent flights, 1930 (courtesy Will Rogers Memorial Museum).

Will Rogers in front of American Airlines aircraft, circa 1930s (courtesy Will Rogers Memorial Museum).

Will Rogers in Ford aircraft, circa 1930s (courtesy Will Rogers Memorial Museum).

Will Rogers munching a snack before boarding a U. S. Mail Express plane, circa 1930s (courtesy Will Rogers Memorial Museum).

Will Rogers, second from left, in front of plane in which Rogers made his only flight from an aircraft carrier, in 1930 (courtesy Will Rogers Memorial Museum).

Will Rogers (r) with Fort Worth Star-Telegram creator and publisher, Amon G. Carter, Sr. (c) in January 1931 (courtesy Will Rogers Memorial Museum).

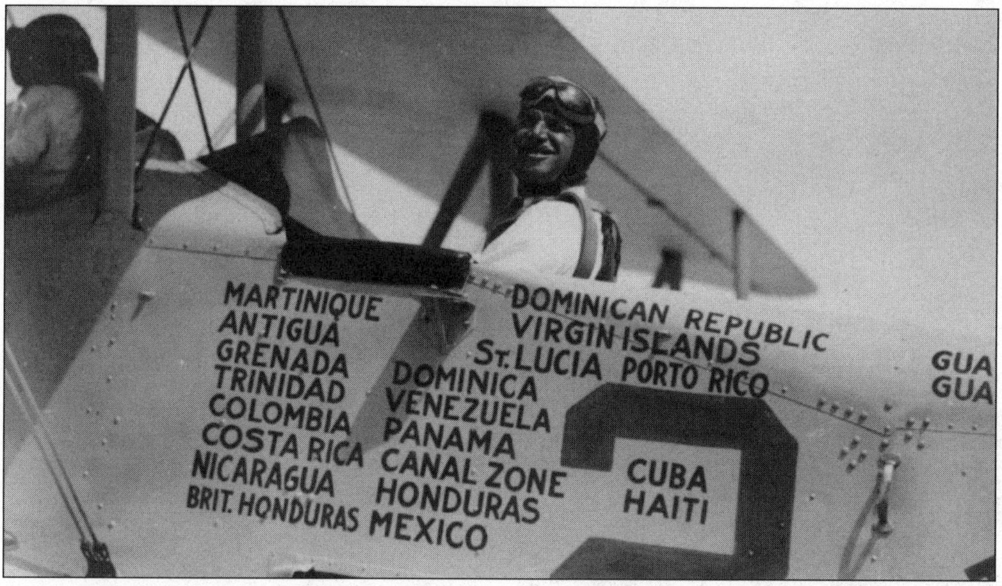

Will Rogers at Panama Canal Zone Naval Base on South American tour to aid Nicaragua earthquake victims in April, 1931 (courtesy Will Rogers Memorial Museum).

"It's my first trip in one where they bundle the wheels up inside the wings. They say they sometimes forget to put 'em down. Believe me Pilot Lee will be reminded of it when we start to land. The wheels are under the wings and the passenger can't see if they are down. I am going to do a little wing walking and go out and see for myself tonight."

—Will Rogers 7-14-1931

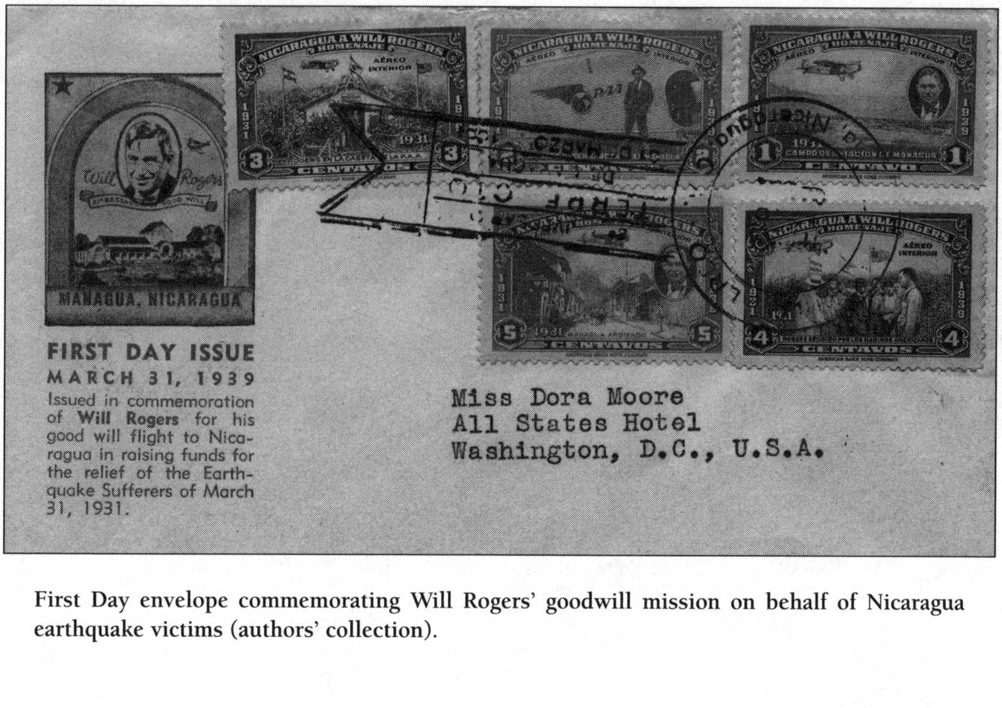

First Day envelope commemorating Will Rogers' goodwill mission on behalf of Nicaragua earthquake victims (authors' collection).

"Amelia (Earhart) Putnam flew across the Atlantic Ocean and then had to call up her husband to see if he thought it would be safe for a married woman to venture into London alone." —Will Rogers 5-23-1932

"Aviation will save this country someday, and I know no politician is going to do it." —Will Rogers 11-6-1932

"Wish we could get our Presidential candidates to travel by plane, but there is no back platform to make the speeches from and there is no plane big enough to carry all their "yes" men." —Will Rogers 11-6-1932

Will Rogers arrives in Chicago from the coast via United Airlines' new three-mile-a-minute plane in April 1933 (courtesy Will Rogers Memorial Museum).

"America developed another Lindbergh, Jimmie Mattern and Amelia Earhart last night when Mrs. Franklin D. Roosevelt finished a transcontinental flight. There is a real boost for aviation." —Will Rogers 6-7-1933

Will Rogers (l), Eleanor Roosevelt (center), and Amon G. Carter, Sr. (r) in June, 1933 (courtesy Will Rogers Memorial Museum).

"There is nothing that will drive you to flying quicker than to have somebody after you." —Will Rogers 8-17-1933

"Roscoe Turner and I just breezed in here—2 hours –400 miles—to do a little stage acting at a benefit. Roscoe's jokes better be good, for with the Democrats doing all that can be done and the Republicans keeping still, why it don't give me much to work on. So my little riddles are not so hot." —Will Rogers 12-12-1933

"Thousands can fly, but few can find a speck in the ocean. You got to be on intimate terms with astronomy. Never mind the carburetors or the feed line or the R.P.M. It's the old man sun, moon and stars that you want to be on speaking terms with."
—Will Rogers 12-5-1934

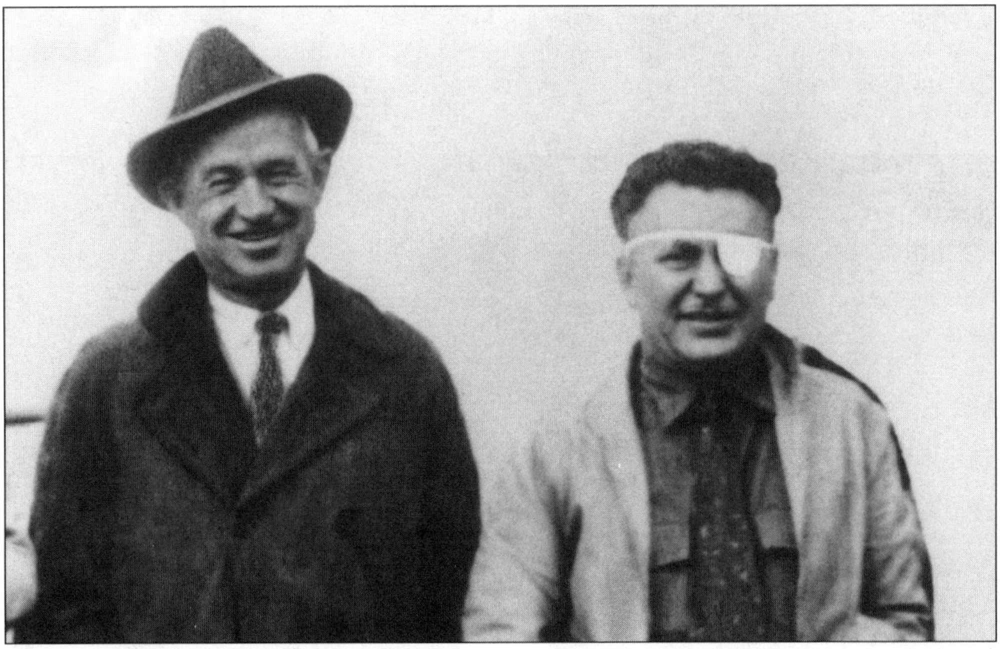

Will Rogers (l) and Wiley Post (r). Will affectionately called Post, "One-Eye, No-Sleep." Post lost his eye in an oil field accident in 1926. Post was an Oklahoma aviator who won the National Air Race for long distance in 1930 and with Australian navigator, Harold Gatty, set the round-the-world flight record in 1931. Wiley Post is enshrined in the Golden Age Section of the National Aviation Hall of Fame (courtesy Will Rogers Memorial Museum).

Will Rogers (r) and Wiley Post (l) (courtesy Will Rogers Memorial Museum).

Will Rogers on wing of Orion-Explorer in Juneau, Alaska on August 9, 1935, (courtesy Will Rogers Memorial Museum).

"Bad weather. Not a plane mushed out of Juneau yesterday. Had a great visit last night. Rex Beach, a mighty dear old friend, arrived from Vancouver...The first movie I ever made was in '18, an Alaskan story by Rex called *Laughing Bill Hyde*." —Will Rogers 8-9-1935

"We are sure having a great time. If we hear of whales or polar bears in the Artic, or a big herd of caribou or reindeer we fly over and see it...Say there is a horse here; the furthest north of any horse, and he eats fish and travels on snowshoes. Maybe Point Barrow today."
—Will Rogers 8-12-35

Will Rogers at ABC House, Aklavik, Northwest Territories, Canada during August 10-12, 1935, (courtesy Will Rogers Memorial Museum)

"Well, we had a day off today and nothing to do, so we went flying with friend Joe Crosson, Alaska's crack pilot." —Will Rogers 8-14-1935

Crash site ending the lives of Will Rogers and Wiley Post at Point Barrow, Alaska on August 15, 1935. Joe Crosson flew the bodies of Rogers and Post to Seattle from Point Barrow (courtesy Will Rogers Memorial Museum).

Will's legacy lives on at the Will Rogers Memorial Museum in Claremore, Oklahoma. Check out the museum website at www.willrogers.com and plan your trip. In the meantime, enjoy some of Will's wit and wisdom.

—Everybody is ignorant, only on different subjects.
—There is nothing as stupid as an educated man if you get him off the thing he was educated in.
—This would be a great time in the world for some man to come along who knew something.
—Every war has been preceded by a peace conference. That's what starts the next war.
—I'm more concerned with the return of my money than the return on my money.
—Don't gamble; take all your savings and buy some good stock, and hold it till it goes up, then sell it. If it don't go up, don't buy it.
—Congress has got more fiction in it in a day than writers can think of in a year.
—We should never blame government for not doing something. It's when they do something is when they become dangerous.
—It's awful hard to get people interested in corruption unless they get some of it.
—A fanatic is always the fellow that is on the opposite side.
—It costs ten times more to govern than it used to, and we are not governed one-tenth as good.
—Once a man holds a public office he is absolutely no good for honest work.
—There are only a few original jokes, and most of them are in Congress.